Times A-Changin'

OXFORD STUDIES IN MUSIC THEORY

Series Editor Steven Rings

Studies in Music with Text, David Lewin

Metric Manipulations in Haydn and Mozart: Chamber Music for Strings, 1787–1791, Danuta Mirka

Songs in Motion: Rhythm and Meter in the German Lied, Yonatan Malin

A Geometry of Music: Harmony and Counterpoint in the Extended Common Practice, Dmitri Tymoczko

In the Process of Becoming: Analytic and Philosophical Perspectives on Form in Early Nineteenth-Century Music, Janet Schmalfeldt

Tonality and Transformation, Steven Rings

Audacious Euphony: Chromatic Harmony and the Triad's Second Nature, Richard Cohn

Music as Discourse: Semiotic Adventures in Romantic Music, Kofi Agawu

Beating Time and Measuring Music in the Early Modern Era, Roger Mathew Grant

Mahler's Symphonic Sonatas, Seth Monahan

Pieces of Tradition: An Analysis of Contemporary Tonal Music, Daniel Harrison

Music at Hand: Instruments, Bodies, and Cognition, Jonathan De Souza

Foundations of Musical Grammar, Lawrence M. Zbikowski

Organized Time: Rhythm, Tonality, and Form, Jason Yust

Flow: The Rhythmic Voice in Rap Music, Mitchell Ohriner

Performing Knowledge: Twentieth-Century Music in Analysis and Performance, Daphne Leong

Enacting Musical Time: The Bodily Experience of New Music, Mariusz Kozak

Hearing Homophony: Tonal Expectation at the Turn of the Seventeenth Century, Megan Kaes Long

Form as Harmony in Rock Music, Drew Nobile

Desire in Chromatic Harmony: A Psychodynamic Exploration of Fin de Siècle *Tonality*, Kenneth M. Smith

A Blaze of Light in Every Word: Analyzing the Popular Singing Voice, Victoria Malawey

Sweet Thing: The History and Musical Structure of a Shared American Vernacular Form, Nicholas Stoia

Hypermetric Manipulations in Haydn and Mozart: Chamber Music for Strings, 1787–1791, Danuta Mirka

How Sonata Forms: A Bottom-Up Approach to Musical Form, Yoel Greenberg

Exploring Musical Spaces: A Synthesis of Mathematical Approaches, Julian Hook

The Musical Language of Italian Opera, 1813–1859, William Rothstein

Tonality: An Owner's Manual, Dmitri Tymoczko

Times A-Changin': Flexible Meter as Self-Expression in Singer-Songwriter Music, Nancy Murphy

Times A-Changin'

Flexible Meter as Self-Expression in Singer-Songwriter Music

NANCY MURPHY

OXFORD
UNIVERSITY PRESS

Oxford University Press is a department of the University of Oxford. It furthers the University's objective of excellence in research, scholarship, and education by publishing worldwide. Oxford is a registered trade mark of Oxford University Press in the UK and certain other countries.

Published in the United States of America by Oxford University Press 198 Madison Avenue, New York, NY 10016, United States of America.

© Oxford University Press 2023

All rights reserved. No part of this publication may be reproduced, stored in a retrieval system, or transmitted, in any form or by any means, without the prior permission in writing of Oxford University Press, or as expressly permitted by law, by license, or under terms agreed with the appropriate reproduction rights organization. Inquiries concerning reproduction outside the scope of the above should be sent to the Rights Department, Oxford University Press, at the address above.

You must not circulate this work in any other form and you must impose this same condition on any acquirer.

Library of Congress Cataloging-in-Publication Data
Names: Murphy, Nancy (Nancy Elizabeth) author.
Title: Times a-changin' : flexible meter as self-expression in singer-songwriter music / Nancy Murphy.
Description: [1.] | New York : Oxford University Press, 2023. |
Series: Oxford studies in music theory |
Includes bibliographical references and index.
Identifiers: LCCN 2023006287 (print) | LCCN 2023006288 (ebook) |
ISBN 9780197635216 (hardback) | ISBN 9780197635230 (epub) | ISBN 9780197635247
Subjects: LCSH: Musical meter and rhythm. |
Popular music—1961–1970–Analysis, appreciation. |
Popular music—1971–1980–Analysis, appreciation. |
Mitchell, Joni—Criticism and interpretation. |
Sainte-Marie, Buffy—Criticism and interpretation. |
Dylan, Bob, 1941—Criticism and interpretation. |
Stevens, Cat, 1948—Criticism and interpretation. |
Simon, Paul, 1941—Criticism and interpretation.
Classification: LCC ML3850 .M815 2023 (print) | LCC ML3850 (ebook) |
DDC 782.42164/1226—dc23/eng/20230210
LC record available at https://lccn.loc.gov/2023006287
LC ebook record available at https://lccn.loc.gov/2023006288

DOI: 10.1093/oso/9780197635216.001.0001

Printed by Integrated Books International, United States of America

Contents

List of Figures	ix
Acknowledgments	xi

1. The Self-Expressive Rhetoric of Flexible Meter	1
Self-Expressive Features	2
Self-Presentation	3
Lyrics	3
Techniques of Vocal Production	4
Flexible Meter	5
Flexible Meter and "The Fiddle and the Drum"	5
The Challenges of Metric Flexibility	7
Responding to Singer-Songwriter Self-Expression	8
Self-Expression and the Singer-Songwriter	10
The 1960s Protest Song	11
1970s Introspective Songwriting	13
Expectations for Singer-Songwriter Music	14
Self-Expression	14
The Impression of Authenticity	15
"Authenticity" in Popular Music	15
"Authenticity" in Singer-Songwriter Music	17
Bob Dylan and the Folk Revival	18
The Ballad Tradition	19
The Delta Blues	20
Flexible Meter as Self-Expression in Singer-Songwriter Music	21
Political and Confessional Singer-Songwriter Music	22
2. The Theory of Flexible Meter	27
Types of Flexible Meter	27
Regular Meter	31
Meter in Rock Music	33
Reinterpreted Meter	34
Omitted and Added Beats	34
Reinterpreted Meter: Mitchell, "Lesson in Survival"	36
Grouping Parallelism and Simon's "The Sound of Silence"	37
Lost Meter	38
Regular and Lost Meter: Mitchell, "Woodstock"	40

vi CONTENTS

Ambiguous Meter	42
Metric Process	43
Metric Projection Symbols	44
Realized and Unrealized Durations	46
Hiatus and Lost Meter in Mitchell's "Blue"	47
Ambiguous Meter: Sainte-Marie's "Sir Patrick Spens"	48
Metric Potential	49
The Aspects of Meter	50
Shifts Between Metric Types	51

3. Regular and Reinterpreted Meter — 54

Regular Meter	54
Mitchell, "Little Green"	55
Reinterpreted Meter	57
Joni Mitchell's Rhapsodic Sentiments	58
"A Case of You"	58
"All I Want"	60
Paul Simon: Reinterpreted Meter Expressing Enigmatic Lyrics	63
"The Sound of Silence"	63
"April Come She Will"	66
Simon's Solo Singer-Songwriter Style	66
Cat Stevens's Introspection	67
"The Wind"	68
"Into White"	68
"Katmandu"	71
Stevens's Introspection	73
A Closer Look: Joni Mitchell's "Lesson in Survival"	74
Lyrics and Form	74
B Sections: Melodic Descent	75
C Sections: Escape and Freedom	79
D Section: Dreams	82
Flexible Meter and Meaning	84

4. Self-Expressive Innovations: Lost Meter — 86

Bob Dylan's "Only a Pawn in Their Game"	87
Formal Flexibility	88
Consistently Flexible Form	90
Flexible Meter	91
Self-Expressive Flexibility	94
Later Verses	95
Performance Frequency	97
The Impression of Spontaneity	98
Cat Stevens's "Time"	99
Meaning of "Time"	100
Irregular Hierarchy	101

The Limits of Reinterpreted Meter	103
Loose Metric Process	105
Synthesized Flexible Meter	108
Metrically Regular Ending	108
Introspective Temporalities	109
Joni Mitchell's "Blue"	110
Central Relationship	110
Lyrics and Accompaniment	111
Reinterpreted Meter: Narrative Space	112
Expressively Lost Meter	112
First Statement of "Blue"	116
Restored Regularity	118
Reinterpreted Then Lost Meter	118
An Expressive Ending	120
Musical and Creative Freedom	122
5. Intensifying "Imperfection": Ambiguous Meter	**125**
Bob Dylan's "Down the Highway"	127
The Blues Model	128
Stressed Events	129
Flexible First Line	131
Metric Orientation	131
Loose Metric Structure	133
Second Line	133
Third Line	134
Flexible Blues	134
"Imperfect" Metric Flexibility	136
Bob Dylan's "Restless Farewell"	137
Influence from "The Parting Glass"	138
Stressed Events	139
Opening Line	140
Second Line	142
Third and Fourth Lines	143
Fifth Line	144
Flexible Effects	146
Self-Presentation and "Authenticity"	146
Restless Metric Imperfection	147
Joni Mitchell's "The Fiddle and the Drum"	148
First Vocal Fragment	149
Second Fragment	149
Metric Emergence	151
Expressive Emergence	153
Self-Presentation and Flexible Meter	153
Buffy Sainte-Marie's "Sir Patrick Spens"	154
Ballad Narrative	156

viii CONTENTS

Instrumentation	156
Stressed Events	157
Vocal Entry and Narrator Authority	159
Folk Song Adaptations	161

6. What Happens Next to Self-Expressive Flexible Meter? 164

Beyond 1972	164
Ensemble Careers	165
Future Singer-Songwriters	166
Buffy Sainte-Marie's "My Country 'Tis of Thy People You're Dying" (1966)	167
Self-Presentation	168
Activist Music	169
Lyrics	169
Vocal Production	171
Flexible Meter	172
"My Country" (1966, *Rainbow Quest*)	175
Expressive Voice	175
"My Country" (2017, *Medicine Songs*)	176
Self-Expressive Impact	180
Conclusion: Flexible Meter as Self-Expression	181

Bibliography	183
Index	197

Figures

1.1 Mitchell, "The Fiddle and the Drum" (0:00–0:23)	6
2.1 Five Types of Flexible Meter	29
2.2 Dot notation for metric hierarchy	32
2.3 Five-layer metric hierarchy	33
2.4 Metrical reinterpretation symbols in a dot diagram	35
2.5 Mitchell, "Lesson in Survival" (0:35–0:43)	36
2.6 Simon, "The Sound of Silence" (0:00–0:39)	38
2.7 Mitchell, "Woodstock," introduction (0:00–0:46)	41
2.8 Summary of Hasty's symbols	45
2.9 Realized Durations, Hiatus, and Unrealized Durations	47
2.10 Mitchell, "Blue," first vocal phrase (0:12–0:21)	48
2.11 Sainte-Marie, "Sir Patrick Spens," introduction (0:00–0:13)	49
2.12 Aspects of Meter	51
2.13 Linear conception of the Aspects of Meter	52
3.1 Mitchell, "Little Green" (0:22–0:43)	56
3.2 Mitchell, "A Case of You," lyrics, end of stanza 1	58
3.3 Mitchell, "A Case of You," metrical reinterpretation (0:40–1:04)	59
3.4 Mitchell, "All I Want" (0:21–0:34)	61
3.5 Mitchell, "All I Want" (0:34–0:47)	62
3.6 Simon, "The Sound of Silence" (0:00–0:39)	64
3.7 Simon, "The Sound of Silence," Reinterpreted Meter, verses 2–5	65
3.8 Simon, "April Come She Will" (0:20–0:37)	67
3.9 Stevens, "The Wind" (0:29–0:49)	69
3.10 Stevens, "Into White" (0:30–0:50)	70
3.11 Stevens, "Katmandu," introduction (0:08–0:16)	72
3.12 Stevens, "Katmandu" (0:16–0:42)	73
3.13 Mitchell, "Lesson in Survival," verses and sections	75
3.14 Mitchell, "Lesson in Survival," verse 1, A and B sections (0:06–0:29)	76
3.15 Mitchell, "Lesson in Survival," verse 2, B melodic descent (1:18–1:27)	78
3.16 Mitchell, "Lesson in Survival," verse 3, B section (2:20–2:26)	78
3.17 Mitchell, "Lesson in Survival," verse 1, C section (0:36–0:44)	79
3.18 Mitchell, "Lesson in Survival," verse 2, C section (1:32–1:45)	80
3.19 Mitchell, "Lesson in Survival," verse 3, C section (2:29–3:11)	81
3.20 Mitchell, "Lesson in Survival," verse 1, D section (0:53–1:00)	83
3.21 Mitchell, "Lesson in Survival," verse 2, D section (1:52–2:01)	83
3.22 Mitchell, "Lesson in Survival," verse 3, D section (2:51–4:06)	84
4.1 Dylan, "Only a Pawn in their Game," verse 1 lyrics (0:00–0:30)	88

X FIGURES

4.2 Dylan, "Only a Pawn in their Game," *c* line melodic motives 89

4.3 Dylan, "Only a Pawn in their Game," verse 3 *d* lines and refrain 90

4.4 Dylan, "Only a Pawn in their Game," first phrase (0:00–0:08) 92

4.5 Dylan, "Only a Pawn in their Game," *b* and *c*1 lines (0:07–0:17) 93

4.6 Dylan, "Only a Pawn in their Game," final verse *b* and *c*1 lines (2:58–3:10) 96

4.7 Stevens, "Time," introduction as a Reinterpreted Meter (0:00–0:19) 102

4.8 Stevens, "Time," first vocal phrases as a Reinterpreted Meter (0:19–0:36) 104

4.9 Stevens, "Time," first vocal phrase with metric projections (0:19–0:27) 106

4.10 Stevens, "Time," return to $\frac{4}{4}$ meter (0:44–1:06) 109

4.11 Mitchell, "Blue," expressive extension on "sail away" (0:32–0:45) 113

4.12 Mitchell, "Blue," expressive extension on "space to fill in" (0:53–1:06) 114

4.13 Mitchell, "Blue," formal structure and timings 115

4.14 Mitchell, "Blue," prototype *a* and *b* phrases with similar motives and contour 115

4.15 Mitchell, "Blue," *a*1 phrase (0:12–0:32) 117

4.16 Mitchell, "Blue," *b*2 phrase (1:12–1:29) 119

4.17 Mitchell, "Blue," second half of *a*4 (2:16–2:32) 121

5.1 Dylan, "Down the Highway," first stanza 128

5.2 Dylan, "Down the Highway," performed dynamic accents in stanza 1 129

5.3 Dylan, "Down the Highway," tactus beat interpretation (0:00–0:14) 130

5.4 Dylan, "Down the Highway," line 1 (0:00–0:14) 132

5.5 Dylan, "Down the Highway," line 2 (0:14–0:24) 132

5.6 Dylan, "Down the Highway," line 3 (0:24–0:34) 135

5.7 Blues harmonic structure 136

5.8 The Clancy Brothers, "The Parting Glass" (*Come Fill Your Glass with Us*, 1959) lyrics and four-beat metric structure (verse 1) 139

5.9 Dylan, "Restless Farewell," lyrics and possible four-beat metric structure (verse 1) 140

5.10 Dylan, "Restless Farewell," phrase 1 (0:00–0:08) 141

5.11 Dylan, "Restless Farewell," phrase 2 (0:08–1:15) 142

5.12 Dylan, "Restless Farewell," phrases 3 and 4 (0:15–0:29) 144

5.13 Dylan, "Restless Farewell," phrases 5 and 6 (0:29–0:41) 145

5.14 Mitchell, "The Fiddle and the Drum," first and second vocal units (0:00–0:13) 150

5.15 Mitchell, "The Fiddle and the Drum," fifth and sixth vocal units (0:23–0:31) 152

5.16 Sainte-Marie, "Sir Patrick Spens," introduction (0:00–0:17) 158

5.17 Sainte-Marie, "Sir Patrick Spens," first vocal phrase (0:20–0:35) 160

6.1 Sainte-Marie, "My Country" (*Little Wheel Spin and Spin*, 1966) (0:00–0:54) 173

6.2 Sainte-Marie, "My Country" (*Medicine Songs*, 2017) (0:00–0:44) 178

6.3 Sainte-Marie, "My Country" (*Medicine Songs*, 2017) (3:50–3:56) 179

6.4 Sainte-Marie, "My Country" (*Medicine Songs*, 2017) (4:24–4:33) 180

Acknowledgments

I would first like to extend my thanks to the students and faculty at the University of Houston for their support of this research during my time there. Particular thanks to Timothy Koozin, who encouraged me to write a book in the first place. Thanks to my Spring 2021 Singer-Songwriter class who helped me develop broader ideas about this self-expressive tradition and its impacts on twenty-first-century popular music. Many thanks as well to my colleagues at the University of Michigan, especially Karen Fournier, Leah Frederick, Patricia Hall, Marc Hannaford, Áine Heneghan, Diane Oliva, René Rusch, and Henry Stoll. for their encouragement and support of this project in the final stages. Thank you to the School of Music, Theatre & Dance for their support for the publication of this manuscript.

I developed the initial ideas for this research during my doctoral degree at the University of British Columbia. My sincere appreciation goes to my adviser John Roeder for his insights, guidance, and kindness during the origins of this project and beyond. Many thanks to the scholarly community at UBC, particularly my professors Alan Dodson, Nathan Hesselink, Richard Kurth, and Michael Tenzer, and peers Robin Attas, Kristi Hardman, Kimberly Hieb, and Grant Sawatzky.

My time at the University of Chicago had a deep influence on the trajectory and development of this work. I am so grateful for my experiences with the intellectual community I encountered there. Particular thanks to John Lawrence for his insights into my work and to Rebecca Flore for her encouraging and careful editing of this manuscript.

I am very grateful to the faculty at UChicago for their impact on this project. Many thanks to Larry Zbikowski, who talked me through his vision for how my research could become a monograph. Thank you to Jennifer Iverson for her encouragement, mentorship, advice, and belief that this manuscript would be a good fit for Oxford. Thanks most of all to Steve Rings, who has supported my work for many years and helped to develop and define this project.

Thank you to everyone at Oxford, especially Norm Hirschy, Steve Rings (as series editor), Sean Decker, Laura Santo, and Kavitha Yuvaraj for their

xii ACKNOWLEDGMENTS

assistance. Many thanks to my fellow authors in the Oxford Studies in Music Theory Series, Megan Kaes Long, Drew Nobile, and Mitch Ohriner, who were so helpful and supportive with my questions at every stage of writing this book. A huge thank you to the members of my writing group, Megan Lavengood and Olivia Lucas, for their feedback on chapter drafts. Several chapters in particular would not be what they are today without Olivia's brilliant and valuable insights. I am also grateful to the anonymous readers of this manuscript and to audiences who responded to portions of this book at conferences and at colloquia hosted by Northwestern University, Louisiana State University, and the Society for Music Analysis.

Versions of some of the analyses in this manuscript originally appeared as "The Times are A-Changin': Metric Flexibility and Text Expression in 1960s and 1970s Singer-Songwriter Music," *Music Theory Spectrum* 44, no. 1 (2022): 17–40. These are adapted here with permission.

My family has provided unconditional support and love throughout the process of writing this book. Thank you to Mom, Dad, Katie, Steve, Jimmy, Kat, Julia, Tessa, Mia, and Lily. Many thanks to Reg, Kay, Matthew, Amanda, and the MacLeod, Zapolski, and Tubbs families. To my dearest friends Barbara Dietlinger and Tara Boyle: your empathy, reassurance, and camaraderie were essential to the development and completion of this manuscript and to maintaining my sanity during the process. Thank you for your continual support and friendship. And finally, I extend my deepest gratitude to my husband, Joshua Klopfenstein, whose encouragement, editing, and support of every kind made this book possible.

1

The Self-Expressive Rhetoric
of Flexible Meter

It is 1969 and Joni Mitchell is on television, standing empty-handed in the middle of a circular stage that is adorned with psychedelic colors. She is wearing a long, hunter-green dress, surrounded by an audience sitting cross-legged on the floor. She waits for television host Dick Cavett to introduce her next performance.[1] The show is filming on the day after the 1969 Woodstock music festival, an event that Mitchell was initially scheduled to attend but from which she was held back by her management to ensure she could per-form on The Dick Cavett Show the next day.[2] The host introduces Mitchell and jokes with her about singing a cappella wondering aloud if someone stole her guitar. The singer laughs politely in response, denies any theft, and then proceeds to her performance, explaining to the audience that she will be singing a "song for America" that she wrote "as a Canadian living in this country." With her hands clasped behind her back, she performs "The Fiddle and the Drum" with no accompaniment, channeling the folk performance tradition on which the song is based.[3]

This song about military participation is a rare political statement from Mitchell, who, unlike her peers Bob Dylan and Buffy Sainte-Marie, had

---

[1] The episode was recorded on August 18, 1969, and broadcast the next day. Mitchell's performance of "The Fiddle and the Drum" starts just before the forty-minute mark without commercials (1969). Cavett's show rarely included shots of the audience, preferring a focus on the interview; but "The Woodstock Show" (as it came to be known) was an outlier in presentation and format, featuring entirely musical guests, with Cavett in atypically casual attire. Katherine Monk (2012, 94) describes the episode as feeling like "something of a Woodstock after-party."

[2] O'Brien (2001, 101). Cavett does not introduce his other guests (and Woodstock attendees) David Crosby and Stephen Stills at the beginning of the show (1969), suggesting they were, indeed, late for the Cavett Show performance, as Mitchell's producers feared she might be. They show up around twenty-five minutes into the recording and mention to Cavett that they still have mud on their pants from the festival performance.

[3] This is the fourth song that she performed for this episode of Cavett's show, after "Chelsea Morning," "Willy," and "For Free." Whitesell (2008, 42) places "The Fiddle and the Drum" in a cate-gory of songs that deal "in anonymous archetypal emotions, as if in conscious imitation of a timeless folk repertory."

Times A-Changin'. Nancy Murphy, Oxford University Press. © Oxford University Press 2023.
DOI: 10.1093/oso/9780197635216.003.0001

2 TIMES A-CHANGIN'

released only this one "protest song" by 1969.[4] But the song's message was not a particularly risky proclamation. Her antiwar narrative echoed the opinions of the young Cavett Show audience that night, aligning with an established trend of resistance against the war in Vietnam.[5] Similar to the way that Mitchell's song "Woodstock" would eventually capture the spirit of an event she did not attend, "The Fiddle and the Drum" characterizes a popular antiwar sentiment in the public consciousness of the late 1960s.[6]

Self-Expressive Features

I see Mitchell's performance of "The Fiddle and the Drum" on Cavett's show providing an important demonstration about what the label "singer-songwriter" might mean when applied to a solo artist during this period. In 1969, the folk traditions favored by the emergent 1960s singer-songwriters transitioned to the confessional songwriting practices of the 1970s. Most singer-songwriter music features a solo singer with a single accompaniment instrument (usually guitar), lyrical topics of personal significance, and the overall impression that songs are vehicles for personal expression. In the decade from 1962 to 1972, artists like Mitchell and Dylan, among others, developed methods of self-expression in performance that were in dialogue with the traditional music popular in the mid-century folk revival. The term "self-expression" captures the impression that in singer-songwriter music, something of the "self" was being communicated to audiences through

[4] Dylan's initial coffeehouse performances and first few albums included multiple tracks that became prototypes of the 1960s topical protest song, commenting especially on civil rights in the 1960s. But Dylan disliked being labeled as a protest singer, mentioning in *Chronicles, Volume One* (2004a, 82–83) that "topical songs weren't protest songs" and "rebellion songs" were what really interested him. Sainte-Marie wrote many of her own "activist songs" that provided commentary on the mistreatment of Indigenous people in North America, particularly Native Americans. For more on Sainte-Marie's career as an activist and protest singer, see Warner (2018). Earlier in the show, Mitchell and Cavett discuss that she is not very political, which she claims is the result of not understanding politics, singing instead about love and things she does know. She also states that Canada is not a very political country. A year later she released one of her most popular, radio-friendly songs, "Big Yellow Taxi," which is an environmentalist anthem and the third-most-covered song in her repertoire (behind only "Both Sides, Now" and "River").

[5] Warner (2018, 15) suggests that Sainte-Marie's 1964 song "Universal Soldier" was actually one of the first songs that was written about the Vietnam War, "warning people about what was happening in Vietnam before most fully realized the extent of the conflict" a few years ahead of the antiwar sentiment reaching an "all-time high."

[6] Mitchell claims she was able to encapsulate the experience of the Woodstock festival because she was longing to be there herself—her distance from it gave her this perspective. Mitchell's commentary on this is reproduced in O'Brien (2001, 101).

performance. Mitchell's 1969 Cavett Show performance of "The Fiddle and the Drum" demonstrates what I interpret as four central components of self-expression in 1960s and 1970s singer-songwriter music: self-presentation (which shapes the reception of performance persona), personal lyrics, striking techniques of vocal production, and flexible meter.

Self-Presentation

First, the visual components of this television appearance allow Mitchell's audience access to the markers of her self-presentation. These include decisions made about her hair, the presence or absence of makeup, and clothing, as well as Mitchell's body language, demeanor, and banter between songs, which may have been rehearsed or improvised.[7] (This self-presentation also includes decisions the Cavett Show producers made about filming and editing her performance.) Alongside aural musical cues, Mitchell's self-presentation as a thin, white, straight, solo, female singer-songwriter contributes to the formation of her persona and the public reception of her music in the context of contemporaneous attitudes toward race, gender, and sexual orientation.

Lyrics

The second feature that her 1969 performances demonstrate is the self-expressive importance of singer-songwriter lyrics. In the song's two stanzas, Mitchell interrogates her friend, "Johnny," about his military participation, gradually shifting her attention to asking "America" why it, too, has traded

---

[7] In Mitchell's case, these visual cues sometimes distracted her critics from focusing on the musical features of her performance. Indeed, reviewers of her early coffeehouse gigs seemed unable to discuss her performances without some mention of her appearance and behavior, commenting on her nervous shyness, on indicators of her fragility, and on qualities of her femininity and her apparent level of attractiveness. Hoskins (2017, 99) reproduces a *New York Times* article by Ian Dove, in which Dove describes Mitchell as looking "flaxen-haired and frail" in the 1960s. Hoskins (2017, 58) also includes an article by Michael Watts of *Melody Maker* that recounts Mitchell "looking vulnerable and dreamy," while relating her appearance to his readers as "rather severe in an attractive sort of way." Watts goes on to describe her as having an "open face" and a body, the "seeming fragility" of which "inspires a feeling of instinctive protectiveness." Such commentary reflects ideas about gender and sexuality in the late 1960s and gives some indication of how public reception of a songwriter's persona might interact with their techniques of self-expression. (Many of these features of Mitchell's self-presentation and persona become even more foregrounded in discussions of her introspective album *Blue* in 1971.)

the communal fiddle for the military drum.[8] Mitchell offers a clear antiwar message here, and the song's first-person perspective gives the impression that the lyrics reveal her own opinions about war. The concept of songs as vehicles for personal, political, or introspective truths is not unique to singer-songwriter music, but is a fundamental and well-studied component of self-expression in this songwriting tradition.[9]

Techniques of Vocal Production

A lesser studied, but no less important, aspect of Mitchell's performance is her vocal production techniques, which comprises the third feature of singer-songwriter self-expression. In Mitchell's case, her vocals typically display mesmerizing timbral techniques and shifts of register that add layers of complexity above her otherwise simple accompaniment patterns.[10] By comparison, her vocal production for "The Fiddle and the Drum" is stark in its simplicity and limited melodic contour. Here, the rhetorical import of her song's message is highlighted by a direct address and a simple singing style; a rhapsodic vocal line is absent. In singer-songwriter music more broadly, idiomatic techniques of vocal production are linked with a singer-songwriter's self-presentation and delivery of lyrics. For example, Bob Dylan's imitations of Woody Guthrie's drawl intentionally invites comparisons to the legendary folk singer; Buffy Sainte-Marie's striking vocal timbre and vibrato mark her voice as inimitable within the singer-songwriter tradition.[11] I address vocal techniques briefly in the present study, but this is a rich area for future inquiry into singer-songwriter self-expression.[12]

[8] "Johnny" is a stereotypical name for a soldier, equivalent to Buffy Sainte-Marie's "Universal Soldier."

[9] Dylan's winning a 2008 Pulitzer Prize and a 2016 Nobel Prize in Literature gives some indication about how the lyrics in singer-songwriter music are valued. Published volumes of lyrics for artists like Mitchell (2019) and Dylan (2004b) show how important these lyrics are as poetic texts outside of their musical settings.

[10] Whitesell (2008) and Sonenberg (2003) observe Mitchell's piano technique, including extended harmonic structures.

[11] Some of Steven Rings's work on singer-songwriters addresses vocal production; see his (2013) investigation of Dylan's "It's Alright, Ma (I'm Only Bleeding)" and his brief but insightful (2015) analysis of Sainte-Marie's "Cod'ine." For more on the popular music singing voice, see Malawey (2020).

[12] Malawey (2020) provides an apparatus for such an inquiry, offering a systematic and conceptual model for analyzing vocal delivery.

Flexible Meter

The fourth feature of singer-songwriter self-expression is the most overlooked in this music and is the focus of the present study: flexible meter. For several artists in the 1960s and 1970s, flexible meter is a critical self-expressive feature, made easily available to these artists because of their self-accompanied musical textures. These singers could accommodate creative improvisational whims in performance, sometimes as an in-the-moment response to lyrical content. By shifting patterns of voice and accompaniment, these artists at times created unpredictable, irregular, malleable metric structures that form a musical rhetoric for this performance tradition. Songs deliver lyrical messages, allowing for seemingly improvised flights of vocal rhapsody that help to craft the performance persona of each artist and showcase their techniques of vocal production and individual musical styles. For the singer-songwriters in this study, flexible meter is a critical component of the rhetoric of self-expression in performance.

Flexible Meter and "The Fiddle and the Drum"

But what is *flexible meter*? I theorize the term more fully in Chapter 2 as it connects to metric theory. For the moment, I define it as a metric structure that contains malleable performance timings, either in the form of ambiguous or vague meter or as vacillations between ambiguous and regular meter. This kind of unpredictable timing makes it difficult to tap, clap, or conduct along with a performance because these timings evade steady rhythmic patterns. (If you try to tap along to the beat when meter is flexible, it is often challenging to predict when the next beat will occur.) In singer-songwriter music, flexible meter can arise as a dissolving of predictable rhythmic patterns in metric regularity into ambiguous or vague contexts, or it can occur when these looser contexts begin to regularize into more predictable patterns.[13] Flexible meter accommodates the potential for meter to shift from predictable to unpredictable patterns and vice versa.

To demonstrate how important flexible meter is in Joni Mitchell's self-expressive performance, I want to take a closer look at her 1969 versions of

---

[13] It is also possible for a song to have entirely ambiguous or vague meter without regularizing. But this scenario is quite rare in singer-songwriter music.

"The Fiddle and the Drum." In this song, there is an unpredictable timing technique that Mitchell employs both on her *Clouds* studio recording and on The Dick Cavett Show performance discussed in the opening of this chapter. Mitchell's rhetoric includes metric flexibility, a push and pull of timing that serves to highlight her song's antiwar message. Interrogating "Johnny" and "America," her lyrics repeat the phrase "And so once again" as pleas to the song's subjects, positioning Mitchell as a gentle admonisher of war through a desire to understand why it is necessary. Within these repeated pleas, Mitchell's timing is strikingly flexible. Listening to the opening phrases of the *Clouds* studio recording, the fragments of her vocal line are so spaced apart that it might initially seem like the song does not have a clear meter. Taking a closer look at the stressed events in this passage helps to uncover *why* the meter is unclear. There are obvious stresses on the words "so," the second syllable of "again," the first syllable of "Johnny," and so on, which create two-stress patterns for each vocal fragment (as shown in Figure 1.1). The transcription includes a plausible key signature and pitches, with the melody noteheads spaced proportionally to their sounding length. Slurs indicate that each note is sustained until the next onset; solid lines show the longer duration of sustained pitches at the end of each vocal fragment. But these two-stress patterns cannot join together to be counted as combined units—they are interrupted by Mitchell's sustaining the last pitch of each fragment and leaving space between the units.

There is a possible expressive rationale for this kind of fragmented opening to "The Fiddle and the Drum." The metric rhetoric of this fragmentation reinforces the pleading of Mitchell's lyrics. The inability for the song to settle into a meter underscores her restlessness in not understanding the need for military violence. But an even more compelling rationale emerges later in the song, when Mitchell sings about raising weapons and marching into war (beginning at 0:23 in the studio recording). Whether an in-the-moment decision, or a preplanned metric trajectory, Mitchell's timings tighten so that

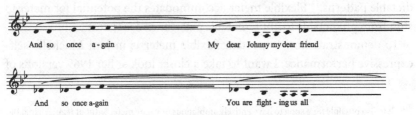

Figure 1.1 Mitchell, "The Fiddle and the Drum" (0:00–0:23)

the fragments are no longer interrupted by long durations, and her meter becomes regular. It is striking that this occurs as she describes a marching into battle, with her more regular rhythms implying a duple regularity of steady bodily motion.[14] The metric flexibility of her opening fragments is set into relief by the clear meter of later passages in the song. And these performance decisions illustrate a strong correlation between metric malleability and self-expression in Mitchell's performances. That this flexibility also occurs in other singer-songwriter music in the 1960s and 1970s suggests that flexible meter is a rhetoric of self-expression in this performance practice more broadly.

The Challenges of Metric Flexibility

The malleable metric setting of "The Fiddle and the Drum" draws attention to how Mitchell uses flexible meter as a technique of self-expression in performance. But from the perspective of metric analysis, this malleability presents a challenge. There is no single theory of meter that can accommodate all of the timings that Mitchell offers in this song. There are theories of meter that account for regularity like the one presented in Fred Lerdahl and Ray Jackendoff's *A Generative Theory of Tonal Music*, and some that can represent some irregularity in the form of missing or added beats, as explored by meter scholars like Gretchen Horlacher.[15] There is even a theory of meter—as proposed in Christopher Hasty's *Meter as Rhythm*—that works well to account for passages that lack clear meter.[16] But there is no metric theory that captures these possibilities as related within a single, malleable framework.[17]

Complicating this problem further is the fact that the experience of meter in "The Fiddle and the Drum" is antithetical to the expectations for regular rhythms and clear meter in popular music performances.[18] This might lead

[14] This section is explored in more detail in Chapter 5.
[15] See Lerdahl and Jackendoff (1983) and Horlacher (1995).
[16] See Hasty (1997).
[17] Mirka (2009) and Rockwell (2011) come close, but without as much accommodation of metric ambiguity as the singer-songwriter repertoire needs.
[18] There are, of course, many examples of popular music in which metric irregularity is more typical. Some genres, especially metal and progressive rock, commonly illustrate irregular, changing, and asymmetrical groupings. Sometimes there is even metric irregularity built into rock performances in the form of changing meter or grouping, which is not the same process as flexible meter. For some examples of irregularity in popular music, see Biamonte (2014), Pieslak (2007), Lucas (2018), and Everett (2009a). In many of these cases, the music is still often classified as metric because there is typically regularity at some level in the performance, most often with a regular tactus or subtactus level active during metric or hypermetric disruptions.

8 TIMES A-CHANGIN'

a listener to hastily categorize Mitchell's performance as "ametric" (having no meter) and end the line of inquiry there. In some popular songs, metric irregularity can call into question "How is the meter irregular or disrupted?" Performances like Mitchell's, however, have the potential to instead invite the question "Is there meter at all?"

There is an important distinction between these two questions. The former seems to invite further investigation in assuming there will be some kind of organization of beats into larger metric groups even if that meter is irregular or disrupted. The latter, on the other hand, seems poised to dismiss the possibility of metric analysis based on ambiguity or vagueness. It is no surprise, then, that the latter of these two questions is an underexplored area of meter analysis, and there has been little analytic attention paid to songs like "The Fiddle and the Drum" that do not initially have a clear meter.

While it may be tempting to classify the opening of Mitchell's song as lacking meter, her performance in this section is not entirely devoid of metric cues. And searching for these cues gives insights into the techniques of metric flexibility that are used for self-expression in singer-songwriter performances. "The Fiddle and the Drum" offers textual and musical stresses of varying weights with different timespans between them, which without Mitchell's interruptions would be easily classified as metrically regular. To label this performance as ametric would overlook the possibility of seeing these metric cues between the flexible and regular passages as related. There is a malleability to Mitchell's performance timings that correlates with the typical timing expressivity found in musical performance, but she also takes those timings to extremes. Her performance vacillates between a metrically loose opening section and subsequent passages of regularity that highlight expressive moments in her antiwar narrative. She has intensified expressive timing to create a flexible meter that is an essential feature of her self-expressive rhetoric in performances of this song.

Responding to Singer-Songwriter Self-Expression

The timings of "The Fiddle and the Drum" exemplify the need for a more flexible approach to meter, one that responds to the malleable metric settings this self-expressive performance tradition presents. Such a theory

THE SELF-EXPRESSIVE RHETORIC OF FLEXIBLE METER   9

would also respond to similar timing flexibilities by other performers in the singer-songwriter tradition between 1962 and 1972, many of whom were performing at coffeehouses in New York's Greenwich Village. Here several artists, including popular musicians like Joni Mitchell and Bob Dylan, incorporated metric flexibility as an important feature of self-expression in performance. Alongside Mitchell and Dylan, this malleable meter can be found in songs by Paul Simon in the mid-1960s, Buffy Sainte-Marie from the mid-to-late 1960s, and Cat Stevens beginning in the 1970s.[19] While much critical attention has been paid to this music, particularly to how its song lyrics respond to the sociocultural context of this period, few studies are concerned with how these artists deliver those lyrics.[20] That is, there has been little analytic attention to the rhetoric of self-expression within this singer-songwriter performance practice.[21]

The flexible work of these five artists includes stylistic features of solo music like expressive timing that puts their work in dialogue with self-expressive folk-revival performance traditions. These traditions include seventeenth-century ballads from England and Scotland alongside American ballads from the twentieth century, old-time and country music, and the Delta blues. Like some of these traditional genres, singer-songwriters take timings to extremes and shift between passages of regular accompaniment patterns and more unpredictable, ambiguous rhythms. From the lens of metric theory, this performance practice demonstrates a flexible meter that encompasses all possible metric scenarios from a multi-leveled hierarchy of regular meter, to the more malleable but still regular hierarchy of expressive timing, to unpredictable rhythmic patterns with unclear, vague, or ambiguous meter. Locally, the flexible singer-songwriter meter can serve to highlight important lyrical content—specific imagery and sentiments of singer-songwriter narratives. But flexible meter also more broadly signals the rhapsodic, spontaneous, and "imperfect" aesthetic associated with this period of singer-songwriter music. In this book, I argue that the seemingly spontaneous moments of

[19] As I explore in the final chapter of this study, some of Sainte-Marie's metric flexibility shows up in later performances as well, but it is less prevalent.

[20] Bentley (2016b), for example, situates singer-songwriters as commentators on society and culture in the 1970s.

[21] Whitesell (2008, 3) positions his Joni Mitchell monograph as a solution to the prevalence of attention to only her lyrics in the popular press. His book addresses various stylistic, lyrical, and compositional features of Mitchell's songs. In *Chronicles* (2004, 119), Dylan complains about critical attention paid only to his lyrics, arguing that his "songs were more than just words." Neal's (2002) music-theoretical work on Jimmie Rodgers explores his irregular phrase structure and hypermeter alongside lyrical narratives as important and original features of Rodgers's song structure.

10   TIMES A-CHANGIN'

flexible meter in these performances are critical features of the poetics of self-expression in 1960s and 1970s singer-songwriter music.

In the next two sections of this chapter, I explore some general features of self-expression in singer-songwriter music and then focus on the flexible metric features of the five singer-songwriters that form the core of this study: Joni Mitchell, Bob Dylan, Buffy Sainte-Marie, Cat Stevens, and Paul Simon. In the first section I explore the concept of self-expression in connection with the emergence of the term "singer-songwriter" in the 1960s and 1970s. This discussion points out some of the general trends of singer-songwriter music during this period and the features of self-expression—particularly self-presentation, lyrics, and vocal production—that we might expect from artists labeled as singer-songwriters. In the second section I focus on the flexible meter of the artists in this study by positioning Bob Dylan as a central figure in the development of metrically flexible singer-songwriter music. Dylan occupies a unique position as an emerging songwriter, whose immersion in the folk-revival styles of the early twentieth century resulted in a malleable metric rhetoric that was both new and embedded in a music-historical dialogue. In developing a musical style in the spirit of his influences, one that gives the impression of his music being truly "authentic" and "unmediated," Dylan helped to develop techniques of metric flexibility that permeate the singer-songwriter music of the five artists in this study. Although many resources cover topics from both of these sections in depth, this overview recasts these discussions through the lens of flexible meter and provides context for the individual expressive styles explored in the chapters that follow.

Self-Expression and the Singer-Songwriter

The term "singer-songwriter" arose in the late 1960s as a way to describe solo, acoustic artists who, like Joni Mitchell, wrote and performed their own music on topics of personal significance.[22] Scholars suggest that Bob Dylan, Paul Simon, and Joni Mitchell were among the first, most well-known artists

---

[22] As I explore further, several of these artists (particularly Dylan, Mitchell, Sainte-Marie, and Simon) came to be known for their original compositions and began their careers by adapting traditional songwriting, typically in coffeehouse performances.

to whom the label singer-songwriter was applied in an attempt to capture the distinct "aesthetic space" inhabited by these artists, defined neither as commercial pop stars, nor as "high culture" composers.[23] As a type of popular music, singer-songwriter music was intended for public or private listening, rather than dancing, and it valorized "literate verbal texts and individual expressive styles" designed within a flexible musical setting that encouraged listeners' attention to the subtleties of song construction.[24]

The 1960s Protest Song

In the 1960s, this expressive personal songwriting was linked to communal issues, politics, and social justice, which continued the American folk tradition of community engagement. In the early twentieth century, the pro-union songs of artists like Pete Seeger and Woody Guthrie modeled this type of political songwriting that included adaptations of traditional songs for social-justice causes. Songwriters like Bob Dylan began contributing work to this folk canon in the form of "topical protest songs" like his "Oxford Town" and "The Lonesome Death of Hattie Carroll," among others, that addressed civil-rights issues at the time of their writing and release.[25] Dylan also wrote songs like "The Times They Are A-Changin'" that more enigmatically captured the public sentiment about cultural change in this decade. Singer-songwriter lyrics responded to the emerging countercultural ideologies of the 1960s, which were themselves a reaction to 1950s ideas about race, sex, and gender roles. Many viewed this music as commentary on the confusing political climate of this time, in some ways reflecting the emotional needs of the public consciousness.

With these songs offering new ideas and perspectives, listeners began looking to singer-songwriters for commentary on social events.

[23] See Whitesell (2008, 7) and Bennighof (2007, xi). Retrospectively, the singer-songwriter designation was assigned more broadly to include artists as far back as the early twentieth century, including Delta bluesmen like Son House and Robert Johnson and country singer Jimmie Rodgers.

[24] Whitesell (2008, 7).

[25] Bentley (2016a, 417) sees singer-songwriters growing out of the folk revival, a period that "invested in maintaining American vernacular music practices." Bentley cites the "wave of artists interested in contributing original compositions to the folk canon" as the branch of the folk revival from which the singer-songwriter movement emerged. Artists like Joan Baez, who revived traditional folk songs like "We Shall Overcome," demonstrated the communal aesthetic of the period but did not contribute original compositions. For more on Dylan's early protest songs see Harvey (2001).

12 TIMES A-CHANGIN'

At the 1963 March on Washington, audiences could hear Dylan sing "Only a Pawn in Their Game," which offered a new perspective on the racist murder of civil-rights leader Medgar Evers. At Greenwich Village coffeehouses, audiences could find the Cree singer Buffy Sainte-Marie performing antiwar songs like "Universal Soldier" and hear lyrics protesting the mistreatment of Indigenous people in North America.[26] Songs like "Now That the Buffalo's Gone," her first widely popular Native American protest song, offered an education to her listeners by objecting to "the hypocrisy of Americans who lamented the nation's past injustices while allowing current ones" against Indigenous people.[27] On Paul Simon's 1965 solo album *The Paul Simon Songbook*, listeners could also hear Simon try out some protest songwriting.[28] While the whole album showcases a stripped-down singer-songwriter aesthetic, with quiet acoustic guitar accompaniment and solo singing, it also shows Simon experimenting with topical and antiwar protest music on the tracks "A Church Is Burning" and "The Side of a Hill."[29] Alongside songs like Mitchell's "The Fiddle and the Drum," topical protest songs acted as vehicles for these artists to express their opinions about issues important to them and their audiences during the 1960s.

[26] Sainte-Marie was born in 1941 on the Piapot Cree First Nations reserve in the Canadian province of Saskatchewan before being adopted by an American family (of Mi'kmaq descent) in Massachusetts. She later rediscovered her Indigenous heritage with a return to the Canadian reserve in 1964. Her work as a social advocate has always included Indigenous rights. For more on Sainte-Marie's biography, see Stonechild (2012) and Warner (2018). Shelton's (1963) review of Sainte-Marie's performance at the Gaslight Cafe describes her as "one of the most promising new talents on the folk scene" with songs that "are impressive musically as well as for revealing the world-awareness of the writer."

[27] Stonechild (2012, 11). Sainte-Marie wrote several other songs criticizing American mistreatment of Indigenous people, including "My Country 'Tis of Thy People You're Dying" (explored in Chapter 6), which borrows text and melody from the American patriotic song "My Country 'Tis of Thee" to point out the "genocide basic to this country's birth" and the hypocrisy of teaching that American history began with the arrival of European colonists. In her *Village Voice* interview (2017), Sainte-Marie said she prefers to call these songs "Activist Songs," which "spell out solutions," instead of protest songs, which in her view only "spell out problems."

[28] By 1965, Simon was not yet a household name. His 1964 album with Art Garfunkel (*Wednesday Morning, 3 A.M.*) was initially unsuccessful until the overdubbed "folk rock" version of "The Sound of Silence" was released (without the duo's knowledge) in 1965, while Simon was touring in England. For more on the history of this song, see Stephan-Robinson (2009, 4).

[29] Simon's self-accompanied singer-songwriter period was relatively brief compared to the other artists in this study. His later work with Garfunkel is classified in a folk-rock genre that includes fewer cases of flexible meter. Several scholars, including Russell (1997, 595), credit the influence of folk revivalists, particularly Bob Dylan's "poetic invention and social commentary," with the shift in Simon's songwriting from "bouncy pop music" of his early days in the duo Tom and Jerry, to "the troubling events of the civil rights movement."

1970s Introspective Songwriting

In the 1970s, there was a shift away from protest songwriting (from which Dylan himself had already departed in the mid-1960s) to a more introspective or "confessional" songwriting mode. This change in singer-songwriter music aligned with a broader cultural shift in American thought at the turn of the decade, from the communalist ideology of the 1960s to the rise of individualism in the 1970s.[30] Many sources cite the folk period as one of musical and stylistic growth for singer-songwriters, but point to the confessional period as the archetype of singer-songwriter music.[31] It is in this latter category that Joni Mitchell's songwriting is more typically situated, with her 1971 album *Blue* positioned as the zenith of confessional songwriting. Her first-person songs like "All I Want," "A Case of You," and "Blue" are thought to be autobiographical accounts of her romantic history.[32] Listeners feel a sense of being let in on Mitchell's personal secrets when listening to her introspective songwriting.

It was in this 1970s confessional songwriting period that Cat Stevens found a re-entry into the music industry after his career as a young pop star and a year-long hiatus from the industry to recover from tuberculosis.[33] He reappeared in 1970 and released three albums in the first two years of the new decade—*Mona Bone Jakon* (1970a), *Tea for the Tillerman* (1970b), and *Teaser and the Firecat* (1971)—with songs that "perfectly caught the mood" of the beginning of the 1970s.[34] His song "Peace Train" (from *Teaser and the Firecat*) became an anthem for his audiences, and songs like "The Wind," "Into White," and "Time" reflected Stevens's new, more introspective and

---

[30] Bentley (2016b, iii) views singer-songwriter music from this lens of it reflecting a cultural history. She proposes that the musical aesthetic of confessional singer-songwriter music that promoted self-reflection "encapsulated the rise of individualism" in the 1970s. For an investigation of "first-person music" and the influence of psychological trends (like Arthur Janov's book, *Primal Therapy*) on 1970s rock, see Tochka (2020).

[31] Shumway (2016, 11) suggests that "the category and perception of a class of performers known as singer-songwriters did not emerge into public consciousness until after 1968" with "no usage prior to the early 1970s"; his work associates this songwriting practice with a direct address. Bentley (2016b, 137–252) defines singer-songwriters as established in the confessional songwriting movement in 1970s Los Angeles, particularly in Laurel Canyon. Her work investigates "discourses of authenticity surrounding the singer-songwriter as intimate, vulnerable, and personal," associated with social movements like second-wave feminism and resistance against the Vietnam War.

[32] In some cases, the romantic subjects of her songs have been identified. For example, "Willy" is believed to address her relationship with CSNY's Graham Nash (O'Brien 2001, 110); "A Case of You" was reportedly inspired by Canadian poet and songwriter Leonard Cohen (Monk 2012, 146).

[33] For more on Stevens's background, see Islam (2014).

[34] Yentob (2006).

14 TIMES A-CHANGIN'

religious philosophies. In Mitchell's and Stevens's confessional songwriting, listeners got the impression that these songs were expressing the inner self, with performances as acts of self-expression.

Expectations for Singer-Songwriter Music

Applying the label of singer-songwriter to artists in the 1960s and 1970s implies a set of criteria for how their music will sound and what it might offer to its listeners. The term typically designates a self-accompanied musical texture with artists performing original songs that contain lyrics of some significance to themselves and their listeners. The term is associated in particular with an aesthetic of musical self-expression that generates an empathetic response with audiences and gives the impression of an "authentic" and "unmediated" performance practice in which songs are vehicles for personal truths. To label an artist as a singer-songwriter creates expectations that their music will offer "authentic" self-expression.

Self-Expression

These last two terms deserve a little unpacking here. I have thus far used "self-expression" to signal an impression that these artists are sharing something of themselves in performance. My use of the term relates to how it is explored in Mitchell S. Green's book *Self-Expression*, in which he describes it as a showing of thought, feeling, or experience that is either voluntary or spontaneous and that signals a cognitive, affective, or qualitative state that can only otherwise be known through introspection.[35] Green's definition is helpful in that it draws out the communicative importance of self-expression without exclusively relying on conscious intention on the part of (in this case) the performer. This allows for the possibility that techniques of self-expression in singer-songwriter music like flexible meter could occur as a spontaneous event, potentially in response to sentiments that a song's lyrics and meaning might evoke.[36]

[35] Green (2007, 38–39).
[36] That said, some instances of flexible meter seem pre-planned and occur in identical ways in multiple performances of a song. This is the case with "The Sound of Silence," as I explore more in Chapter 3.

THE SELF-EXPRESSIVE RHETORIC OF FLEXIBLE METER   15

The Impression of Authenticity

But what might it mean for these musical acts of self-expression to be "authentic"? A short answer is that we can never be sure that they are. Musical performance is, after all, a performance, and these artists, however authentic their acts of performance may seem, are entertainers. (Of course, this is not how folk revivalists in the 1960s viewed musical performance: the commercial success of the mainstream entertainment industry is antithetical to folk music values.[37]) A longer answer to the question of what makes artists and their music seem authentic has been explored in various popular music studies, and I will not reproduce the entirety of that discussion here. But from the perspective of singer-songwriter music, there are a few central components that relate to the four features explored earlier (self-presentation, personal lyrics, vocal production, and flexible meter) that project an authenticity of self-expression in this music.

"Authenticity" in Popular Music

As a first step, it is worth summarizing what some popular music sources have to say about the perception of authenticity in singer-songwriter music. For Simon Frith, authenticity in popular music denotes a type of realism that goes beyond simply using first-person perspectives in song lyrics. In this view, artists like Bob Dylan, who drew from "classic balladry, from the beat poets, from 150 years of Bohemian romantic verse," ushered in a welcome change from the "lyrical banality" of rock music stemming from the Tin Pan Alley songwriting tradition.[38] Frith indicates that repertoire like Dylan's improved popular music lyrics, particularly because of its connections to "authentic," self-expressive folk traditions.

> This was to suggest a new criterion of realism—truth-to-personal experience or truth-to feeling, a truth measured by the private use of words, the self-conscious use of language. And truth-to-feeling became a measure of the listener too . . . Alan Lomax had once written that the "authentic"

---

[37] Bentley (2016b, 51) notes that Joan Baez's career, for example, was a paragon of valuing political commitment over commercial success, with the artist reportedly turning down $100,000 worth of concert dates in one year in favor of touring mostly on college campuses.

[38] Frith (1988, 117).

16 TIMES A-CHANGIN'

folk singer had to "experience the feelings behind his art" . . . the good rock singer made the listener experience those feelings too.[39]

This commentary valorizes the self-expressive possibilities of a tradition like singer-songwriter music, the lyrics of which seemed to allow artists to communicate realism to their audiences.

When authenticity arises in discussions of post-1950s popular music, it often occurs with some reference to singer-songwriter music. For example, in Allan Moore's discussion of authenticity in rock, he clarifies the term by relating it to the singer-songwriter tradition.

> In rock discourse, the term [authenticity] has frequently been used to define a *style* of writing or performing, particularly anything associated with the practices of the singer/songwriter, where attributes of intimacy (just Joni Mitchell and her zither) and immediacy (in the sense of unmediated forms of sound production) tend to connote authenticity.[40]

Moore's definition highlights the typical melody-and-accompaniment texture of singer-songwriter music and references mediation—in the sense that singer-songwriter music seems unmediated—as an important feature of how authenticity is perceived in singer-songwriter music.

The unmediated sound production Moore references denotes the typical acoustic accompaniment of this repertoire. This texture gives the impression that there is a direct line of communication between the artist and audience, not mediated by the technologies necessary for genres like rock music that might use electric guitars and synthesizers. But of course, technology mediates all forms of popular music. In many cases technological interventions are necessary to disseminate music to audiences, whether that be through amplification in coffeehouses and concerts, or through the recording equipment used to create studio albums, or through the headphones and speakers that listeners use to hear this music at home. But the *impression* is one of direct address, of the singer-songwriter sharing something of themselves with their listeners without any mediation. This impression is so prevalent in singer-songwriter music that it is often considered central to the perception of authenticity from artists labeled as singer-songwriters.

[39] Frith (1988, 118).
[40] Moore (2001, 11).

Performance locations can also contribute to the perception of unmediated performance. Christa Anne Bentley's work on the Troubadour night club in Los Angeles argues that the club venue's size fostered an intimate environment between artist and audience.[41] With the club being such an important venue for Los Angeles singer-songwriters, its intimacy resulted in the conception of the term singer-songwriter becoming "imbued with meanings based on audience perceptions of intimate performance, storytelling, an artist's vulnerability, and a sense of immediacy between the listener and the artist's persona."[42] She cites 1970s artists like Joni Mitchell, James Taylor, Jackson Browne, and Carole King as examples of California-based, confessional singer-songwriters who offer signals about these meanings through the club's venue alongside musical features like lyrics, visual cues, and individual self-expressive styles.

"Authenticity" in Singer-Songwriter Music

Bentley's conception of a singer-songwriter brings up ideas of intimacy and immediacy that are in many ways determined by location, mediation, and texture. Conceptions of storytelling and vulnerability are in dialogue with the self-expressive features explored in the beginning of this chapter and are important to the impression of authenticity in singer-songwriter music. For these artists to be perceived as trustworthy narrators, they must project an "aura of authenticity" in performance that helps to persuade their audiences that the self-expressive features of their performances are believable.[43] In other words, in addition to *what* they say in these performances, there is import to *how* they say it. Their rhetoric must persuade audiences that their musical utterances are truly self-expressive. In addition to the features of self-expression discussed earlier, one of the ways that this perception of authenticity was established in singer-songwriter music was through connections to traditional sources in the folk revival that were widely considered "authentic" expressive acts. Since Bob Dylan was a key figure in the transition of folk-song performance to singer-songwriter music, I will turn now to an

---

[41] Bentley (2016a)

[42] Bentley (2016a, 79).

[43] Everett (2009b, 381) describes singer-songwriter music as projecting an "aura of authenticity" because their songs derived "from a gut-produced extension of true values without either the commercial potential that comes with writing credit or the chintz of artificial overproduction."

18   TIMES A-CHANGIN'

exploration of his positioning during this period and how the rhetoric of self-expressive metric flexibility likely found its way into singer-songwriter music through Dylan and his many traditional musical influences.[44]

Bob Dylan and the Folk Revival

In the early 1960s, Bob Dylan occupied a unique position in the folk revival at the intersection of adapted and original songwriting.[45] Dylan was a "sponge" for traditional styles like ballads, old-time, country, and the Delta blues within the Greenwich Village coffeehouse scene.[46] Yet Dylan's early self-expressive style might have been as inauthentic as possible. His mimicry of Woody Guthrie's nasal vocal techniques and hillbilly clothing resulted in an enigmatic self-presentation that was at best a misrepresentation of Dylan's middle-class, Minnesota upbringing or at worst was an attempt to intentionally hide it entirely in favor of fashioning himself as the logical heir to the musical traditions of his Southern idols.[47] Yet, somewhat ironically, Dylan's resulting "aesthetic of imperfection" became part of a broader "shambolic" performance style that audiences viewed as signaling the singer's authenticity.[48]

Regardless of intent, Dylan's adoption of the musical styles of artists like Guthrie situated him in dialogue with these seemingly authentic folk

[44] While many scholars (especially Harvey 2001) examine Dylan's influences during his "formative period," few acknowledge the impact of flexible meter on his unique self-expressive style. One exception is Ford (2012). There are some brief mentions of Dylan's metric style in some early reviews, alongside commentary about general features of the singer's shambolic performance style. For example, in Shelton's (1961) *New York Times* review of Dylan's performance at Gertie's Folk City, the critic describes Dylan's "messy hair" and loose-fitting clothing. Shelton evaluates the singer's voice as "anything but pretty" and notes the flexibly timed and improvisational aspects of the song performances, including "elasticized phrases" that are "drawn out until you think they may snap." He positions these features of Dylan's music as markers of the singer's emerging talent.

[45] Scholars note a development of the singer-songwriter movement from the American folk revival. Bentley (2016b, 417) suggests that it was from the period of maintaining American vernacular music that inspired artists to contribute original compositions to the folk canon, and thus the singer-songwriter movement emerged.

[46] Harvey (2001) traces the source material for the songs in Dylan's "formative" period as stemming from songs in these musical traditions. Harvey notes sources from the Child Ballads, Harry Smith's *Anthology of American Folk Music* (1997), country singers like Jimmie Rodgers, and bluesmen like Blind Lemon Jefferson, among others.

[47] Rings (2013, [34]) discusses Dylan's vocal production as influenced by Guthrie. *Newsweek* (1963) criticized Dylan for embellishing his personal history. Harvey (2001) suggests that songs like "Restless Farewell" can be viewed as Dylan reacting to this article. I explore this song and its lyrics as a response to *Newsweek* in Chapter 5.

[48] Rings (2013, [3]), citing Gracyk (2006) and Gioia (1998).

THE SELF-EXPRESSIVE RHETORIC OF FLEXIBLE METER   19

traditions. In the process, Dylan was knowingly or not adopting an unpredictable metric style. On his debut album (*Bob Dylan*, 1962), nearly every case of flexible meter can be tied to a traditional source. In the song "Talkin' New York," for example, Dylan mimics the talking blues style he absorbed from listening to Guthrie's music.[49] His rhythms are mostly regular, but then beats are added and omitted in unexpected places, enlivening the repetitive strophic song form.[50] This metric unpredictability was a standard practice of talking blues songs that Dylan likely learned by studying and copying Guthrie's performing techniques.[51]

The Ballad Tradition

But Guthrie was not the only source for Dylan's adoption of a flexible metric practice. Another likely influence was the British and American ballad tradition, which was a central thread of the New York City folk revival.[52] The metric irregularity that Dylan adopted from these songs was viewed as an important feature of ballad singing.[53] For example, in Olive Dame Campbell and Cecil Sharp's early twentieth-century collection of Appalachian ballads, Sharp's introduction to the collection notes the practice of mountain singers disrupting metric regularity through techniques of spontaneous variation

---

[49] For more detail about "Talkin' New York" in connection to Guthrie's talking blues, see Murphy (2015, 82–86).

[50] A similar flexibility occurs in "I Shall Be Free No. 10" from *Another Side of Bob Dylan* (1964b) in which Dylan rambles through seemingly improvised lyrics and prolongs certain harmonies in his I–IV–V–I progression with added beats in unexpected places.

[51] He may also have learned this technique of strophic song variation through the suggestions in Pete Seeger's introduction to the Woody Guthrie songbook *From California to the New York Island*. Dylan's copy of the book included a highlighted passage in which Seeger notes a practice of American ballad singers holding melody notes in "unexpected places" with a continuation of even-tempo guitar strumming. Seeger notes that such irregularities add beats to measures but also add interest to strophic song performance, ensuring "no two verses sounded alike." The highlighted passage in Dylan's copy is reproduced in Heylin (2001, 82) and referenced in Rings (2013). In Murphy (2018), I note that this practice of holding out long notes over a continuation in the accompaniment creates composed-out (or performed-out) fermatas that were common to the folk revival and included in several of Dylan's songs, like "Man of Constant Sorrow" and "I Shall Be Free No. 10."

[52] For Dylan's *Bob Dylan* sessions, he recorded the Child ballad (No. 243) "The House Carpenter," which is also featured on Harry Smith's *Anthology of American Folk Music*. Harvey (2001, 44) notes this was recorded in Session II for the album and later included on *The Bootleg Series* and suggests that Dylan's version had no single source, but was an amalgam of "elements easily accessible to folk revivalists."

[53] Dylan's recording of "Gospel Plow" on his debut album was his version of this song from the Child ballads.

for compelling effects.[54] He describes these techniques as charming, fascinating, and "magical," suggesting that there is something beyond just interest that is created when metric flexibility occurs.[55]

The Delta Blues

These expressive possibilities of flexible meter are never more prominent than when they occur in the Delta blues repertoire, another of Dylan's major influences in the 1960s. As commercial recordings from the early twentieth-century blues became more widely available, the folk revivalists incorporated Delta blues songs into their repertoire at coffeehouse performances. In Dylan's adapted versions, he retains the flexible metric style of the bluesmen he most admired. On his debut album, he includes songs he credits to fixtures in the Delta blues tradition: Bukka White's "Fixin' to Die" and Blind Lemon Jefferson's "See That My Grave Is Kept Clean." In both songs, we can hear the influence of the flexible blues rhetoric, with loose phrase structures that seem to suggest Dylan was so wrapped up in his self-expressive vocal performance that he neglected to keep time.

Yet "keeping time" does not seem to be a requirement for the Delta blues. Indeed, some studies of this blues music position metric flexibility as occurring because of just this: an "authentic" lack of attention to counting. Ted Gioia, for example, proposes that metric irregularities arose in the Delta blues because a practice of self-expression within that genre that ignores precise counting in favor of concentrating on sentiment. He suggests,

> ... the Delta blues players ... who rarely counted "correctly" in their songs, adding or subtracting beats from the supposed twelve-bar structure ... nonetheless maintained an ineffable rightness in their *feeling* for the music.[56]

While it is still possible to evoke this kind of "feeling" in music with regular meter, there is a frequent correlation between metric irregularity and self-expression in the Delta blues repertoire.

---

[54] Campbell and Sharp (1917, x) mention that the improvisatory disruptions to regular meter helped to break up the "monotonous regularity of the phrases" and produced a "freedom from rule which is very pleasing." In this passage, Sharp references the eight transcriptions of the song "The Wife of Usher's Well" (No. 19 in the collection), seven of which contain metric irregularities.

[55] Campbell and Sharp (1917, x).

[56] Gioia (2008, 11).

The irregular meter in the Delta blues is among several markers of authenticity in this repertoire that can be found in Dylan's early 1960s recordings, alongside other stylistic features like a rough vocal production, mistakes in performance, and so on. As Gioia notes, these features of blues production are not "inadequacies" or "limitations to be lamented," but are instead "rather inseparable from their brilliance."[57] Indeed, the features of metric imperfection in blues performance were praised as markers of authentic self-expression in the genre, later adopted by artists like Bob Dylan in the folk revival. This adoption was likely motivated in part by admiration but could also have been a deliberate attempt at self-positioning, with Dylan seeking to connect his output with "authentic" performance traditions. He followed his peers in exploring these traditions and absorbed features of their seemingly authentic performances, like flexible meter, into his own original songwriting.

Flexible Meter as Self-Expression in Singer-Songwriter Music

Throughout this study, I position the presence of flexible meter in singer-songwriter music as the result of self-expressive decisions. But I do not mean this to suggest these decisions were always intentional. Some of the nuances of flexible meter in singer-songwriter music are coordinated, pre-planned structures, and some are the result of spur-of-the-moment decisions, subject to the whims of a particular performer. Since it is often difficult and sometimes impossible to differentiate between planning and spontaneity, I focus my attention on the effect—how the resulting timings convey ideas about self-expression. That said, there may be some conscious intention on the part of these artists to have included flexible meter both as a technique of self-expression *and* as a way to align their output with self-expressive traditions. In Bob Dylan's case, flexible meter highlights lyrical meaning and also marks his music as "authentic" through a dialogue with precedents in the self-expressive traditions of the folk revival.

A similar dialogue is occurring with Joni Mitchell's "The Fiddle and the Drum." The flexible meter in her performances of this song signifies her

---

[57] Gioia (2008, 73).

22 TIMES A-CHANGIN'

connection with the solo, self-expressive genres like folk and ballad singing that preceded her appearance on The Dick Cavett Show. The timings are marked as authentic and self-expressive because of the network of signifiers they engage, which position Mitchell in dialogue with previous "authentic" musical traditions. In other words, her use of flexible meter in "The Fiddle and the Drum" connects it to techniques of self-expression already deemed "authentic" in other genres. Flexible meter signals that Mitchell's self-expressive performance is "authentic" as well. It is not meter alone that does this work. But examining flexible meter as a signifier of authentic self-expression establishes its importance as a marker of inclusion in the singer-songwriter tradition.[58]

Political and Confessional Singer-Songwriter Music

The five singer-songwriters at the center of this study—Dylan, Sainte-Marie, Simon, Mitchell, and Stevens—each adopted self-expressive features of the singer-songwriter style that found precedents in the traditional music in the folk revival. Dylan and Mitchell represent two broad categories of self-expressive singer-songwriter music. The first, with Dylan as the representative, includes music either adapting or drawing from traditional sources with political or topical themes, and incorporating metric flexibility both as a dialogue with stylistic influences and as a way to signal an authentic performance practice. The second is exemplified by Mitchell's confessional songwriting period, with lyrics seeming to reveal personal truths in performances with rhapsodic timing flexibilities. The other singer-songwriters in this study with self-expressive metric flexibility are in some ways in dialogue with this two-part organization. Stevens, for example, includes metric flexibility in songs on his 1970s introspective albums that demonstrate some awareness of the emerging confessional songwriting traditions and the self-expressive rhetoric therein. Sainte-Marie's flexible meter occurs in her folk-song adaptations, on the same albums as her most popular political songwriting. (Interestingly,

---

[58] Moore (2001, 182) suggests that for self-expression to be meaningful for the listener, it must be encoded in a way that is interpretable by the listener, with a clear system of signs "between the listeners' interpretation and the performers' intention." But he acknowledges that interactions between the performer and listener are mediated by the "ephemerality" of music, the interpretation of lyrics, and interventions of popular music production. He concludes that communication is not guaranteed between the performer and listener.

THE SELF-EXPRESSIVE RHETORIC OF FLEXIBLE METER 23

malleable meter rarely occurs in her political song performances beyond an expressively timed regular meter.) Simon is known mostly as not performing solo, gaining prominence in his work with Art Garfunkel. Simon's metric rhetoric is limited to a few songs that are shared between his 1965 album *The Paul Simon Songbook* and Simon & Garfunkel records. There is evidence to suggest that he was influenced by Dylan's music and likely absorbed a flexible metric rhetoric from him and the surrounding genres that also influenced Dylan's work.[59]

For each artist, their metrically flexible singer-songwriter period encompasses a different span between 1962 and 1972. For Dylan, flexible meter mostly occurs on his early albums, between 1962 and 1965. Simon's metric flexibility is short-lived, centering around his 1965 solo album. Sainte-Marie includes metric flexibility on songs from her 1964 debut album until 1969. Stevens's flexible meter occurs on his 1970 and 1971 albums, and Mitchell's ranges from her 1969 debut to 1972's *For the Roses*, peaking on her 1971 album *Blue*.

In all of these cases, the move away from malleable meter in singer-songwriter music corresponds to the inclusion of more instruments. Though it is possible to have metric irregularity in ensemble performances, it does not seem to continue in work by these artists beyond the early 1970s.[60] Flexible meter as self-expression arises as a unique feature of this solo-performance tradition. Or to put this another way, timing flexibility is an essential component of the self-expressive rhetoric of solo singer-songwriter music of this era.

***

In the preceding discussion, I position the five singer-songwriters in this study as innovators in developing new techniques of self-expression in singer-songwriter music. While critical attention is paid to the performance persona, lyrics, and (to a somewhat lesser degree) vocal production of these

---

[59] Dylan's influence on Simon is indicated by explicit references to the former in Simon's parody song "A Simple Desultory Philippic (or How I Was Lyndon Johnson'd into Submission)," first recorded on *The Paul Simon Songbook*. The song imitates Dylan's early style, perhaps, as Brackett (1995, 166) suggests, a parody of Dylan's "Subterranean Homesick Blues," which also features a "rapid-fire succession of ultra-short rhyming phrases" and a nasal vocal timbre.

[60] Chapter 6 explores one exception to this in Sainte-Marie's repertoire, when she revives and intensifies her flexible metric rhetoric for a performance of "My Country 'Tis of Thy People You're Dying" for her 2017 album *Medicine Songs*. Examples of irregular meter in ensemble performances also occur in other repertoires. For example, Everett (2009a) explores metric irregularity (in the form of "free" phrase rhythms) in the Beatles' repertoire.

24 TIMES A-CHANGIN'

artists, few scholars are concerned with the techniques of their musical rhetoric.

In Chapter 2, I offer the theory of flexible meter as a solution to the challenges to metric analysis that singer-songwriter music presents. To investigate flexible meter in this repertoire necessitates that my work be in dialogue with theories of meter that are designed for Western art-music, which have more recently been applied to popular repertoires.[61] But the self-expressive metric extremes present a change for metric analysis because no single metric theory accounts for all of the meter this music presents. The theory of flexible meter asks what happens when metric theory can respond to the timings of the singer-songwriter repertoire. With flexible meter, metric cues (stressed events in the voice and accompaniment) are shared by all possible metric scenarios. When singer-songwriters shift their performance timings, these shifts can be understood as a tightening or loosening of those cues. Flexible meter allows for a precise understanding of the techniques of metric disruption (of the metric "imperfection" offered by this repertoire) that signal the broader aesthetic of the intimate and imperfect singer-songwriter performance practice.[62]

This second chapter outlines the methodology for flexible meter first through an interrogation of the components of existing metric theories and how they address or do not address self-expressive metric ambiguity. I draw together theories of regular metric hierarchy, metrical reinterpretation, metric entrainment, and meter as process, to propose a new theory that accounts for metric contexts of more extreme ambiguity in connection with the self-expressive singer-songwriter performance practice.[63] I then propose five types of flexible meter, which account for *Ideal, Regular, Reinterpreted, Lost,* and *Ambiguous Meter.* The singer-songwriter repertoire may engage one of these metric types at a time, may shift from regularity to ambiguity, or may shift from ambiguity to regularity, demonstrating an emerging meter. The type of flexible meter or the vacillation between types has important impacts on self-expression in the singer-songwriter repertoire.

---

[61] Notable applications of existing metric theory to popular music include, but are not limited to, Biamonte (2014), Butler (2001), Attas (2015), Butterfield (2006), and Rockwell (2011).

[62] Rings (2013, [3]) cites several scholars who define an "aesthetic of imperfection" surrounding Dylan's performance practice, which is often "lauded by fans as a marker of authenticity."

[63] A similar fusion of metric theories arises in Mirka (2009) and Rockwell (2011), but they account for a narrower range of metric possibilities.

In Chapter 3, I examine the prevalence of Reinterpreted Meter in this singer-songwriter repertoire as a signal of metric influence and self-expressive style. I offer one example of Regular Meter through a brief examination of Joni Mitchell's song "Little Green" and how her 1971 studio recording demonstrates metric highlighting of a covert narrative meaning. I then proceed to the chapter's main focus: Reinterpreted Meter, which shows how the stylistic metric flexibility in this repertoire demonstrates a self-expressive performance practice. My analyses in this chapter modify existing theories of metrical reinterpretation to account for two irregular structures in these songs: extra strumming (added beats) to an otherwise regular meter, which offers time for reflection; or removed strumming (omitted beats), which forces the narrative forward. In their inclusion of metrical reinterpretations, the singer-songwriters in this chapter—Mitchell, Simon, and Stevens—highlight important moments in their song narratives and signal their broadly flexible, self-expressive performance practice.

In Chapter 4, I analyze singer-songwriter music that showcases the loosening of metric cues that results in Lost Meter. These examples from Dylan, Stevens, and Mitchell offer some metric regularity, but they thwart these structures with passages so flexible that the perception of Regular Meter is temporarily lost. I position these techniques of metric disruption as these artists taking the structures of metrical reinterpretation to extremes in an exploration of rhapsodic, unpredictable, and intentionally disruptive performance practices. I examine technical timing details through the lens of flexible meter, determining how metric regularity is established, lost, and eventually restored. These techniques of metric flexibility demonstrate that these singer-songwriters are taking metric precedents to extremes in their development of individual expressive styles in performance.

The final analytic chapter, Chapter 5, demonstrates the loosest metric type offered by the rhetorically flexible meter in singer-songwriter music: Ambiguous Meter. In this type of flexible meter, timing is too extreme to create a regular, multi-leveled metric hierarchy; the rhetorical denial of metric regularity results in highly Ambiguous metric contexts. In this chapter I analyze four songs by three artists—Dylan, Mitchell, and Sainte-Marie—to show how each songwriter adapts source material and influences in order to create contexts of self-expressive Ambiguous Meter. For each song, I explore how passages of extreme metric ambiguity and vagueness reflect individual self-expressive narratives of introspection and politics and a broader fashioning of performance persona.

26 TIMES A-CHANGIN'

In the concluding chapter (Chapter 6), I synthesize the importance of flexible meter as self-expression in this formative singer-songwriter period between 1962 and 1972. I propose that the extremes of metric flexibility showcased during this decade are not carried forward as stylistic metric features of mainstream English language singer-songwriter music.[64] Subsequent trends in the singer-songwriter tradition generally do not engage with the levels of metric flexibility beyond expressively timed regular meter in service of highlighting personal lyrics. The presence of flexible meter in the 1960s and 1970s is, therefore, a unique feature of this formative singer-songwriter period in popular music.

Though flexible meter falls out of favor when singer-songwriters routinely prefer ensemble textures, it is always available to these artists as an option for self-expressive performance. By way of example, I offer a brief analysis of Buffy Sainte-Marie's flexible rhetoric in her 2017 version of the 1966 solo song "My Country 'Tis of Thy People You're Dying." Her 1966 performances of the song include flexible timing, with Lost Meter in the first verse giving way to expressively timed Regular Meter for the rest of the song. The impression that her self-expressive features give is one of barely repressed fury at the acts of abuse against Native Americans that she recounts in her lyrics. Her 2017 rewrite of the song shifts the perspective to the ways that Canada has oppressed its Indigenous population. Whether or not lyrics about her birth country stirred something in Sainte-Marie's recording, the 2017 version of the song takes the 1966 timings to extremes, pushing and pulling to breaking points. With this example, I show the powerful expressive impact of more flexible meter added to singer-songwriter performance: how it can shape the impact of lyrical reception and vocal techniques, and of our understanding of singer-songwriter persona of some of the most important socio-musical voices of the 1960s and 1970s.

This study will investigate the details of singer-songwriter performances to illustrate the techniques by which they use flexible meter for self-expression. It examines aspects from the four main features of self-expression in this repertoire, but its primary aim is to position flexible meter as a critical component of the rhetoric of self-expression in music by these five artists between 1962 and 1972.

---

[64] For this I mainly focus on popular music from the United States, the United Kingdom, and Canada.

2

The Theory of Flexible Meter

In this chapter, I introduce the theory of flexible meter as a solution to the issues that arise when analyzing meter and timing in songs like Joni Mitchell's "The Fiddle and the Drum." This theory asks some important questions about what a theory of meter can include. What happens when metric theory can respond to all of the timings in the self-expressive singer-songwriter repertoire? How can metric theory account for meter that is more malleable than theories currently accommodate? What can such a theory do to conceptualize ambiguity and vagueness not as devoid of meter but as related to regularity, as the metric equivalent of continental drift? The theory of flexible meter recasts metric structure as having the *potential* to shift between predictable regularity and unpredictable ambiguity. With flexible meter, metric cues are shared by all possible metric scenarios. When singer-songwriters shift their performance timings, these shifts can be understood as a tightening or loosening of those cues. Flexible meter allows for a precise understanding of the techniques of metric disruption (metric "imperfection") offered by this repertoire that signal the broader aesthetic of the seemingly authentic, intimate, and imperfect singer-songwriter performance practice.

Types of Flexible Meter

To build a theory of meter that responds to the flexibility of the singer-songwriter repertoire, I must follow Wallace Berry's proposal that "meter is *not* to be equated with regularity, so that metric fluctuation, however extreme is not 'meterlessness.'"[1] Certainly, some of Berry's point with this statement was to acknowledge standard timing fluctuations in performance that fall under the category of expressive timing or *tempo rubato*.[2] But his proposal

---

[1] Berry (1976, 318).

[2] For more on expressive timing as a critical concept, see Ohriner (2019). For studies of expressive timing in connection to hypermeter, see Dodson (2002) and Dodson (2011); for dialogue between timing and grouping, see Dodson (2008) and Ohriner (2012); and for work on expressive timing and tactus, see Martens (2011) and Martens (2012).

Times A-Changin'. Nancy Murphy, Oxford University Press. © Oxford University Press 2023.
DOI: 10.1093/oso/9780197635216.003.0002

28 TIMES A-CHANGIN'

can also underlie a more malleable approach to meter that encompasses all metric possibilities between metric regularity and ambiguity and includes a focus on *metric cues*—stressed musical events that contribute to the hierarchic organization of musical rhythm.

To build a framework to account for the possibilities of more flexible metric structures, I propose *five types of flexible meter* that accommodate the metric realities of the singer-songwriter repertoire. These five types are summarized in Figure 2.1. *Ideal* and *Regular Meter* act as predictable, consistent metric hierarchies, free from interruption. Ideal Meter represents a chronometric prototype in which rhythms are precisely, mathematically equal (isochronous)—a type of meter rarely created by human performers without some technological mediation. Regular Meter, by contrast, accounts for natural rhythmic variation and expressive timing that occur in musical performance by live or recorded performers. *Reinterpreted* and *Lost Meter* are interrupted types in which meter is mostly Regular but some passages occur in which regularity cannot continue. In Reinterpreted Meter, regularity is interrupted by beats added to or removed from an otherwise Regular metric context. After this small accommodation through metrical reinterpretation, Regular Meter continues. In Lost Meter, a similar process of interruption occurs, but in this type of flexible meter, timings are so extreme that the perception of regularity is lost into ambiguity. Lost Meter occurs when a context of Regular Meter dissolves into passages of *hiatus* before regularity returns again. In some singer-songwriter music, however, this expectation for Regular Meter to return is not present—either because it was never achieved initially or because no regularity ever emerges. These situations demonstrate *Ambiguous Meter*, which features techniques like *Unrealized Durations* (timespans with clear onsets but unclear or absent end points) that include metric cues but do not yield metric regularity. Ambiguous Meter differs from Lost Meter in that, retrospectively, there is no expectation of meter returning. In Lost Meter, a listener can anticipate metric regularity returning after moments of expressive hiatus. In Ambiguous Meter, there is no such expectation. Attention is given to metric cues that give some indications about stress and duration, with no expectation for these to emerge into metric regularity. There is *potential* for regularity to emerge but no realization of that potential and no expectation for Regular Meter to return.

All five of these types of flexible meter share metric cues. When singer-songwriters manipulate their performance timings, shifting between

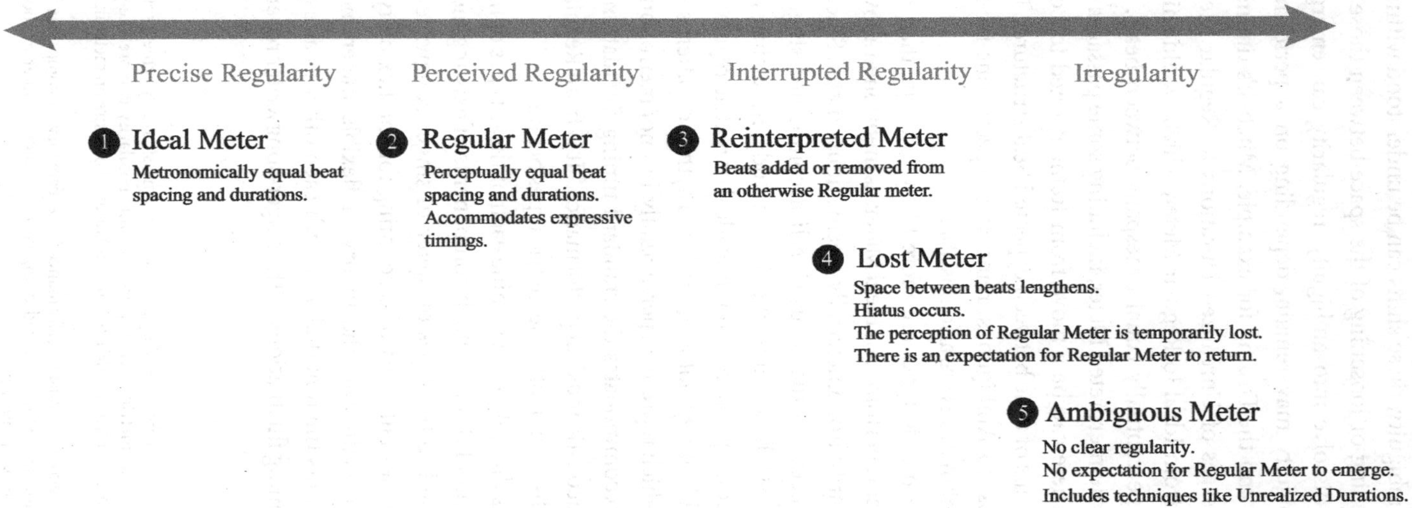

Precise Regularity · **Perceived Regularity** · **Interrupted Regularity** · **Irregularity**

1 Ideal Meter
Metronomically equal beat spacing and durations.

2 Regular Meter
Perceptually equal beat spacing and durations. Accommodates expressive timings.

3 Reinterpreted Meter
Beats added or removed from an otherwise Regular meter.

4 Lost Meter
Space between beats lengthens.
Hiatus occurs.
The perception of Regular Meter is temporarily lost.
There is an expectation for Regular Meter to return.

5 Ambiguous Meter
No clear regularity.
No expectation for Regular Meter to emerge.
Includes techniques like Unrealized Durations.

Figure 2.1 Five Types of Flexible Meter

regularity and ambiguity, these shifts can be understood within this framework as a tightening or loosening of the space between those cues. Metric regularity may dissolve into ambiguity, regularity can emerge from ambiguity, or ambiguity may remain, depending on a performer's timings. (In "The Fiddle and the Drum," for example, Mitchell's timings shift from Ambiguous passages of Unrealized Durations to Regular Meter.) Flexible meter can drift from Ideal to Regular Meter, which would shift from metronomically to perceptually equal timespans between beats. It can move from Regular to Reinterpreted Meter, including some passages with extra or omitted beats. There can be a move from Reinterpreted to Lost Meter including larger spans of time between expected beat structures. Or meter can change from Lost to Ambiguous, removing expectations for metric regularity. Other combinations are also possible.

Some of these metric types are more likely to occur than others in the singer-songwriter repertoire. An Ideal Meter, as mentioned above, represents a precisely regular (chronometrically isochronous) meter. Since this type of meter does not occur in the acoustic, self-accompanied singer-songwriter repertoire, I will not discuss it further in this study; nevertheless, this metric type serves as a conceptual, metronomic ideal of metric regularity.[3] Timings that instead yield *conceptually* equivalent rhythmic patterns demonstrate Regular Meter, which represents perceptually, but not metronomically, equal groupings and accommodates the standard timing fluctuations like *rubato* associated with acoustic musical performance.[4] It is from Regular Meter that my subsequent discussion of these metric types begins.

In the sections that follow, I examine each of these types of meter in turn. Within each section I discuss which components of existing metric theories do well to respond to the types of meter in singer-songwriter music, and where these theories fall short of accounting for the flexibility of this repertoire. Then I explain how the theory of flexible meter modifies these approaches and puts them in dialogue with each other as a response to the more extreme timing fluctuations of the singer-songwriter repertoire.

---

[3] The acoustic performance practice of singer-songwriter music rarely achieves the chronometric isochrony required for this metric level. This metronomic regularity is more likely to be found in genres like electronic dance music (EDM), techno, and house. For more on meter in EDM, see Butler (2006).

[4] When I refer to "acoustic music performance," the category encompasses musical sounds produced by live performers without the aid of digital electronics or other methods of producing chronometrically isochronous pulse layers.

THE THEORY OF FLEXIBLE METER   31

Regular Meter

In contrast to the metronomic precision of Ideal Meter, Regular Meter is very common in the singer-songwriter repertoire, even from artists other than the five singer-songwriters examined in this study.[5] Regular Meter is also the type proposed in theories of hierarchic meter designed for Western art music. Such theories offer a comprehensive approach to metric regularity in the theory of metric hierarchy developed in Lerdahl and Jackendoff's *A Generative Theory of Tonal Music* (hereafter *GTTM*). The approach to hierarchic meter—or "grid based" meter—presented in *GTTM* is prevalent in the music-theoretic literature that conceptualizes the time-point elements in a metrical pattern as beats that organize into a layered hierarchy. The authors describe metric structure as the strong-weak organization of beats within a metric hierarchy of two or more levels of equally spaced beats.[6] Their dot notation illustrates these beats in two possible diagrams. Figure 2.2a illustrates as dots arranged hierarchically in a duple or quadruple metric structure. Dots at levels 1–3 are organized as patterns of alternating strong and weak beats. Figure 2.2b shows a triple grouping of beats in dot notation in which beats are organized into patterns of strong-weak-weak. In both dot diagrams, strong beats at one level are also beats at the next lower level.[7] These dot diagrams represent patterns of accent and grouping heard in or inferred from musical rhythms in performance.[8]

This dot notation does well to capture patterns of Regular Meter and hypermeter.[9] Beats occur predictably at perceptually regular timespans,

---

[5] To choose which artists to include in this study, I only considered those whose music displayed meter more flexible than Regular Meter including Reinterpretations, Lost Meter, and Ambiguous Meter, and whose music included this flexible meter within vocal phrases. As a result, prominent singer-songwriters like Carole King, James Taylor, Leonard Cohen, and Joan Baez were left out because their music is mostly Regular or only included irregularity between vocal phrases.

[6] Lerdahl and Jackendoff (1983, 19).

[7] Lerdahl and Jackendoff (1983, 19).

[8] In score-based music, it is possible to conceptualize the meter as a dot diagram looking only at the score and not by referring to a specific performance. For popular music, where scores are not prevalent, such information must be determined from analyzing recorded performances. See Cook (2012), and other essays in the April 2012 issue of *Music Theory Online*, for ideas about situating performance as central to informing analysis.

[9] The definition of hypermeter here follows the one presented in Rothstein (1989, 12), where he encourages the "conceptual combination of measures on a metrical basis," which includes "both the recurrence of equal-sized measure groups and a definite pattern of alternation between strong and weak measures." Notated measures group together to form hypermeasures, the downbeats of which are hyperbeats, with strong hyperbeats labeled as hyperdownbeats. To this I add the caveat that hypermeter may include any level above the tactus, which may or may not align with the notated measure lengths.

Figure 2.2 Dot notation for metric hierarchy

and listeners can entrain to these predictable rhythms and anticipate when the next beat will occur. Theories of metric entrainment observe such processes of anticipating beats, studying how mental and physical regularities align with musical periodicities and help listeners to direct attention and predict the timing of subsequent event onsets.[10] Entrainment theories engage with the research that empirically determines the perceptual limits of meter.

The number of layers in a metric hierarchy depends on how salient the metrical signal is in the music.[11] Figure 2.3 shows a hierarchic representation of meter in which the third of the five lines includes the tactus beat, the beat layer most likely to align with entrainment patterns like foot tapping or conducting. The upper lines are levels of tactus-beat subdivisions, and the lower two lines represent metric and hypermetric groupings of the tactus-beat level. Though there is some disagreement about the number of beat layers necessary for a well-formed meter, I would accept two layers as demonstrating hierarchy, but acknowledge that more layers yield more salient hierarchies.[12] Three layers is ideal, with one as the tactus, one grouping tactus beats, and one subdividing the tactus. Figure 2.3 illustrates a possible five-layer metric hierarchy with the tactus as the middle layer.[13]

---

[10] See London (2012) and his citations of several empirical studies of beat entrainment. Other research on this topic in the field of perception and cognition includes, for example, Parncutt (1994), Repp (1998, 2005), Large and Palmer (2002), Jones et al. (2002), Huron (2006), and London (2019).

[11] London (2012, 190) suggests that composers and performers sometimes "play with our metric abilities," inviting but then thwarting our ability to perceive a specific number of metric levels.

[12] Temperley (2001, 39) proposes five layers: a tactus, two layers above, and two layers below. London (2012, 16) states that two levels are necessary, but prefers three: the tactus, one level grouping tactus beats, and one level subdividing them. Lester (1986, 47) and Yeston (1976, 66) each propose two layers: the tactus and one slower level of tactus groupings.

[13] Lerdahl and Jackendoff (1983, 21) suggest that a metric hierarchy could "theoretically be built up to the level of the whole piece" but that it should only include perceptually relevant layers, though they do not quantify these perceptual limits. The arrows in Figure 2.3 illustrate the fading of perceptual acuity as the listener "processes away from the tactus in either direction." The layers closest to the tactus feature the most strict regularities of structure, while at larger levels the meter is more likely to be heard as grouping structures, which the authors suggest are "rarely regular." Lerdahl and Jackendoff, therefore, consider meter to be a relatively local phenomenon.

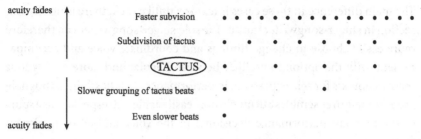

Figure 2.3 Five-layer metric hierarchy

Meter in Rock Music

Though designed for Western art music, theories of Regular Meter often apply well to popular music. And there are many similarities between the Regular Meter of singer-songwriter music and that of related popular repertoires like rock. Consistent with its origins in twentieth-century dance music, rock often presents a Regular Meter that is "overtly iterated in the accompaniment patterns."[14] Drums usually establish regular rhythms, which in many songs mark each beat of the meter, with occasional syncopation.[15] The regularity of percussion rhythms is often reinforced by the rhythm section (bass, guitar, keyboard, etc.), which together typically creates a consistent pulse layer at the tactus level, with a regular alternation of strong and weak beats suggesting a metric hierarchy. Repeating patterns for a rock groove collectively establish and sustain lower levels of pulse, giving rise to meter and hypermeter, with typical groupings of four-bar units.[16] Even in cases where deviations from these four-bar units occur, such deviations are often observed as expansions or contractions of prototypical unit lengths.[17]

The expectation for metric regularity in popular music is also present in the examples from the singer-songwriter repertoire that demonstrate Regular Meter. But there are many examples that thwart this expectation. The flexible meter in singer-songwriter music, especially the extremes of metric ambiguity, would require preparation and coordination to occur in rock music.

---

[14] Biamonte (2014, [1.4]).

[15] Everett (2008, 8).

[16] Rock's typical instrumentation separates the melody from the groove; the rhythm section, as Everett (2008, 8) describes, articulates "the music's foundation, providing the metric framework against which all pitched instruments and vocals find their place" and have more varied rhythms.

[17] For example, in Everett (2009), many instances of irregular meter in songs by the Beatles are observed in relation to possible four-bar units.

34 TIMES A-CHANGIN'

The main difference in these cases is texture: unlike rock, there is no rhythm section in singer-songwriter music. The solo singer-songwriter can therefore more easily choose to change timings and coordinate voice and accompaniment, with the option to vacillate between Regular and more Ambiguous metric contexts for self-expression in performance. This flexibility is possible to coordinate in ensembles but much more easily achieved (especially as a spur-of-the-moment performance decisions) in the voice-and-accompaniment texture of singer-songwriter music.[18]

Reinterpreted Meter

Within the system of metric hierarchy that accounts for Regular Meter, there are some ways to respond analytically when meter is disrupted. Different theories of Regular Meter are more or less flexible about the predictability of beats in various levels of a hierarchic structure. Lerdahl and Jackendoff, for example, are stringent in requiring equal rhythmic proportions in layers closest to and including the tactus.[19] In their view, well-formed meter demonstrates consistent groupings of beats in either twos or threes on a given level by the next-slower level. Any disruption to these regular beats is understood as the result of conflict among grouping preferences. As is often the case in interrupted meter, decisions about grouping necessitate the restructuring of a metric hierarchy, through *metrical reinterpretation*. For singer-songwriter music that contains such processes, these would demonstrate the flexible metric type called *Reinterpreted Meter*.

Omitted and Added Beats

Gretchen Horlacher's research on meter in Stravinsky's *Les Noces* provides a framework for examining reinterpretations in singer-songwriter music.[20]

---

[18] For some examples of irregular meter coordinated in ensemble situations, see N. Mitchell (2019) and Everett (2009).

[19] Lerdahl and Jackendoff (1983, 21).

[20] Horlacher (1995) examines how Stravinsky creates metric accent and grouping in the absence of periodicity. She finds that when beats are removed from or added to an initial motivic pattern, there is a break in periodic meter at the pulse and measure level. Her analysis then relies on grouping parallelism to characterize the meter of Stravinsky's motives. Her work contrasts previous studies of meter in that it accommodates reinterpretations at all metric levels.

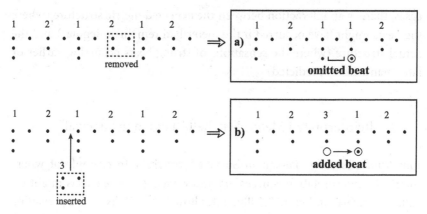

Figure 2.4 Metrical reinterpretation symbols in a dot diagram

Following Horlacher, I define two types of metrical reinterpretations that are prominent in singer-songwriter meter: *omitted beats* (removed from an otherwise Regular Meter) and *added beats* (inserted into a Regular Meter). To illustrate these two reinterpretations, I borrow two symbols from Horlacher's work that show omitted and added beats as modifications to a dot diagram.[21] Figure 2.4 illustrates these two possibilities in a metric hierarchy with beats either added or omitted. In an omission, a beat is removed (along with any faster beat levels) from a hierarchy. Figure 2.4a illustrates an omitted beat in the middle layer of the dot diagram. I include numbers above the staff to illustrate a possible simple duple conception of this scenario. In it, a tactus beat is removed from a measure along with its subdivisions (outlined in the dotted line box on the left side of the diagram). This beat would have been the second of a plausible two-beat bar. Omitting it results in two successive downbeats.[22] In the boxed portion of Figure 2.4a, the circled dot indicates the arrival of a beat earlier than expected, with the square bracket signaling an omission. In situations with added beats, a downbeat will occur later than expected. Figure 2.4b shows the process of beats being added to a metric hierarchy. On the right side of this figure, an empty circle indicates the expected beat—had the meter remained regular—and the arrow signals the eventual arrival of the beat later than expected at the circled beat location. In both

---

[21] These are included in the categories of "metric shifts" in Horlacher's study (1995, 296), but I prefer the term metrical reinterpretations.
[22] For further discussion of successive downbeats, see Rothstein (1989, 58–63).

cases, there is an interaction between the expected metric structure (where the beats might have occurred if the meter had remained Regular) and the actual structure (where the sensations of strong beats occurring earlier or later than initially predicted).

Reinterpreted Meter: Mitchell, "Lesson in Survival"

Joni Mitchell's song "Lesson in Survival" provides an example of where metrical reinterpretation is necessary and what expressive effects might result. The excerpt in Figure 2.5 illustrates how Mitchell disrupts a prevailing ¾ meter. She withholds a possible strong beat at the end of the excerpt's second measure by not changing harmony on that beat (where she did in the previous measures). This expected downbeat (that would have retained the ¾ meter) occurs instead a half note later, giving the impression that the musical events at the word "know" should be assigned metric accents. In the dot diagram, I use Horlacher's symbols to illustrate this as a metric addition of a half-note beat value, delaying of the would-be strong beat by a half-note duration. At the lowest (breve) level of the dot diagram, this can be read as a shortening of a possible two-bar unit from eight quarter-note beats to six. The ¾ bar could have lasted for eight quarter-note beats, but the reinterpretation and subsequent stressed event in the third bar of this excerpt suggest that this is instead a shortened metric unit. I illustrate this as an omitted beat in the lowest level of the dot diagram. (In this and many other cases, there is no change to the meter at the fastest levels above the irregularity; however, omitted and added beats may also impact reinterpretations at all metric levels.) Both conceptions—the added beat and omitted beat—yield a strong

Figure 2.5 Mitchell, "Lesson in Survival" (0:35–0:43)

THE THEORY OF FLEXIBLE METER   37

beat on the downbeat of the third measure of this excerpt, as Mitchell sings the word "know." In Chapter 3, I interpret this passage as a moment of self-discovery, an awareness of the dawning realization of what the song's narrator needs to survive her relationship. The metric emphasis created by the Reinterpreted Meter helps to highlight this perspective as it occurs here and throughout the song.

Grouping Parallelism and Simon's "The Sound of Silence"

In some cases, decisions about interpreting and reinterpreting meter rely on grouping parallelism, in which there is often a preference for motives with distinct initial metric identities to retain those identities in subsequent repetitions.[23] For meter, parallelism suggests that repetitions should be given the same placement in a metric hierarchy; so, for example, what was first considered a downbeat should also be a downbeat when repeated. In Regular Meter, parallelism yields similar metric profiles without disruptions to the metric hierarchy. However, the decision to retain an initial metric identity occasionally results in beats added to or removed from an otherwise Regular Meter and metrical reinterpretation must occur. An example of this arises in Paul Simon's "The Sound of Silence" (Figure 2.6). In m. 15, when Simon and Art Garfunkel sing the word "silence" it aligns with the same tonic harmony as m. 1. Since I consider the m. 1 accompaniment in to begin with a downbeat, it therefore has metric accent, which I show with three levels of dots in the diagram. The reappearance of this accompaniment in m. 15 encourages a parallel metric reading. As such, I also include three levels of dots below the downbeat of m. 15 to give it metric accent as well. But in this case, to retain this metric identity requires a metrical reinterpretation in m. 14—in this case, added beats.[24] The expressive impact of this reinterpretation is that the

---

[23] The principle of parallelism appears as the sixth grouping preference rule in Lerdahl and Jackendoff (1983, 75). This preference rule is of significance for many of my grouping decisions in this study. It encourages the grouping of parallel units according to similarities of rhythm, internal grouping, and pitch contour. This preference rule extends to meter as well, supporting a reading of parallel groups with parallel metric structures.

[24] As I explain more in Chapter 3 (alongside an interpretation of the self-expressive rationale for this metric type), this reinterpretation results in the possible metric accent (with three levels of dots) in m. 14 being shifted forward to m. 15 (alongside the reinterpretation in m. 13), which changes the meaning of the text at this moment.

Figure 2.6 Simon, "The Sound of Silence" (0:00–0:39)

word "silence" is given metric accent, suggesting it is more important than the word "sound" that preceded it and for which metric accent was withheld.

Other scenarios for metric and hypermetric reinterpretations can also occur. As another example, Reinterpreted Meter might arise when a metric unit elides (borrowing grouping terminology) or overlaps with another metric unit. In flexible meter, Reinterpreted Meter accounts for any situation when beats are added to or removed from any level of metric hierarchy in an otherwise Regular metric context.

Lost Meter

While metrical reinterpretations do well to account for small disruptions to Regular Meter, there are some scenarios in the singer-songwriter

THE THEORY OF FLEXIBLE METER   39

repertoire when meter is interrupted to such a degree that it can no longer be conceptualized as Reinterpreted Meter. In such scenarios, the fourth type of flexible meter, *Lost Meter*, is helpful to encompass these more extreme timings in this music. In this metric type, meter is mostly Regular, but timings in certain passages are so flexible that metric hierarchy cannot simply be reinterpreted; instead these passages create the impression of Regular Meter being temporarily abandoned.[25] Lost Meter accounts for scenarios in which an otherwise Regular Meter slips into metric hiatus (temporary ambiguity) with the expectation that Regular Meter will eventually be restored.

Theories of metric regularity and reinterpretation that rely on dot diagrams are not well suited to accommodate the flexibility that Lost Meter presents. Some theories discuss features related to those that result in Lost Meter. Without directly addressing metric loss, many studies of meter *do* discuss the ability for listeners to accommodate changes of tempo, expressive timing, and fermatas in performance.[26] Lerdahl and Jackendoff, for example, state that a "certain amount of metric inexactness is tolerated" in the presence of tempo fluctuations.[27] When performers add small temporal variabilities, listeners can understand these as "local deviations: that do not break down metric regularity."[28] These attitudes are shared by other studies. William Benjamin and Jonathan Kramer both separately argue that meter is tolerant to tempo variations.[29] Similarly, in passages with a fermata, Benjamin states that listeners experience a "kind of standing still of counting, in which the counter stops, but keeps track" of where we were in the count.[30]

But how long can listeners stop counting? When instead is the perception of Regular Meter simply Lost? Horlacher proposes the concept of metric *dissolution* to affirm that it might be possible to lose periodic regularity.[31] Benjamin does not indicate a limit for how long the listener can stop counting

---

[25] Mirka (2009, 20) describes similar scenarios as a "bewilderment" or "losing one's bearings," which occurs when an analysis "has been selected by the processor and generates expectations, but then a surprising event arrives" causing a clear sense of meter to be replaced by metric ambiguity or vagueness.

[26] These timing phenomena may be explicitly indicated by a composer or result from interpretive decisions made by the performer. In singer-songwriter music, these are typically the same individual. For more on how singer-songwriter music challenges the perceptions of composer, performer, and score, see Murphy (2020).

[27] Lerdahl and Jackendoff (1983, 70).

[28] Lerdahl and Jackendoff (1983, 70).

[29] Benjamin (1984, 398); Kramer (1988, 99).

[30] Benjamin (1984, 397).

[31] Horlacher (2000/2001, 271) defines metrical dissolution (through analyses of Steve Reich's music) as a process of established levels of counting eventually dissolving "when metrical cues

40 TIMES A-CHANGIN'

before losing metric positioning.[32] In these cases, it is helpful to draw from studies of metric entrainment to theorize these perceptual limits, to quantify when meter might be perceived as Lost. London proposes a range of 100 milliseconds (ms) to 5 or 6 seconds as the temporal envelope for entrainment.[33] He also references 200–2000 ms as a proposed range for successive note onsets, and this is the range taken up by Yonatan Malin in his discussions of metric entrainment and perception.[34] I use this envelope as a guide: if the inter-onset intervals (IOIs) between beats exceed the range of perceptual regularity on either end, this would be considered Lost Meter. When IOI values lie within these perceptual limits (from 100 ms to a few seconds), but give the impression of breaking Regular Meter beyond Reinterpretation, I rely on contextual cues, considering the relative IOI values of surrounding durations to measure the degree of metric salience and whether or not meter sounds Lost. In some situations, I find that contextually longer durations disrupt regularity enough to create Lost Meter even when these durations exist within the temporal envelope for entrainment.

Regular and Lost Meter: Mitchell, "Woodstock"

The Wurlitzer introduction to Joni Mitchell's song "Woodstock" provides a helpful synthesis for the discussion so far, illustrating Regular and Lost Meter. The excerpt that comprises the first few systems of my transcription are expressively timed in Mitchell's performance, but demonstrate enough Regular Meter to establish quarter-note tactus beats. The final system of Figure 2.7 (beginning in m. 14) also illustrates a passage of Regular

---

disappear or contradict one another" amid Reich's repetition of motivic units. As an opposite process, metrical emergence occurs when sporadic cues result in initial uncertainty, but if cues "eventually articulate the missing level(s)," it leads "us to experience a process of growth as the metrical identity of a repeated motive is enriched." Horlacher's dissolution is a related process to Lost Meter; however, in singer-songwriter contexts it is only the disappearance of metric cues that causes the loss of meter and not contradicting motivic repetitions.

[32] There are many interesting cases of long, drawn-out notes that do not disrupt metric positioning. One example from the singer-songwriter repertoire is Dylan's song "Freight Train Blues" (starting at 1:11 in the studio recording), where he sustains a tonic upbeat for sixteen beats before proceeding to the next vocal downbeat, all over a steady pulse in the guitar accompaniment. In Murphy (2018), I examine similar occurrences in traditional folk songs and early Bob Dylan songs as *performed-out fermatas*, in reference to the *composed-out fermatas* discussed in Rothstein (1989, 80–87).

[33] London (2012, 46).

[34] London (2012, 31); Malin (2010, 44–45).

Figure 2.7 Mitchell, "Woodstock," introduction (0:00–0:46)

Meter, with consistent tactus beats grouped into $\frac{4}{4}$. These quarter-note beats are reinforced by the rhythms of the right hand and subdivided by the eighth notes in the left hand. In systems 3 and 4, however, Mitchell's rhythms challenge representation as a Regular metric hierarchy, or even as a Reinterpreted hierarchy.[35] Instead, the IOIs (shown in ms values over

---

[35] As I explore in Murphy (2015, 52–56), commercial sheet music fails to capture the nuances of Mitchell's flexible meter in this introduction to "Woodstock," in some cases completely regularizing the rhythms. In other score representations, like the transcription from Dunn (2023), fermata symbols attempt to capture timing nuances, succeeding in at least highlighting parallel passages by using parallel rhythmic patterns.

42 TIMES A-CHANGIN'

dotted lines below the staff) of these durations push durational relativity to its limits. In some cases, the onsets are 2–3 seconds apart, resisting grouping with surrounding onsets into a representation in Regular Meter. I have spaced the durations in this transcription proportionally, so that longer durations between onsets are farther apart on the staff. Mitchell's performance at times gives the impression of a sense of meter either nearly or completely Lost. But these passages of extreme timing are not unrelated to the regularity that follows. Using parallelism to compare passages of this introduction gives insight into viewing the more extreme timings of flexible meter as something like a continental drift from regularity. For example, m. 12 and m. 13 have similar content to that of m. 14 but are spaced apart in duration: the third and fourth whole notes of mm. 12–13 are longer-duration versions of the right hand's quarter notes in m. 14. Viewing this passage (mm. 12–14) as an example of nearly Lost Meter, m. 12 and m. 13 can be understood as four-beat units (shown with the numbers above the staff) that offer the same metric cues as the four beats of m. 14 but with longer durations between the cues.[36] The looser, more spaced-apart onsets of mm. 12–13 have the potential to snap into predictable regularity, a potential that is eventually achieved from m. 14 onward. In this introduction, Mitchell showcases the timing possibilities of flexible meter within her self-accompanied performance, shifting from a malleable metric setting to one with more predictable, more easily entrained Regular Meter. Viewing the introduction to "Woodstock" as flexible meter allows for a dialogue between the looser and more Regular structures as related within the same metric framework.

Ambiguous Meter

For situations, like Mitchell's "Woodstock" introduction, in which metric cues exceed or push the limits of perceptual salience, metric theorists like Lerdahl and Jackendoff describe such cases as not having metric structure, since no metric hierarchy can be extrapolated from the musical signal.[37] Horlacher

---

[36] There are differences in the accompaniment as well once Mitchell settles into metric regularity. Other transcriptions of the "Woodstock" introduction do not assign similar metric identities to parallel motivic material. The transcription here and in Murphy (2015, 55) takes steps to remedy this issue.

[37] Lerdahl and Jackendoff (1983, 18).

THE THEORY OF FLEXIBLE METER   43

observes this perspective in most metric theories: if meter is defined as regularly spaced beats at many levels, a lack of periodicity is "tantamount to saying this music is not *metric* at all."[38] Despite this view, there is still the possibility to hear some semblance of meter within these looser structures. When meter is Lost or Ambiguous and Regular Meter is not present, I argue that this does not mean that all cues for meter have disappeared. This music instead calls for a different framework. In these more extreme moments of flexible timing, Christopher Hasty's theory of metric process, or metric *projection*, can provide tools for analyzing Lost Meter as well as the most extreme metric type in singer-songwriter music: *Ambiguous Meter*. I find Hasty's projective meter to be particularly well suited to analyzing metric ambiguity because his theory focuses on metric cues even in the absence of periodic regularity.[39] Using components of Hasty's theory helps to conceptualize metric cues as having metric potential, a potential in which these cues could organize into Regular Meter, whether realized or not.[40]

Metric Process

The key feature of metric projection is its in-time approach to meter that observes the unfolding of durations. It focuses on the timespans between events and proposes that when a duration between two events is heard, a listener imagines (projects) a reproduction of that duration that may or may not occur. This is a process of hearing and casting forward that attends to rhythms as they unfold in time. As such, this theory does well to account for more Ambiguous metric contexts, in which durations may be heard between events, but it is not clear whether more events will occur to reproduce similar durations in the future. Hasty's theory proposes an in-time listening experience, allowing for the imagining of possibilities, and makes present the expressive impact of fulfilled or unfulfilled "projected potential."[41]

---

[38] Horlacher (1995, 289–90).

[39] See Hasty (1997). Knowles (2016) finds a similar benefit for using the theory of meter as process to analyze what she defines as "post-tonal, unmetered music." My use of Hasty's theory contrasts the application of metric process thus far in popular music, which (with the exception of Rockwell 2011) focuses on repetition and regularity in groove-based music. See Attas (2011), Attas (2015), and Butler (2006).

[40] Hasty (1997).

[41] There are several other theories of meter that explore beats as temporal spreads rather than points in time; see, for example, Hosken's theory of beat pockets (2021), Ito's focal impulse theory (2020), and Danielsen's theory of beat bins (2010).

44 TIMES A-CHANGIN'

In not relying on regularity for defining meter, this process-based theory provides an apparatus through which extremes in flexible timing can be examined as metric. However, in deliberately disentangling his work from theories of metric hierarchy, Hasty loses important connections to other metric theories, particularly in how the cues he explores for metric projection can relate to the cues in Regular Meter.[42] The result of metric projection losing dialogue with other theories is that there are several related theories of hierarchic meter and a method well suited for metric ambiguity, but no single theory that synthesizes these various methodologies in a way that responds to the self-expressive metric possibilities of singer-songwriter music.[43] Flexible meter restores a dialogue between these two approaches.

Metric Projection Symbols

The theory of metric process has been explored extensively, and I need not reproduce the entirety of those discussions here, especially since so many applications of Hasty's theory, especially those analyzing popular music, explore metric regularity.[44] However, several details of the theory of metric projection will be useful for the metrically ambiguous examples in this study. I summarize the necessary symbols and terminology in Figure 2.8.[45] Following Hasty, I illustrate a metric projection (or projected duration) using a solid arrow and a letter label, usually beginning with Q and progressing through the rest of the alphabet. The next duration has potential to repeat the first. I indicate these projected durations using a dotted curved line and a prime symbol beside the letter it reproduces, as in Q', the possible reproduction of the Q duration. The top rows of Figure 2.8 show three scenarios that

---

[42] Hasty (1997, x) mentions as early as his preface that his beginnings and continuations are not to be confused with strong and weak beats.

[43] Mirka (2009) and Rockwell (2011) take important steps toward such a synthesis. But since neither of their repertoires demonstrates metric ambiguity similar to that of the singer-songwriter repertoire, their theories do not account for ambiguity in the same way.

[44] For more on the theory of metric projection, see Hasty (1997), Roeder (1998), and the adaptations of Hasty's theory to popular music cited earlier.

[45] This is not an exhaustive list of possible metric scenarios but a summary of those used in this study. For two more categories, see Murphy (2015, 33); both diagrams are adapted from Roeder (2015). My focus is on the durational projection component of *Meter as Rhythm*, so I will not be including beginning (|), anacrusis (/), or continuation (\) symbols in this discussion because I mostly do not employ these in my analyses. Instead, I contextualize Hasty's concepts as stressed and unstressed events, assigning metric positions with a Regular Meter or offering numerical notations when necessary for hypermetric positions.

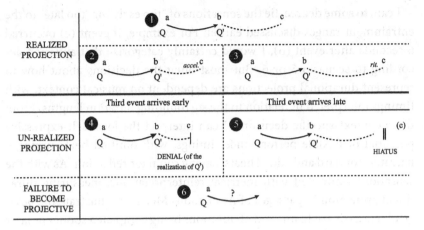

Figure 2.8 Summary of Hasty's symbols

illustrate realized metric projections. That is, the duration between the first two events (Q) is conceptually equal to the duration between the second and third events (Q'). In scenario 1, the Q and Q' durations are precisely equal, which is a rare occurrence in live performance; in scenarios 2 and 3, the Q' duration is shorter or longer than expected, as illustrated by the *accelerando* and *ritardando* indications, respectively, but still conceptually isochronous to the Q duration.[46] In cases where the Q' reproduction is not realized, the third event (c) arrives either "too early" or "too late," as indicated by scenarios 4 and 5. In scenario 4, the stressed event at (c) interrupts the Q' projection, arriving too soon to be understood as an accelerated realization of Q'.[47] If the third event is too late to be considered as following scenario 3, a *hiatus* occurs between the moment where Q' could have been realized and any stress that would indicate a new series of projections. Following Hasty, I indicate a hiatus with ||, and it is typically followed by a third event (c), but much too late. The final row of Figure 2.8 illustrates the symbols used when a stressed event at (a) indicates a duration, but no second event (b) occurs to confirm its timespan. I show this using a question mark above a solid arrow, with no Q' duration following.

---

[46] As a personal preference, I use *ritardando* (notated as *rit.*) in my diagrams instead of the *rallentando* (*rall.*) indications in Hasty (1997).
[47] The placement of scenario 4 on the chart below scenario 2 indicates that the interrupted projection is a more extreme case of the accelerated realization.

46   TIMES A-CHANGIN'

I can, to some degree, tie the sensations of "too early" or "too late" to the entrainment ranges discussed earlier. For example, if event (c) occurred 6 seconds after event (b), I would certainly categorize that situation according to scenario 5 or 6. But most often the decisions about how to represent durational projections are dependent on musical context, with timings interpreted in relation to the surrounding duration lengths. From these context-specific decisions, I can interpret the local self-expressive potential of flexible performance timings, with omitted beats urging a narrative forward and added beats leaving room for reflection. As with the sensations associated with metrical reinterpretations, measuring durational projection in passages of Ambiguous Meter can illustrate the powerful sensations of hiatus and of durations being completed sooner or later than expected.[48]

Realized and Unrealized Durations

These symbols also relate to features of Regular, Lost, and Ambiguous Meter. In Figure 2.9, I show how scenarios 1–3 are types of Regular Meter that demonstrate realized durations. These are durations that occur between beats of a Regular metric grid. Dot diagrams already capture these sensations of regularity, with beats occurring at regular intervals, thus realizing projected durations. I will therefore not use these projection symbols to indicate Regular Meter.[49] (In this diagram, I have made scenario 4 transparent because this is not a likely occurrence in either Realized or Unrealized Durations. I found these scenarios most common in Reinterpreted Meter, where a metric shift in a dot diagram more accurately captures those occurrences.) Scenario 5 demonstrates the hiatus found in Lost Meter, when realized durations dissolve into the sensation of halted regularity when a third event does not occur to confirm the second duration. In scenario 6, a second event does not occur, resulting in an *Unrealized*

---

[48] Roeder (1998, [2.3]) agrees that perceptions of "too short" or "too long" have potential for their expressive or analytic significance. Hasty (1997, 159) builds descriptions of "sensation" into his analytic language; for example, describing the timings of his recompositions of a J. S. Bach Courante, he suggests that "a sense of urgency" is associated with the beginning of the second measure "as if this articulation, on the heels of the abrupt leap preceding it, happened in some sense too soon."

[49] Mirka (2009, 35) also comments on avoiding using realized projection symbols, since full sets of projection arrows would overlap and become cumbersome "because the same set of projection arises every time."

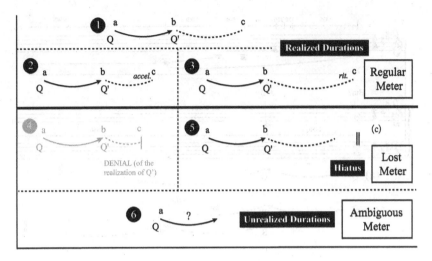

Figure 2.9 Realized Durations, Hiatus, and Unrealized Durations

Duration: a duration with no clear end point, which then cannot reproduce. Unrealized Durations are the most common way for Ambiguous Meter to manifest in singer-songwriter music. This technique accounts for durations that are too long to be perceived as predictable and perceptually Regular. Unrealized Durations could arise both during passages of temporary ambiguity in Lost Meter, where there is an expectation that metric regularity will eventually be restored, and also in Ambiguous metric contexts in which there is no certainty that meter will emerge. But Lost Meter more often reaches hiatus (and not Unrealized Durations) before Regular Meter is regained.

Hiatus and Lost Meter in Mitchell's "Blue"

One provocative example of hiatus occurring in Lost Meter is the first vocal phrase of Mitchell's song "Blue," a passage of which is shown in Figure 2.10. After the Regular Meter of her piano introduction (not shown), Mitchell's first vocal phrase begins to loosen the meter. The space between her half-note chords in the piano's right hand lengthens, and her vocal line prolongs rhythms by holding out notes longer than expected. The result is that the Regular Meter of the introduction becomes Lost. Durations can only be heard initially, and then there is a sense of hiatus before Mitchell resumes

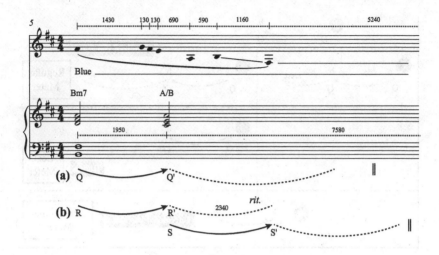

Figure 2.10 Mitchell, "Blue," first vocal phrase (0:12–0:21)

the next line of the lyrics ("songs are like tattoos").[50] I interpret the dissolution of Regular Meter into Lost Meter as reflecting Mitchell getting caught up in the recollection of her lost love, whom she nicknames "Blue." This is, again, an example of a singer-songwriter exploring the metrically flexible self-expressive possibilities of her solo performance, in which her piano accompaniment slows with her vocal line to allow time and space within the meter for this recollection.

Ambiguous Meter: Sainte-Marie's "Sir Patrick Spens"

The more extreme timing of Buffy Sainte-Marie's song "Sir Patrick Spens" demonstrates Unrealized Durations in a context of Ambiguous Meter.[51] The timings of the double bass onsets initially feature a hiatus but then dissolve into further ambiguity when Unrealized Durations begin to occur (as shown with the R arrow). This ambiguity is simultaneous with another technique of Ambiguous Meter I call *Ungrouped Beats*. With Ungrouped Beats, relatively fast beat layers outline a salient pulse, but the durations are too

---

[50] As I explore further in Chapter 4, the arrows below the staff offer two ways to view the rhythms of this passage as metric processes. Both of these possibilities result in a possible next event never arriving, as illustrated by the hiatus symbols (‖) at the end of the measure.

[51] I return to this example in more detail in Chapter 5.

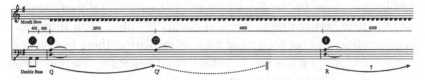

Figure 2.11 Sainte-Marie, "Sir Patrick Spens," introduction (0:00–0:13)

short to group into a generative pattern of strong and weak beats. The result is an Ambiguous metric context that relies on cues from other sources (other than this fast pulse layer) to generate metric salience. In the passage shown in Figure 2.11, the strumming pattern of Sainte-Marie's mouthbow yields durations in such quick succession that no larger grouping patterns can be generated.[52] The mouthbow illustrates a salient but not generative beat level—similar to various types of drumrolls—that does not group into hierarchic meter.[53] To hear any cues for meter, attention must shift to the double bass instrument and the onsets it provides. But since these are Unrealized Durations, it results in a highly Ambiguous metric context. The required attention to Sainte-Marie's vocal line gives agency to her voice as both the narrator and the primary generator of metric orientation within this song, and the Ambiguous Meter foreshadows the tragic narrative of Sir Patrick Spens's fatal sea voyage.

Metric Potential

The five types of flexible meter outlined in this chapter account for the malleable metric scenarios I have observed in singer-songwriter music. This repertoire presents Regular Meter, meter that is mostly predictable with passages that either need to be Reinterpreted or give the impression of meter being Lost, and contexts in which meter is Ambiguous, demonstrating techniques like Unrealized Durations that challenge perceptions of and expectations for regularity emerging. Performances may illustrate only one of these types of meter, as in the consistent Regular Meter of songs like "Little Green" (explored in Chapter 3), or the

---

[52] The mouthbow is a traditional instrument Sainte-Marie used in some of her 1960s recordings. I further investigate this instrument, how it is played, and its likely origins in Chapter 5.

[53] As I explore in Chapter 5, this is due in part to difficulties in consistently relating the mouthbow onsets to the onsets of the double bass rhythms.

50 TIMES A-CHANGIN'

Ambiguous Meter in "Sir Patrick Spens" (Chapter 5). Or performances may vacillate between these types, as occurs in "Blue," with shifts from Regular Meter to Lost Meter and back to regularity. These five types of meter represent possible metric behaviors in this music. Flexible meter is focused on metric potential: the possibility for meter to, for example, shift from Ambiguous to Regular Meter. These metric types account for whether that potential is realized. When, for example, a passage of metrically Ambiguous Unrealized Durations tightens in timing and becomes metrically Regular (as occurs in "The Fiddle and the Drum"), that potential is activated. As we shall see in the analytic chapters that follow, such shifts from Ambiguous or Lost to Regular Meter, or from Regular to Lost or Ambiguous Meter, are some of the most striking techniques of self-expression in the singer-songwriter repertoire.

The Aspects of Meter

A fundamental component in observing metric potential relies on the presence and recognition of metric cues: the *aspects of meter*.[54] These are components of types of flexible meter: *stress*, an accented event onset; *duration*, the timespan between two stresses; *pulse*, a regular series of stresses and durations; *strong-weak organization of beats* within that pulse, where every other beat is heard as stronger than the other; and *metric hierarchy*, which occurs as a multi-leveled organization of pulse layers.[55] I summarize these aspects of meter in Figure 2.12.

In Regular and Reinterpreted Meter, these metric cues are all present. But only some of the aspects of meter are possible within the other metric types. In Lost Meter, the pulse is disrupted at some point so that hearing durations between stresses is pushed to extremes and hiatus occurs. In Ambiguous Meter, techniques like Unrealized Durations are prominent because stressed events are positioned too far apart and the IOI value between durations is too long. These aspects of meter are built into

---

[54] Berry (1976, 318) offers a similar list (his "primary questions") for analyzing meter. Schachter (1999, 79–117) explores aspects of meter with some related features of metrical accent, levels of pulse, and durational levels.

[55] It is also possible for triple groupings to emerge from a pulse layer, in which case the beats would organize into a *strong-weak-weak* pattern. I have not theorized this possibility further because duple structures are more prevalent in my chosen repertoire.

Stress: created by accentual cues (events) in performance. These stresses can be conceived of as beats within a metric hierarchy or as onsets of durations that may or may not become projective.

Duration: the timespan between two stressed events.

Pulse: emerges when a level of equally spaced beats is created between at least three events. For example, when the duration between events (a) and (b) is reproduced between events (b) and (c).

Strong-Weak Organization: occurs when a fourth event, (d), is articulated and creates duple pairings that can organize into strong and weak events.

Metric Hierarchy: a multi-layered organization of beats. If a strong-weak pattern emerges, the strong beats in the pattern will emerge as another metric layer, creating a metric hierarchy. The more layers that emerge, the more salient the hierarchy.

Figure 2.12 Aspects of Meter

hierarchic structures, but become increasingly applicable for analyzing more Ambiguous metric contexts.

Shifts Between Metric Types

I want to return now to Example 2.8 to show how the aspects of meter arise in the types of flexible meter and when it might be necessary to make the shift between the metric types. In all scenarios in Example 2.8, a stress marks the onset of event (a). This stressed event can correspond to a beat in a hierarchic dot diagram or to the onset of a yet-to-be determined timespan. If two stressed events occur in succession, they mark the boundaries of a duration (the onset and end point), illustrated in scenarios 1–5 between events (a) and (b). In a hierarchic meter, durations are reproduced so that they are perceptually equal timespans between beats. Such a meter would align with scenario 1 but is much more easily represented by a hierarchic dot diagram. In more flexible scenarios, like scenario 6 from Example 2.8, no duration is salient because no second stressed event (b) occurs, thereby yielding an Unrealized Duration. For examples like scenarios 1–3, the arrival of the third event (c)—at a timespan conceptually equal to that between (a) and (b)—means a pulse layer has emerged. In scenarios 4–6, a pulse would fail to emerge because the third event (c) arrives too early (as in scenario 4) or too late or not at all (as represented in scenarios 5 and 6). When a pulse is sustained long enough, a pattern of strong and weak organization of beats can emerge, yielding scenarios 1–3 and therefore generating a salient Regular Meter.

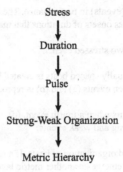

Figure 2.13 Linear conception of the Aspects of Meter

There can be a linearity to the stages of salience of these aspects of meter, as shown with the arrows in Figure 2.13, which is positioned directionally from stress to hierarchy. That is, it could be possible in a passage of emerging meter for loosely spaced stresses to tighten in timing to create realized durations. These successive durations could then create a pulse layer, which, once established, might yield a series of strong and weak beats that can subsequently be understood as Regular hierarchic meter. Reversing the process results in Lost and Ambiguous Meter. Further still, it is possible for the motion into and out of meter to not be so clearly defined, snapping dramatically from ambiguity to regularity or vice versa. The theory of flexible meter can accommodate such changes, accounting for and organizing metric cues into whatever meter the performer's timings manifest in a given moment. Flexible meter provides a language with which to describe various types of self-expressive metric cues, not simply those that create Regular metric hierarchy. With flexible meter, a dialogue between metric possibilities is established, and a single theory of meter can accommodate Regular, Reinterpreted, Lost, and Ambiguous metric contexts. This theory responds to the potential for shifts between different types of meter, thereby yielding timing possibilities at either end of metric extremes: (1) for Ambiguous Meter to tighten and become Regular, demonstrating the emerging meter I explore in Chapter 5 with songs like Mitchell's "The Fiddle and the Drum," and (2) for Regular Meter to loosen and yield to hiatus, a process of Lost Meter featured in songs like Bob Dylan's "Only a Pawn in their Game" explored in Chapter 4.[56] These timing

---

[56] Horlacher (2000/2001, 296) notes that "emerging and dissolving meters" in Steve Reich's music are striking, especially when they "engage tactus and measure, where we direct our primary counting

THE THEORY OF FLEXIBLE METER 53

possibilities highlight the flexible metric rhetoric of the singer-songwriter performance practice and the malleability of this synthesized approach to theorizing meter.

By accommodating metric ambiguity alongside metric regularity within a single theory, I can parse out the details of meter to understand and appreciate the type of meter occurring, the changes to that metric type, and how performance timings impact lyrical reception, interpretation, and the shaping of the unique self-expressive styles of the artists in this study. In the chapters that follow, I apply this malleable metric theory to examples from the singer-songwriter repertoire from Regular and Reinterpreted Meter (Chapter 3) to Lost Meter (Chapter 4), and Ambiguous Meter with Unrealized Durations and/or Ungrouped Beats (Chapter 5).

***

A quick note about transcription before moving on to the analytic chapters. The transcriptions in this study are all my own and are based on cues for stresses and groupings from recorded performance. Since the repertoire in this study is popular music and descriptive printed scores are not common, it is my role as analyst and transcriber to decide how to interpret meter.[57] As such, the analytic transcriptions in this study should be considered ways of hearing performance timings as various types of flexible meter and not as definitive, prescriptive scores. All transcriptions refer to the studio-recording performance unless otherwise indicated. In some cases, this is the only recorded performance of the song. In others, many performances exist, but the studio recording likely has the widest dissemination.

efforts." Knowles (2016, 50–1) describes Horlacher's "metrical dissolution" as the reversal of "metrical emergence" (where cues appear and encourage the listener to count a consistent pulse) in which "levels of counting dissolve as metrical cues disappear or begin to conflict with each other." Lopez (2020) analyzes the opening flute solo of Copland's *Duo for Flute and Piano* and observes how changes of tempo can impact the perception of meter, ambiguity, and vagueness.

[57] For more on metric transcription, see Murphy (2020). For an explanation of the differences between prescriptive and descriptive transcriptions, see Seeger (1958, 184).

3

Regular and Reinterpreted Meter

Drawing on the stylistic, cultural, and historical context of Chapter 1 and the methodology outlined in Chapter 2, this chapter begins my case studies of flexible meter in singer-songwriter music. Across the next three chapters I illustrate the connection between flexible meter and self-expression in examples with increasing metric malleability. I explore songs from the singer-songwriter repertoire that demonstrate several types of flexible meter, including contexts with Regular Meter, Reinterpreted Meter, fluctuations between Regular Meter and Lost Meter, and Ambiguous Meter with extreme levels of metric flexibility. In this chapter, I explore the individual expressive styles of Joni Mitchell, Paul Simon, and Cat Stevens through their use of Reinterpreted Meter. I begin by observing one example of Regular Meter to illustrate the relationship between meter and text in those contexts.[1]

Regular Meter

In Chapter 2, I describe Regular Meter as a metric scenario in which there are hierarchic patterns of rhythms, the beats of which are perceptually but not chronometrically equidistant.[2] Regular Meter can accommodate the standard timing fluctuations that are associated with minor human variation in performance. This perceptually regular metric hierarchy of two or more layers constitutes an essential system of measurement that anchors the timing of musical events and makes possible the powerful sensations of alignment or syncopation that can be heard once metric regularity is established.[3]

---

[1] I will not be examining Ideal Meter in this study because it is purely conceptual for this acoustic repertoire. This is because singer-songwriter music is self-accompanied, with minor human variations yielding timings that are not precisely regular. In the 1960s and 1970s, this repertoire did not include electronic mediation to create precise timings.

[2] This differentiates Regular Meter from Ideal Meter, the latter of which has precisely equal rhythms.

[3] Lester (1986, 120–23).

Times A-Changin'. Nancy Murphy, Oxford University Press. © Oxford University Press 2023.
DOI: 10.1093/oso/9780197635216.003.0003

Mitchell, "Little Green"

In contexts of Regular Meter, singer-songwriters can manipulate the placement of important words in their lyrics to align with metric accents, thereby giving them emphasis in performance. How a listener might interpret lyrical meaning is impacted by how the performer aligns or misaligns important words from metric or hypermetric accents. In the case of Joni Mitchell's song "Little Green," metric emphasis of important words points to a covert autobiographical association for the songwriter hidden from her audiences at the time of the song's release.

"Little Green" appears on Mitchell's 1971 album *Blue*, but it was one of her first original songs written in the mid-1960s.[4] Mitchell sings of a baby "born with the moon in cancer" to a father who traveled west and a mother (herself a "child with a child pretending") lying to her parents about the pregnancy and birth. The song climaxes as adoption papers are signed, and the mother feels sad and sorry but "not ashamed." To Mitchell's 1971 audiences, the song is a mournful tale sung about an unspecified mother.[5] But "Little Green" was more personal than audiences knew at this time. Its lyrics were "painfully autobiographical," written a year after Mitchell had a baby—a daughter named Kelly, suggesting an association with a specific shade of green—whom Mitchell gave up for adoption in 1965.[6] This information was not revealed publicly until 1997, when Mitchell began searching for her now-adult child.[7] The mournful lyrics take on new meaning with this discovery. References to "green" signal images of nature ("Like the color when the spring is born" and "Like the nights when the northern lights perform"), inexperience ("Like the children who've made her"), and also the secret association with her daughter's name ("Little green, have a happy ending"). While other songs on Mitchell's album *Blue* were praised in 1971 for their personal, vulnerable subject matter, "Little Green" was covertly the most personal song on the album.

I see an important connection between this meaning and Mitchell's self-expressive placement of the word "green" on hyperdownbeats in her studio-recording performance.[8] Her meter is Regular at all hierarchic levels,

---

[4] O'Brien (2001, 77).

[5] This was not an uncommon narrative perspective for Mitchell, whose songs like "Marcie" and "Nathan La Franeer" are third-person accounts of fascinating individuals.

[6] O'Brien (2001, 77).

[7] Whitesell (2008, 58); Johnson and Hawalsheka (1997).

[8] Performing the song live in the 1960s, Mitchell sometimes changed the lines "little green" to "Kelly green," further emphasizing their secretive meaning.

Figure 3.1 Mitchell, "Little Green" (0:22–0:43)

matching the prototypical metric hierarchy explored in Chapter 2. The accompaniment establishes a tactus beat that I interpret as a quarter note in $\frac{4}{4}$ (Figure 3.1), with guitar strumming rhythms articulating eighth-note subdivisions.

The tactus beats group easily into hypermetric units at the half- and whole-note levels. Rather than include a dot diagram below the staff, I provide numbers above to denote units of four half-note hyperbeats. Three statements of the word "green" are enclosed in boxes where they align with hyperdownbeats, the first of each group of four half-note beats. By assigning "green" to (hyper)metric accents, Mitchell reinforces the import of her subject matter through meter-text alignment. Revealing the song's meaning in the 1990s gives even greater importance to her metric accents on "green" on her 1971 studio-recording performance. I see these moments of metric emphasis on the painful secret of Mitchell's baby as a hidden call for understanding her private pain. Though this is not an example of metric flexibility,

REGULAR AND REINTERPRETED METER   57

it demonstrates an important connection between Regular Meter and self-expression in the singer-songwriter repertoire.

Reinterpreted Meter

Many songs from the 1960s and 1970s singer-songwriter repertoire demonstrate the kind of self-expression through meter-text alignment shown in "Little Green." But since theories of metric hierarchy do so well to account for this type of self-expressive Regular Meter, this will not be a further focus in the present study. Instead, songs with more flexible meter, particularly those that interrupt a metric hierarchy or demonstrate Ambiguous Meter, are the focus. Indeed, there are some compelling examples of each of these flexible metric types in this repertoire. In the remainder of this chapter, I analyze examples of Reinterpreted Meter that occur during important passages in these singer-songwriter lyrics.[9] These examples are by no means the most flexible cases of singer-songwriter meter (those are reserved for later chapters), but they show how metric disruptions, no matter how small or temporary, can serve as techniques of self-expression in this repertoire.

Reinterpreted Meter comprises the third type of flexible meter outlined in Chapter 2. Songs of this metric type are mostly Regular but contain passages of interruption in which grouping cues in performance encourage a conceptualization of beats being added to or removed from the metric hierarchy. Added beats result when an expected beat in the hierarchy does not occur but instead appears later than anticipated, giving a sense of waiting, delay, or suspension of time. Omitted beats occur when stressed events arrive earlier than expected based on the previously established rhythms.[10] These types of reinterpretations express eagerness and a desire to move the narrative forward more quickly. In some passages, reinterpretations

---

[9] Similar techniques are found in other popular music repertoires, too. See, for example, Everett (2009); Neal (2000). But I do not mean to argue that every reinterpretation in popular music has expressive significance. In some cases, for example, added beats between phrases allow a singer to re-group, breathe, or remember the next set of lyrics. In other cases, reinterpretations between phrases—especially those that occur between some phrases and not others—instead generally reflect a highly flexible performance practice rather than a specific music-text connection. This seems to be the case for Bob Dylan's song "With God on Our Side," as explored in Murphy (2020).

[10] Neal (2000, 134–37) finds similar sensations associated with hypermetrical reinterpretations in Chris LeDoux's performance of "Cadillac Ranch," in which he manipulates hypermeter as part of a playful interaction with the audience.

58 TIMES A-CHANGIN'

express both types at different levels of the metric hierarchy and represent a general disorientation or unexpected emotions. In the examples that follow, I explore how Reinterpreted Meter occurs at moments of narrative significance and serves to demonstrate the individual expressive style of each artist.

Joni Mitchell's Rhapsodic Sentiments

In Joni Mitchell's early 1970s songs with Reinterpreted Meter, these reinterpretations occur as critical features of her self-expressive rhetoric, highlighting her personal lyrics and artistic freedom. The effect of metrical reinterpretations is a sensation of expressive interpolation, as if Mitchell is suddenly swept up in emotional declarations while singing. Her added beats give time for reflection during moments of self-discovery, while omitted beats often reflect a youthful eagerness to gain experience and wisdom. These expressive techniques of Reinterpreted Meter are present in the two examples that follow: "A Case of You" and "All I Want" both from her 1971 album *Blue*.

"A Case of You"

The song "A Case of You" is an ode to a lost romance, beginning with lyrics that describe a time before love "got lost" and proceeding to a refrain that suggests a once-potent love has since lost its strength ("I could drink a case of you, darling/Still I'd be on my feet"). Mitchell's second stanza illustrates a metrical reinterpretation motivated by a supplemental but emotionally central line in the stanza during which she references the melody of the Canadian national anthem. Figure 3.2 shows the five lines of the stanza in which line 4 stands out for several reasons: it is much shorter than the surrounding lines, it breaks up the prevailing regularity with assonance between "light" and

> On the back of a cartoon coaster
> In the blue TV screen light
> I drew a map of Canada
> Oh Canada
> With your face sketched on it twice

Figure 3.2 Mitchell, "A Case of You," lyrics, end of stanza 1

Figure 3.3 Mitchell, "A Case of You," metrical reinterpretation (0:40–1:04)

"twice." Further, it is syntactically redundant—it could be removed without detriment to the meaning of the surrounding text. This line seems to function as a spontaneous emotional interpolation, a lyrical exclamation of patriotism or of nostalgia for her homeland.

The musical setting echoes this disruption of the poetic structure. My analytic transcription in Figure 3.3 illustrates the Regular Meter and two-bar hypermeter that characterize this passage. The initial arrival on the word "Canada" in m. 24 sounds like a hyperdownbeat at the breve level, which would maintain the established hypermeter. However, the simultaneous stressed events at the final syllable of "Canada" encourage hearing a

60 TIMES A-CHANGIN'

metrical reinterpretation here.[11] This shifts a possible hyperdownbeat to m. 25, supported by a durationally and dynamically accented tonic scale degree after the 3–2–1 descent in the melody and an accented downbeat arrival in the newly added guitar part (played by James Taylor). At the whole-note level, there is an omitted half-note beat; this accounts for the sensations of these m. 25 stresses arriving too early. At the breve level, the hyperdownbeat shifts from the empty circle forward to the circled dot. Added beats at this hypermetric level give Mitchell time for her self-expressive digression. She is taking a moment here to be swept up by her recollections of Canada. Within this verse, her sentiments for her homeland with the twice-sketched face of her former love show a heightened awareness emerging from the poignant superimposition of these two powerfully nostalgic images. The moment of flexible meter (in this case Reinterpreted Meter) demonstrates how the sentimental priorities of her expressive interpolation can disrupt a prevailing meter to powerful effect.

"All I Want"

In a similar pattern of self-expression, the opening song on her album *Blue*— "All I Want"—also demonstrates flexible meter as a reflection of a personal narrative. This song offers another glimpse into Mitchell's psyche on her 1971 album. "All I Want" presents the narrative of Mitchell on a quest for personal freedom.[12] Lloyd Whitesell classifies this as an "ingénue song" in which the intensity comes from Mitchell's "response to life's pleasures and pains, as if experiencing them for the first time," with her exuberance resulting in "phrases that gush out of a stream of insistent repetitions and volatile emotions."[13] Lyrics like "I hate you some, I hate you some/I love you some/I love you when I forget about me" illustrate a growing self-awareness and the sense that in her traveling, the narrator will also experience a personal education.

The sense of eagerness in Mitchell's lyrics for "All I Want" is highlighted by passages of flexible meter that necessitate metrical reinterpretations. The first of these occurs in the passage in Figure 3.4 between the first and the second vocal phrase. I show this Reinterpreted Meter as metric additions at

[11] In the Canadian national anthem, the final syllable of the word "Canada" is also metrically accented. This adds further support to an interpretation of this moment as a hyperdownbeat in Mitchell's song.

[12] Monk (2012, 129) suggests that Mitchell wrote the song based on her trip to Europe in 1970.

[13] Whitesell (2008, 66–67).

REGULAR AND REINTERPRETED METER   61

Figure 3.4 Mitchell, "All I Want" (0:21–0:34)

the whole-note and breve levels of the metric hierarchy, which corresponds to the sense of m. 18 lengthening from a bar of 4 to a bar of 6 beats.[14] These reinterpretations correspond to a rhetorical pause in the lyrics at that moment, to give Mitchell time to explore what she might be "looking for" on the "lonely road" she is traveling.[15] The added beats offer more time to respond to the question "what can it be?"[16]

---

[14] With no stress cue on the third half note of m. 18, I have decided not to give this moment a downbeat in a ⅞ meter like I do later for m. 26 in Figure 3.5. In that passage, there is a vocal stress and dulcimer chord on that beat, suggesting a metric accent.

[15] Neal (2000, 121–22) finds similar moments of suspension in the song "I Don't Have to Wonder" by Garth Brooks, describing sensations of stretching in association with lyrical meaning and a playful performance practice.

[16] At the hypermetric level, there is also a metric omission occurring at this moment that shortens the hypermeasure from 4 measures to 2.5 measures, which adds a layer of temporal disorientation to this moment.

Figure 3.5 Mitchell, "All I Want" (0:34–0:47)

The relocated hyperdownbeats occur at moments that reveal critical narrative information in the song: there is a love interest about whom the narrator has conflicting feelings. Mitchell's reinforcing of the word "hate" on the m. 19 downbeat is echoed in subsequent statements of the word "love." Figure 3.5 illustrates that both "love" and "hate" align with downbeats in the ⁴⁄₄ meter. In m. 23, I have positioned "love" on a hyperdownbeat, which gives this a similar metric emphasis to m. 20. However, since the beat in m. 20 is unexpected, Mitchell's stresses on its arrival offer some self-expressive reasoning: hatred may be the primary emotion and is the impetus for the narrator's solo quest for self-discovery. This disdain for her former love is reinforced in m. 28 when another metrical reinterpretation highlights the word "strong," this time through omitted beats at the whole-note and breve levels. The metric omissions between m. 25 and m. 27 emphasize the eagerness with which Mitchell's narrator desires this strength. She has begun

REGULAR AND REINTERPRETED METER   63

to find an answer to what she is "looking for," and the flexible meter helps propel the lyrics forward so she can eagerly express her newfound personal desires. Both "A Case of You" and "All I Want" illustrate the close coordination between self-expression and flexible meter in Mitchell's studio-recording performances on this confessional singer-songwriter album.

Paul Simon: Reinterpreted Meter Expressing Enigmatic Lyrics

In Paul Simon's singer-songwriter music, lyrics are not as overtly personal as Mitchell's. His songwriting (both solo and with Art Garfunkel) capitalizes on trends in the folk revival, bridging a gap between intimate folk music and the aloof "coolness" of the folk-rock style. I will discuss two of his songs that feature metrical reinterpretations in the form of added and omitted beats: "The Sound of Silence" and "April Come She Will." These instances of Reinterpreted Meter highlight specific passages of Simon's otherwise enigmatic lyrical narratives. The flexible meter in these songs is an exemplar of Simon's 1960s style and one of the ways that this style borrows from the techniques of singer-songwriter self-expression, both in his duets with Art Garfunkel and in his solo performances of these songs on *The Paul Simon Songbook* (1965).

"The Sound of Silence"

In "The Sound of Silence" (recorded by Simon & Garfunkel on *Wednesday Morning, 3 A.M.*), metrical reinterpretations emphasize references to sensory imagery in the lyrics.[17] The text describes the dream images of silent crowds of people with whom the narrator is attempting to communicate. These crowds ignore him and instead silently pray to the "neon god they made."

---

[17] Simon wrote the song in the early 1960s, and he performed it solo and as a duet with Art Garfunkel. The duo's initial acoustic version on *Wednesday Morning, 3 A.M.* (1964) was re-released as a single in 1965, overdubbed with drums and electric bass and guitar. Following this, Simon also recorded a solo acoustic version on *The Paul Simon Songbook*. The duo reunited, after the overdubbed single achieved commercial success, to re-record the song with a folk-rock ensemble on their 1966 album *The Sounds of Silence*. All recordings of the song between 1963 and 1966 feature the same grouping irregularities, which highlight important moments in the lyrical narrative. For a detailed history of the "The Sound of Silence," see Stephan-Robinson (2009, 2–11).

64 TIMES A-CHANGIN'

Figure 3.6 Simon, "The Sound of Silence" (0:00–0:39)

The song begins as shown in Figure 3.6, with a clear ⅜ meter. As it progresses, the grouping of several passages encourages metrical reinterpretations.[18] For example, the change of harmony and the stress at the word "vision" at m. 10 suggest a placement on a metric downbeat, which necessitates a metrical reinterpretation in m. 9: an addition at the whole-note level and a deletion at the breve level. A similar reinterpretation occurs in m. 13, where the strong stresses on the word "sound" encourage hyperdownbeat placement. And this is followed by a further reinterpretation in m. 15 when the accompaniment returns to the motive from m. 1 and the melody for "In restless dreams I walked alone" parallels that of "Hello darkness my old friend." This encourages hearing mm. 19–20 as parallel to mm. 1–2, so that both

---

[18] Since there is no change to the quarter-note level of the metric hierarchy for this song, I have not included it in the dot diagram.

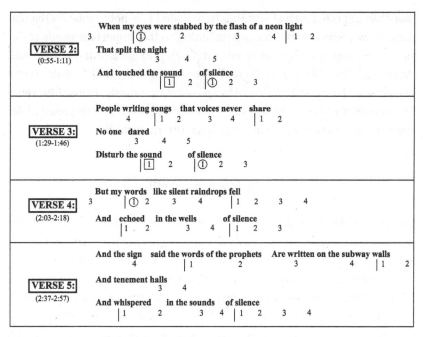

Figure 3.7 Simon, "The Sound of Silence," Reinterpreted Meter, verses 2–5

units begin with a hyperdownbeat.[19] Doing so yields a reinterpretation so that the breve-level hyperdownbeat that *would* have occurred in m. 14 is reinterpreted to m. 15, paralleling m. 1 and resetting the meter so that "alone" occurs on a downbeat of a similar strength to "friend" in m. 2.

These reinterpretations reflect grouping preferences and express the lyrics at these moments. This placement of "silence" on a hyperdownbeat gives it metric emphasis that suggests that "silence" is more important than "sound," as an oxymoronic modifier of the kind of sound being heard. Metric additions occur here to emphasize both titular words and also words pertaining to other senses (like "vision"), marking these as essential to the narrative that will follow.

The metric emphasis on sensory-oriented lyrics is continued into the remaining verses. Figure 3.7 illustrates moments of hypermetric reinterpretations occurring in parallel passages in verses 2 through 5. The numbers indicate half-note beats, which typically group into four-bar hypermetric units. Circles around downbeats indicate that they arrive earlier than expected—when beats of the previous measure are omitted. Downbeats with square boxes indicate a

---

[19] Such a choice engages the grouping parallelism preference discussed in Chapter 2.

66 TIMES A-CHANGIN'

later-than-expected arrival resulting from added half-note beats. As the diagram shows, Simon varies the metric setting so that important words at different moments in each verse receive emphasis through Reinterpreted Meter. Words like "eyes" (verse 2), "sound" (verses 2 and 3), and "words" (verse 4) receive such emphasis, followed by an entirely metrically regular fifth verse. Throughout the song there is a clear connection between Reinterpreted Meter and references to the senses within Simon's performances.[20]

"April Come She Will"

On his song "April Come She Will" (from *The Paul Simon Songbook*, 1965, the meter of which is repeated on 1966's *Sounds of Silence* with Art Garfunkel), Simon's inclusion of flexible meter mimics Mitchell's metric flexibility explored earlier in this chapter. Within his ⅜ meter for this song, Reinterpreted Meter occurs at moments that express themes of time, stasis, and urgency. Like "The Sound of Silence," "April Come She Will" is an enigmatic lyrical narrative: it references a failed relationship over a passage of time with lyrics that hint at, but never reveal, the reason for the relationship's gradual demise. Figure 3.8 includes a passage from verse 1, in which Simon sings about streams swelling with rain and the meter swells like the stream, with added beats expanding a four-bar hypermetric unit to five bars.[21] Similar additions occur in the next two hypermeasures to create five-bar units instead of the more typical four-bar units. These lengthened metric units occur in association with the lyrics "May she will stay" and "Resting in my arms again," further emphasizing the connection between metric flexibility (here as added beats) and sensations of expanded time and space in the lyrics.

Simon's Solo Singer-Songwriter Style

Simon's flexible meter in these two songs serves locally expressive purposes in the meter-text connection: Reinterpreted Meter draws attention to important

---

[20] The same metrical reinterpretations occur on Simon's duet with Art Garfunkel (on *Wednesday Morning, 3 A.M.* and their re-recording on *Sounds of Silence*) and on his solo album *The Paul Simon Songbook*.

[21] This is another example of hypermetric-unit extension common to various genres of popular music. Neal (2000, 34) notes that unit extensions in country music occur to add to general effects of expression, interest, and space for interaction among instruments.

REGULAR AND REINTERPRETED METER 67

Figure 3.8 Simon, "April Come She Will" (0:20–0:37)

moments in the song narratives. But the flexible meter also has a broader purpose for Simon. It shows that he was attuned to solo songwriting trends in the 1960s, like the inclusion of techniques of metric flexibility that occurred in music by solo singer-songwriters during this period. He was not a central figure in the Greenwich Village folk scene the way that Bob Dylan was, but there is evidence here through his own inclusion of flexibility in performances (both in Simon & Garfunkel and as a solo artist) that he understood the musical trends of self-expression in the singer-songwriter tradition. The presence of flexible meter in Simon's songs signals that malleable meter was a critical self-expressive feature in singer-songwriter music and that Simon was to some degree aware of this and ensured that his music in this solo style included it, too.

Cat Stevens's Introspection

For Cat Stevens, who began his career in the late 1960s as a pop star, flexible meter is critical to his musical comeback as a singer-songwriter in the 1970s. Stevens engaged in trends from the introspective singer-songwriter period as part of a musical rebranding underscored by a personal, spiritual transformation. This,

68 TIMES A-CHANGIN'

too, marked his membership in the flexible singer-songwriter performance practice. Several of his 1970s compositions synthesize some of the techniques of metric flexibility examined so far. Three of his songs "The Wind," "Into White," and "Katmandu" are personal narratives of reflection and self-discovery through meditative activities and travel. And in each case, Reinterpreted Meter occurs in service of expressing time or vivid sensory imagery in the lyrics.

"The Wind"

In "The Wind" from his 1971 album *Teaser and the Firecat*, Stevens reflects on his past errors ("I swam upon the devil's lake") but vows never again to repeat the same mistakes. In both verses of "The Wind," Stevens's flexible meter highlights his repetitions of the word "never." After singing about sitting "on the setting sun," Stevens states "never" four times after the phrase "never wanted water once." During the passage in mm. 17–18 of Figure 3.9, the word first appears on a metric accent on beat 3 of m. 17, but this downbeat placement is withheld from subsequent statements. In his final repetitions in mm. 21–22, Stevens's timing yields two metric deletions, which both serve to emphasize the second syllable of his last declamation of the word and reinforce its finality. His metric flexibility in this verse is repeated in the second verse when Stevens sings about swimming "upon the Devil's lake" and vowing to "never make the same mistake." Here the "Devil's lake" seems to serve as a metaphor for Stevens's past life as a teenage pop star, touring with Jimi Hendrix. When he contracted tuberculosis in 1969, the resulting illness and long recovery that followed were the catalyst for Stevens to interrogate his lifestyle, study religion, and investigate his own spirituality.[22] In "The Wind," his word repetitions and Reinterpreted Meter highlight his remorse and emphasize the permanence of this personal transformation.

"Into White"

Similar techniques of self-expression occur in his song "Into White" (from *Tea for the Tillerman*, 1971), where flexible meter highlights the visual

---

[22] The biography on Stevens's (2020) official website offers the following as explanation for the cause of his illness: "In 1968 the heavy work load of touring, media commitments, and the perks

Figure 3.9 Stevens, "The Wind" (0:29–0:49)

70 TIMES A-CHANGIN'

Figure 3.10 Stevens, "Into White" (0:30–0:50)

imagery of color and lights as representative of a spiritual awakening. The song's introduction begins with a ¾ meter. The middle system of Figure 3.10 includes a passage in which the arrival on the word "light" is accented by a

of a pop-star lifestyle took its toll and Cat contracted a potentially fatal bout of tuberculosis which hospitalized him for several months. It was during this time that he began a significant process of inner reflection and meditation."

harmonic change, a long duration, and a higher vocal register. These factors necessitate omitted beats that shorten the hypermeasure. Stevens's voicing creates a cross-relation between the melodic G♯ and the bass's G natural across the measure that intensifies the point of arrival in m. 22.

In the third system, Stevens's timing highlights the syncopated arrival of the word "white" through metric omissions in m. 28, creating a single $\frac{2}{4}$ measure. The sensation here is that the narrative is thrust forward—as if the "emptying into white" is occurring much faster than expected. And this sensation is compounded by Stevens's arrival on the word "white" a quarter-note earlier on E3, then sliding the pitch upward to F♯3. When the introductory material returns in m. 31, it yields a metric addition that shifts the possible hyperdownbeat in m. 29 to m. 31. I see this as allowing time for the emphasized arrival on "white" to register, its color representing a spiritual transformation and the blank slate of a new beginning. The Reinterpreted Meter helps to convey the expressive impact of dissolving the previous lines' imagery into the peaceful white of Stevens's spiritual awakening.

"Katmandu"

I read a similar type of awakening in his song "Katmandu" (from *Mona Bone Jakon*, 1970a), but this time resulting from a change of physical location rather than spiritual state. "Katmandu" explores temporality as a theme both in the lyrics and within the groupings of the performance rhythms. Stevens's narrator describes his cultural experiences in the Nepalese city of Kathmandu as a "strange, bewildering time," which characterizes passages of Reinterpreted Meter in Stevens's performance.[23]

In his guitar introduction, Stevens provides a steady stream of eighth notes with accentual patterns that yield irregular groupings. My analytic transcription in Figure 3.11 shows one interpretation of these groupings. The metric analysis below the staff includes additions and omissions to accommodate metrical reinterpretations that occur between the $\frac{4}{4}$ and $\frac{6}{8}$ metric groupings. In m. 5, this odd grouping organizes into a $\frac{4}{4}$ meter, but new accentual cues yield either a 2 + 2 + 4 grouping of eighth-note beats as I notate on the score

---

[23] In Murphy (2016) I explore temporal themes in "Time," "Katmandu," and "Into White" as reflections of Stevens's 1968 illness and subsequent year-long recovery.

Figure 3.11 Stevens, "Katmandu," introduction (0:08–0:16)

or a 2 + 3 + 3 grouping, which I show below the upper voices of the guitar system. The metric irregularities of this introductory passage (both the irregular meter and the irregular groupings within the $\frac{4}{4}$ meter) initiate the context of metric flexibility to reflect the "bewildering" time that Stevens experiences in Kathmandu.

The first metrical reinterpretation involving the vocal line occurs in mm. 1–15 when Stevens reports that the vast "morning lake" is drinking up the sky; two metric additions occur to accommodate the flexible timing of this passage. These allow time for the listener to imagine this occurrence and its physical and expressive impact. As in the introduction, in other locations metrical reinterpretations reflect the more general theme of bewildering time. One such instance occurs before the refrain as shown in the last few measures of Figure 3.12. The odd accompaniment grouping in m. 16 yields an extra eighth-note sub-tactus beat that shifts the arrival of the final syllable of "Katmandu" at the tactus level of the dot diagram and all higher metric levels. This effect gives emphasis to the specific location of all of Stevens's temporal bewilderment.

Figure 3.12 Stevens, "Katmandu" (0:16–0:42)

Stevens's Introspection

The flexible meter in this song—as well as "The Wind" and "Into White"—illustrates the relationship between Stevens's timing and his self-expression. This shows the way he manipulates the meter of his songs to evoke text and temporal themes. But it also gives some indications about Stevens's personal revelations as he shifted from being a heavily produced teenage pop star to a serious, introspective singer-songwriter. As I explore more in Chapter 4, this shift occurred after

74   TIMES A-CHANGIN'

a serious illness forced Stevens into isolation and resulted in a self-expressive style that aligned with the emerging confessional singer-songwriter tradition. His flexible meter in songs demonstrates some of his musical techniques of self-expression during this period of musical and personal transformation.

A Closer Look: Joni Mitchell's
"Lesson in Survival"

The preceding examples illustrate how the flexible metric structures of Reinterpreted Meter are critical features of text emphasis and self-expression in this singer-songwriter repertoire. To synthesize these findings, I move to a more in-depth case study of metrical reinterpretation as a technique of self-expression in Joni Mitchell's song "Lesson in Survival" from her 1972 album *For the Roses*. This album is a follow-up to her success with 1971's *Blue*, and Mitchell once again delivers personal insights and arranges these ideas within a metrically flexible musical setting. The lyrics for "Lesson in Survival" are a "furrowed brow monologue" in which Mitchell's text resembles speech patterns more than regular poetic structure.[24] In the analysis that follows, I explore the timings of "Lesson in Survival" through the lens of flexible meter and show that the song's metric flexibility is essential to the rhetoric of its conversational lyrical quality.

Lyrics and Form

The narrative of "Lesson in Survival" is initially enigmatic; it is not immediately clear what the "lesson" is, what the narrator means by "survival," and more broadly what this context might mean about Mitchell's personal survival. A clearer meaning is gradually unveiled, with crucial information emerging in a few passages of the lyrics that occupy parallel formal positions in their respective stanzas.[25] In Figure 3.13, I arrange the song's lyrics into three columns (one per verse) and indicate four formal sections (A, B, C, and D) as four rows to organize parallel musical content shared by the three verses. For

---

[24] Whitesell (2008, 41) suggests that in the lyrics for this song, Mitchell demonstrates her ability to mold "poetry out of spontaneous conversation."

[25] A similar technique of metric flexibility in parallel material occurs in "Blue" (another voice-and-piano song) examined in Chapter 4. This is also the case in "Katmandu" (Figure 3.12).

		VERSE 1		VERSE 2		VERSE 3
	0:00–0:06	Piano Introduction	1:00–1:07	Piano Introduction	2:01–2:07	Piano Introduction
A	0:06–0:20	Lesson in survival...	1:07–1:19	Maybe it's paranoia...	2:07–2:20	I went to see a friend tonight...
B	0:20–0:29	You need to believe in something Once I could in our love	1:19–1:27	Oh baby I can't seem to make it With you socially...	2:20–2:29	I came in as bright As a neon light...
C	0:29–0:49	...That's fine sometimes But I know my needs...	1:27–1:52	...Love to see that green water in motion I'm going to get a boat...	2:29–2:51	...Watched them buckle up In his brow
D	0:49–1:00	...Deep kisses And the sun going down	1:52–2:01	Fresh salmon frying And the tide rolling in	2:51–3:11	...Magnet and iron The souls

Figure 3.13 Mitchell, "Lesson in Survival," verses and sections

example, the A section in verse 1 has a similar melody and harmonic progression to the A sections in verses 2 and 3. As the lyrics unfold, Mitchell explains the lesson: that the survival involves overcoming a past relationship and that there are many reasons why it ended. The grey boxes in Figure 3.13 highlight passages where metrical reinterpretations occur in Mitchell's studio-recording performance. These moments of metric flexibility arise within the B and C sections and in the final line of each D section. Though each parallel section has similar musical content, they have varying levels of metric flexibility.[26]

In parallel moments of each verse, Mitchell gives special emphasis, both melodically and metrically, to highlight revelatory passages in the narrative. These instances of metric flexibility illustrate her techniques of text expression through metrical reinterpretation. In the analysis that follows, I examine the B, C, and D sections of each verse to illustrate the parallel moments of flexible meter as connected to her revelations of critical narrative information and of the practice of self-expression in this song.

B Sections: Melodic Descent

The first metrical reinterpretation occurs in the B section of verse 1. I have illustrated this passage in Figure 3.14.[27] In the A section, Mitchell mentions

---

[26] Whitesell (2008, 159) sees this song as generally demonstrative of irregular phrase structure, illustrating at one point a phrase structure with measures grouped in the pattern "2+4+2+3+4+4?"

[27] My musical representation of "Lesson in Survival" was completed in reference to the Blackburn (2023) transcription of the song available on Joni Mitchell's official website. The metric analysis is entirely my own.

"Guru books" and the Bible as formalized paths to faith that have been a poor fit for her, serving only as a reminder that she is "just not good enough." She concedes that there is some benefit to believing "in something" and reveals that she had such a belief in her previous relationship. The first-person pronoun addresses her former partner and suggests that her commitment might not have been reciprocated.

I have included these A and B sections in Figure 3.14. The first four measures of this excerpt establish a four-bar hypermetric unit in the $\frac{4}{4}$ meter. Mitchell's piano accompaniment provides a steady stream of eighth notes that subdivide the quarter-note tactus; half-note chords in the piano's right hand group these tactus beats. In the third bar of the second system, the melodic leap to C#5

Figure 3.14 Mitchell, "Lesson in Survival," verse 1, A and B sections (0:06–0:29)

REGULAR AND REINTERPRETED METER 77

provides a peak of emotional intensity at the transition between the A and B sections that is released in the descending melodic line that follows. This brings metric change and structural uncertainty to the subsequent material. The setting of the line "You need to believe in something/Once I did in our love" aligns each vocal stress with the established quarter-note tactus. Mitchell's text stress, as well as her clear metric arrival on the word "our," results in an extra tactus beat in the preceding measure labeled with a $\frac{5}{4}$ time signature. A metrical reinterpretation is necessary here. My annotations below the staff show the expected location of the hyperbeats at the whole-note and breve levels with an empty circle, and the beats in the subsequent $\frac{4}{4}$ bar occur a quarter note later than expected. Mitchell's timings result in an extended measure as she sings about needing to believe in something (referencing the religious texts in the previous lyrics) and revealing to her listeners that there is a specific love in which she once believed. This gives important context to the narrative information to follow and it is marked for attention with the flexible meter in this passage.

The material in this verse 1 excerpt is paralleled in verse 2, where there is again a melodic leap to C♯5 followed by a descending melody. This time, however, Mitchell's timings do not necessitate a metrical reinterpretation. This passage shown in Figure 3.15 maintains a $\frac{4}{4}$ meter throughout, as Mitchell sings "Oh baby I can't seem to make it with you socially" to pinpoint a failure in the relationship. The content of the final line of this section ("there's this reef around me") speaks to the social limitations the narrator is experiencing. These limitations are mirrored in the metric setting, which is unable to break free from regularity to demonstrate the flexible meter of the parallel sections.

In the third verse's B section, the metrical flexibility returns as Mitchell sings the lines "I came in as bright/As a neon light/And I burned out/Right there before him" to the descending melodic line. In this instance, the descending line depicts the burning out and loss of energy. Mitchell confides in her friend and notices that her visit seems "to darken him" because he presumes "suspicious reasoning" for her ramblings toward him, as if her excited chatter hides larger, more negative emotions. Seeing his brow furrow in concern shows her how poorly she was hiding her emotions; interrogating her feelings further provides impetus to end her romantic relationship. Figure 3.16 illustrates this B section passage in verse 3.[28] Like verse 1,

---

[28] I illustrate the grouping of this added eighth-note beat as 8 + 1 rather than a bar of $\frac{9}{8}$ but this is a notational convenience to denote an $\frac{8}{8}$ ($\frac{4}{4}$) bar with extra eighth note (in a 2 + 2 + 2 + 3 grouping). Blackburn's (2023) transcription shows this as a $\frac{7}{8}$ bar followed by a bar of $\frac{9}{8}$ before the return to $\frac{4}{4}$ at the word "burned."

Figure 3.15 Mitchell, "Lesson in Survival," verse 2, B melodic descent (1:18–1:27)

Figure 3.16 Mitchell, "Lesson in Survival," verse 3, B section (2:20–2:26)

Mitchell's timings shift the expected hyperbeats by the value of an eighth note. This impacts the meter at the quarter-note level and above. Her placement of the word "burned" in alignment with the reinterpreted downbeat and hyperdownbeat provides emphasis to the meaning of this word in contrast with the "bright" in the previous measure. Such emphasis illustrates the negative effects of the narrator's relationship, witnessed by the friend in whom she confides. It is a signal of their eventual breakup, which is an act of self-preservation for Mitchell as the narrator.

C Sections: Escape and Freedom

Within the C sections of each verse, Mitchell includes metric flexibility that highlights either the freedoms the narrator will experience outside the relationship or the realization that she must escape. Each verse's flexible C material features parallel musical content and metric flexibility to highlight Mitchell's self-expressive meaning. The first such passage occurs in verse 1 and illustrates the musical content to follow in parallel sections. Here Mitchell suggests that it was the social aspect of her relationship that isolated her, comparing her confinement to the "double yellow line" that separates opposing lanes of traffic. In her performance, the piano includes a repeated F#2 in the left hand supporting an F# major seventh chord with flattened fifth harmony, and syncopation both in the piano's right hand and in the vocal line. Mitchell's stress on the word "know" results in a $\frac{3}{4}$ measure grouping for the second measure in Figure 3.17. The result is a metrical reinterpretation at the whole-note level, in which the expected beat shown with the empty circle is shifted forward a half-note value. From the perspective of Mitchell's self-expression, this addition to

Figure 3.17 Mitchell, "Lesson in Survival," verse 1, C section (0:36–0:44)

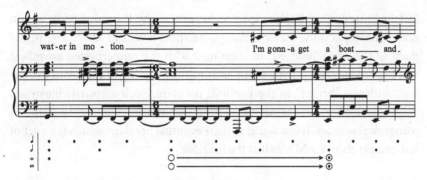

Figure 3.18 Mitchell, "Lesson in Survival," verse 2, C section (1:32–1:45)

the hierarchy allows time for the "fine sometimes" to process and gives her a moment to collect herself before explaining why it is not always fine to have "campers in the kitchen." At the breve hypermetric level, the possible two-bar hypermeasure of 4 half-note beats is shortened to 3 half-note beats. This reflects an eagerness to move the narrative forward so she can express her realization in the subsequent lyrics that she needs more "quiet times." Her meter echoes some of these issues with time.

This parallel moment in the second verse has similar additions in the form of a ⅜ bar and draws on the water imagery occurring throughout the song. Figure 3.18 illustrates this passage in the third verse, when Mitchell sings about loving to "see that green water in motion" and the piano's repeated F♯2 and syncopated rhythms evoke the moving water. The metric effect here is slightly different from the previous verse: in this case the syncopation to the downbeat of the ⅜ bar withholds a clear stress at this moment. I have notated this as a metric downbeat to maintain a ¼ meter as long as possible, but I do not hear hyperdownbeats here, as I represent with open circles in the hierarchy diagram. It is not until the next bar that beats at the whole-note and breve levels can be confirmed.[29] So the sensation here is of time suspended across the ⅜ bar. Only quarter and half-note beats in the meter are salient, and the measure is lengthened to allow the imagery of water and its musical depiction more time to resonate for Mitchell and her listeners.

In the final verse, the flexible C passage illustrates part of the narrator's realization that the waters of this relationship might drown her. This passage

---

[29] But even these are slightly obscured by Mitchell's unexpected emphasis on the word "get" and by the accent on the final beat of the ⅜ bar.

REGULAR AND REINTERPRETED METER 81

Figure 3.19 Mitchell, "Lesson in Survival," verse 3, C section (2:29–3:11)

(shown in Figure 3.19) addresses the narrator's confiding in a friend, telling him the same information she is giving to her audience, and recalls how he reacts. To musically illustrate the "buckle" in his brow, Mitchell returns to the repeated piano F♯2. The right hand in this passage on the quarter note following the word "brow" sustains that harmony, thereby forcing attention to the piano's left hand. The possible hyperdownbeat in the 3/4 bar is not clearly articulated, so I show that beat with an empty circle. It is not until Mitchell's stress on the word "dig" in the final measure of Figure 3.19 that the hypermetric regularity is restored. The result is 6.5 quarter-note beats (or 13 eighth-note beats) between the downbeat of the 3/4 bar and the emphasis on "dig."[30] The Reinterpreted Meter includes an omitted eighth-note beat in the 7/8 bar that results in omissions at the tactus level and the half-note level. Hypermetrically, this is an addition, with the hyperdownbeat withheld in the 4/4 bar until the eventual restored meter. The sensation here is of Mitchell

---

[30] I have notated this as a bar of 3/4 and a bar of 7/8, as is shown in Blackburn's (2023) transcription, but I can also hear a reading that shows a bar of 4/4 followed by a bar of 5/8.

82 TIMES A-CHANGIN'

increasingly obscuring the $\frac{4}{4}$ meter, reflecting the disorienting effect of her friend's reaction to details about her relationship. The flexible meter suggests that the friend's furrowed brow unsettles the narrator—shifting her out of metric regularity—and encourages her to conclude her romantic relationship.

D Section: Dreams

The final section of each verse includes one more instance of self-expressive flexible meter, with the last of these clarifying the relationship's outcome. The D sections of each verse express the narrator's dreams about how the relationship might have satisfied her. In verse 1, this section contains metric flexibility in the passage with the lyrics "the sun going down" as shown in Figure 3.20. Mitchell's timings in this passage result in an extended measure, with an added eighth-note beat to create $\frac{9}{8}$ and an extended hypermetric unit in which a third bar lengthens the two-bar hypermetric unit to three bars. Throughout the same passage, groupings of three eighth notes in the right hand occur against the two-beat groupings in the left hand. This grouping dissonance depicts the "river flowing" that gives the narrator time for quiet contemplation. The metric and hypermetric additions give time for a rhetorical pause with the introduction of this peaceful imagery: with the flowing river, the narrator and her love interest embracing as the sun gradually sets. This is the narrator's ideal reality: a mental state more calm than when there are "campers in the kitchen." The metric flexibility allows for Mitchell to linger on this idealistic imagery before the second verse begins.

At the end of the second verse, Mitchell's narrator is again imagining a romantic ideal. The final lines of the second verse describe a similar fantasy to verse 1; here the couple is rowing a boat, then watching "fresh salmon frying/ And the tide rolling in." Both scenarios express a desire for closeness alongside imagery of open water, which occurs in contrast to the social "reef" she feels is confining her. Mitchell again depicts imagery of water in the final line of this verse, with a renewal of the 3-against-2 grouping, this time with a less clear 2-layer to group against and metric flexibility (Figure 3.21).[31] The groups of three eighth notes evoke a gradual,

incoming tide. In verse 1, Mitchell withholds hyperbeats for a single extended measure; this passage lengthens that process. The hyperbeats are

---

[31] For more on grouping dissonance and n-layers, see Krebs (1999, 23–26).

REGULAR AND REINTERPRETED METER   83

Figure 3.20 Mitchell, "Lesson in Survival," verse 1, D section (0:53–1:00)

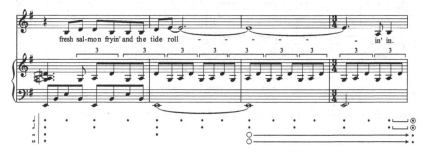

Figure 3.21 Mitchell, "Lesson in Survival," verse 2, D section (1:52–2:01)

withheld for a 2/4 bar and an additional 3/8. I interpret this 3/8 bar as a shortened 2/4, with one tactus beat omitted.[32] So again, there is a sensation of thrusting forward, earlier than expected, with an overall sense of lengthening, lingering on the peaceful imagery.

In the final verse's D section, Mitchell trades water imagery for "magnet and iron" as symbols of her narrator's attraction with the love interest. She exclaims that the emotional investigation into the negative effects of this relationship has made her "heavy company." The final, syntactically broken lines of the lyrics are devoted to the task of terminating their relationship. Mitchell describes souls in love attracted but failed in potential, with her statement "I will always love you" as a declaration of farewell. As she sings "magnet and iron" (Figure 3.22), Mitchell's performance revives the three-beat groupings of the previous D sections, this time evoking the pulsating attraction of the

---

[32] This passage could also be interpreted as a lengthening of the 3/8 bar from Figure 3.18 to 2/4.

84 TIMES A-CHANGIN'

Figure 3.22 Mitchell, "Lesson in Survival," verse 3, D section (2:51–4:06)

two substances. The flexible meter also results in a withheld hyperdownbeat in the first measure of the final system. In this concluding passage of the song, the downbeats shift indefinitely, with the song ending before any accentual cues are able to restore these beats. The effect evokes the lingering attraction of the couple that threatens to upend the lesson in survival.

Flexible Meter and Meaning

Mitchell's flexible meter in the studio recording of "Lesson in Survival" illuminates passages of critical narrative information for her listeners. Reinterpreted Meter in the form of added and removed beats occurs as she reveals what she is surviving (a problematic relationship) and how she feels about it (trapped and desiring personal freedom), describing her desires in connection with water imagery. The excerpts explored here show direct instances of meter-text expression through metrical reinterpretations, which continue similar trends of flexible meter on Mitchell's previous albums. But there is more at play here from the perspective of self-expression. Since many

REGULAR AND REINTERPRETED METER   85

listeners took Mitchell's songs to be autobiographical, these passages of flexible meter indicate a connection between the singer revealing personal truths in her songs and a malleable metric rhetoric that responds to her expressive whims. After the success of her introspective songwriting on *Blue*, Mitchell's audiences were primed to listen for personal revelations in her music. From the lens of confessional songwriting, it is assumed that the narrator is Mitchell herself or at least significant aspects of her personal experience are represented in this song: she is eschewing traditional expectations for domesticity of her gender in favor of personal freedom. "Lesson in Survival" shows the ways that Mitchell continues the rhetoric of self-expression she began on *Blue*, with Reinterpreted Meter highlighting important self-expressive passages in this revelatory song. In her performance, Mitchell reinforces flexible meter as an essential feature of her self-expressive rhetoric in her 1970s songwriting.

***

The examples in this chapter demonstrate an important relationship between metric flexibility and unique styles of self-expression in this repertoire for three of the singer-songwriters in this study. Paul Simon connects his work to the self-expressive practices of the 1960s folk-revival songwriting by including metrical reinterpretations to highlight meaning within his enigmatic lyrics. Unlike other artists in this study, Simon is known more for performing with other musicians than as a soloist. Perhaps because of this Simon takes his flexible meter no further than Reinterpreted Meter, never venturing into contexts of metric ambiguity or vagueness.[33] Cat Stevens immersed himself in 1970s singer-songwriter trends as part of his musical reinvention. In closely tying his work to practices in the introspective period of singer-songwriter music, his work engages metric flexibility as an important stylistic marker, an assured signal of musical and narrative authenticity and sophistication. For Joni Mitchell, including Reinterpreted Meter highlights revelatory passages in her personal lyrics. Metric flexibility in her songs signals a practice of rhapsodic self-expression that by 1972 had become a marker of her performance persona. In Chapter 4, I explore the ways that Mitchell and others move beyond Reinterpreted Meter to the metric rhetoric of Lost Meter for further self-expressive effect.

---

[33] As a result, there are no further examples from Paul Simon in this study. Regarding solo versus ensemble flexibility, Ford (1998, 71) makes a similar claim about the meter of solo Delta blues musicians like Robert Johnson, who "controlled their irregularities with remarkable sense of design" in part because they were soloists. Ford positions this repertoire in contrast to "their contemporaries in Chicago, such as Lonnie Johnson and Leroy Carr, who never drop or add a beat to the twelve-bar formula, mainly because they spent most of their time playing in ensembles."

4

Self-Expressive Innovations: Lost Meter

In the previous chapter, I explored the ways that Reinterpreted Meter is a technique of self-expression in 1960s and 1970s singer-songwriter music. Metrical reinterpretations bring attention to passages in song lyrics concerning time like urgency or stasis and reflect the broader stylistic rhetoric of metric interruption in this repertoire. In this chapter, I explore the self-expressive use of Lost Meter. For the sensations of Regular Meter to be Lost, rather than temporarily disrupted, expressive timing fluctuations must occur that cannot be understood as missing or extra strumming. Instead, the timings are so flexible—the singer is so caught up in a moment of pause—that regularity disappears. But in most examples from the singer-songwriter repertoire, this expressive metric loss is only temporary. Regular Meter is eventually regained through the process of metric emergence in which regularity returns after a brief passage of metric hiatus.[1] After metric loss, loosely spaced metric cues—stresses and durations—gradually or suddenly organize into clear rhythms with patterns of strong and weak beats, which create a conceptual metric hierarchy. The effect is of stability restored after a passage of self-expressive instability.

The expressive impact of Lost Meter is striking when compared with the regularity of surrounding sections, intensifying the self-expressive effects discussed in Chapter 3. In this chapter I explore three songs to showcase how different artists use the more extreme metric flexibility of Lost Meter as a self-expressive metric rhetoric. The first example is Bob Dylan's "Only a Pawn in Their Game," which serves as a characteristic instance of meter Lost and regained, with flexibility dramatically increasing in parallel sections of each stanza. Secondly, I illustrate how the flexible meter of Cat Stevens's "Time" refuses to settle into a single meter or conform to the grouping patterns of Regular Meter. I offer two readings of Stevens's song: one with frequent metrical reinterpretations and one as a series of metric projections. The different interpretations position the song as a point of transition between these two

---

[1] For more on metric emergence, see Horlacher (2000/2001).

Times A-Changin'. Nancy Murphy, Oxford University Press. © Oxford University Press 2023.
DOI: 10.1093/oso/9780197635216.003.0004

SELF-EXPRESSIVE INNOVATIONS: LOST METER 87

metric theories and show how multiple sensations of temporality are essential to understanding Stevens's lyrics and metric style. Lastly, in my analysis of Joni Mitchell's "Blue," I fuse together the theories of hierarchic and process-based meter to analyze passages of Regular and Lost Meter as illustrating themes of freedom in her lyrics that are essential features of her 1970s performance aesthetic. In all three cases, changes in the metric trajectory—from regularity to loss and back—highlight important moments in the lyrical narrative and signal broader self-expressive features of each artist's performance style.

Bob Dylan's "Only a Pawn in Their Game"

At the height of Bob Dylan's protest song period, he included the track "Only a Pawn in Their Game" (hereafter "Only a Pawn") on his 1964 album *The Times They Are A-Changin'*.[2] This song contains a provocative lyrical message and seemingly improvised metric flexibility.[3] Dylan's lyrics address the 1963 murder of NAACP leader Medgar Evers, and his perspective differs from that of his contemporaries who wrote songs on the same topic. Rather than focusing on the victim of the violence, "Only a Pawn" describes a broader perspective: how politicians and policemen used the "poor white man" (in this case, Byron De La Beckwith, Evers's murderer) to enact their racist agenda.[4] Dylan's lyrics address the social stratification of structural racism, with the wealthy white people in power teaching poor white men to hate Black Americans as a distraction, so they "never think straight" about their own status in the larger sociopolitical game.[5]

[2] As mentioned in Chapter 1, Dylan openly disliked the term "protest song" and only acknowledged his status as a "protest singer" in an effort to refute it. He instead referred to himself as a writer of "contemporary songs"; see Scorsese (2005).

[3] It is unclear whether the flexible features of this performance are pre-planned or spontaneous, but they have the effect of spontaneity, which reflects and reinforces Dylan's unpredictable performance persona.

[4] Dylan never mentions De La Beckwith by name, but he is the "pawn" who is sung about. Other mid-1960s songs on this topic focused on Evers as the victim and how his death reflects the urgent civil-rights situation in the American South. For example, Nina Simone's "Mississippi Goddam" (released in 1964 on *Nina Simone in Concert*) is her response to Evers's death. Phil Ochs wrote songs referencing the harsh realities of living under Jim Crow in Mississippi in the 1960s. Several songs—including "Love Me, I'm a Liberal" (*Phil Ochs in* Concert, 1966) and "Too Many Martyrs," also titled "The Ballad of Medgar Evers" (recorded live on *Newport Broadside*, 1964; studio recording on *All the News That's Fit to Sing*, 1964)—reference Evers's murder.

[5] Harvey (2001, 82) encourages such a reading of the lyrics, describing the songwriter's perspective as supporting the common man, "even excusing a racist because he is a hapless pawn," saving condemnation instead for the corrupt officials who condone racism.

88 TIMES A-CHANGIN'

a	A bullet from the back of a bush took Medgar Evers' blood
b	A finger fired the trigger to his name
c1	A handle hid out in the dark
c2	A hand set the spark
d1	Two eyes took the aim
d2	Behind a man's brain
d3	But he can't be blamed
e	He's only a pawn in their game

Figure 4.1 Dylan, "Only a Pawn in their Game," verse 1 lyrics (0:00–0:30)

Dylan's performance engages two types of flexibility in his expression of these lyrics: the first is formal, with varying stanza lengths and an irregular number of line repetitions; the second relates to timing and Dylan's vacillations between Regular Meter and Lost Meter, with shifts to looser metric structures at expressive peaks in his performance. In my analysis, I argue that the song's flexibility is part of Dylan's self-expressive protest-song performance rhetoric. The Lost Meter highlights local details of his storytelling and the features of his unpredictable performance style. In this song, his formal and metric flexibility are manifestations of his broader, "shambolic" persona and imperfect performance aesthetic.[6]

Formal Flexibility

Dylan creates formal flexibility in "Only a Pawn" through unpredictable melodic line repetitions for each verse, which change the length of each strophe. Figure 4.1 shows the structure of the first verse, with five lines categorized as *a–e* based on similar pitch content. Dylan repeats the *c* line twice and the *d* line three times and changes both the number of repeats and the melodic content in subsequent verses. For example, he repeats the *c* lines 1–3 times; all iterations begin with a dyad from E4 to A3 shown in grey boxes in Figure 4.2. Each ends with an E3, typically through a melodic descent from A3 in the dotted line box.[7] For his *d* lines, the rhyme scheme follows

---

[6] This shambolic "aesthetic of imperfection" is the performance persona description coined by Gracyk (2006, 177) and Gioia (1998) and explored by Rings (2013, [3]).

[7] Verses 1 and 4 also include a turn motive D4–C♯4–B3–C♯4 (circled). To simplify this diagram, I have only included the syllable in the lyrics that aligns with the changes in the melody notes. So, if a word or syllable is not present, it is sung to the same pitch as the previous melody note. For example, in verse 1, the first syllable of the word "handle" is sung as an E4 pitch, like the preceding word "A," and is followed by a pitch change to A3 on the word's second syllable.

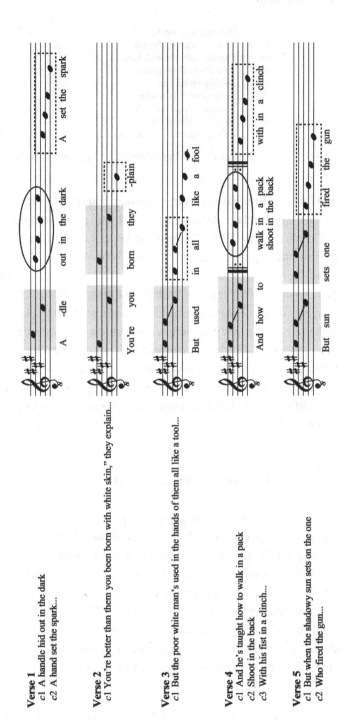

Figure 4.2 Dylan, "Only a Pawn in their Game," *c* line melodic motives

90 TIMES A-CHANGIN'

$d1$	He's taught in his school
$d2$	From the start by the rule
$d3$	That the laws are with'him
$d4$	To protect his white skin
$d5$	To keep up his hate
$d6$	So he never thinks straight
$d7$	'Bout the shape that he's in
$d8$	So it ain't him to blame
e	He's only a pawn in their game

Figure 4.3 Dylan, "Only a Pawn in their Game," verse 3 d lines and refrain

the number of line repetitions, which varies between 3 and 8.[8] In verse 1, the three d lines have words related by assonance or rhyme to the refrain's final word ("game"): "aim," "brain," and "blamed." In verse 3 (Figure 4.3), Dylan initially pairs lines through assonance or rhyme ("school" and "rule," "him" and "skin," and "hate" and "straight"). But despite this predictable couplet pairing, Dylan breaks the pattern in $d7$, with a the word "in" matching the "him/skin" rhyme in the $d3$–$d4$ couplets. He then ends $d8$ with "blame" to rhyme with the refrain. The varying number of melodic repetitions adds to the improvisatory quality of Dylan's performance. It has the effect that Dylan is cycling through his melodies as many times as wanted or needed to tell a certain amount of the story of Evers's murder. The unpredictability of the performance reinforces Dylan's broader unpredictable and imperfect performance aesthetic.

Consistently Flexible Form

There is a sensation with these varying verse lengths that Dylan is making in-the-moment decisions to deliver more or less of the narrative than previous verses, keeping the song's form unpredictable to maintain control of the storytelling pace. However, evidence from different performances of the song suggests that this variable line structure is a fixed component of "Only a Pawn." He has four live performances of the song in 1963 that all have identical lyrics and formal structures to the August 7 studio recording: at Silas Magee's Farm on July 6, his July 26 performance at the Newport Folk Festival, the *Songs of Freedom* TV program recorded on July 30 in New York, and the

---

[8] The number of repetitions of the d line is: 3 for verse 1, 7 for verse 2, 8 for verse 3, 6 for verse 4, and 4 for verse 5.

SELF-EXPRESSIVE INNOVATIONS: LOST METER   91

August 28 performance at the March on Washington.[9] Though the formal structure sounds improvised, it is apparently a pre-planned and stable component that adds interest to his strophic song performance.[10] I conclude from this that Dylan designed the song to seem irregular and spontaneous as a way to reinforce the qualities of "aliveness" associated with his 1960s performance practice.[11] The formal flexibility, then, is part of a broader aesthetic of unpredictability in Dylan's 1960s songwriting.

Flexible Meter

Adding to this, Dylan also includes metric flexibility in his studio-recording performance.[12] He shifts between Regular Meter and loosened, eventually Lost Meter, before regaining regularity. This shift between metric types both illustrates the local details of the song's original, topical lyrics and evokes a sense of spontaneous self-expression in Dylan's broader performance practice.

Each verse of the *Times* studio recording contains a similar metric trajectory: Regular Meter is established in line *a*, then a moment of rhapsodic expressive timing results in Lost Meter between the *b* and *c* lines, and finally, the metric hierarchy is regained in the first *d* line. In the first phrase (Figure 4.4) Dylan introduces the simple triple meter. In my transcription, I represent guitar strums as quarter-note beats, with changes of harmony occurring every dotted half note. The only metric shift in this phrase occurs at the hypermetric level. After a bar of introduction, the first phrase begins in m. 2, and the vocal cadence on scale-degree 3 over tonic harmony arrives in m. 6. This creates a five-bar vocal phrase unit rather than the prototypical four, shown in Figure 4.4 with numbers between the staves that count hyperbeats.

---

[9] These other 1963 performances can be found on Pennebaker (2011), Lerner (2007), Dylan (2013), and Dylan (1964a). Footage from his performance at Silas Magee's Farm in Greenwood, Minnesota, shows only the final two verses, but both have the same verse structure as the *Times* studio recording.

[10] I see this, to some degree, as connected to Dylan's mimicking Woody Guthrie's performance practice for strophic songs, explored in Rings (2013, [24]) and Murphy (2018).

[11] Rings (2013) explores Dylan's "shambolic" performance style; Murphy (2020) examines unpredictability in a duet with Joan Baez.

[12] I have found similar flexibility on other recordings of the song that I examined for this study, and Dylan's timing details vary considerably between each version. To trace the details of all available recordings of "Only a Pawn" is outside the scope of the present study, but a careful consideration of his flexible meter on the *Times* studio recording reveals the expressive effects of his vacillations between the different types of flexible meter. For detailed investigations of multiple performances of a single Dylan song, see Rings (2013).

Figure 4.4 Dylan, "Only a Pawn in their Game," first phrase (0:00–0:08)

In the subsequent phrase, a loss of meter occurs when Dylan's timings expressively disrupt the established hierarchy with tempo fluctuations and increased rhythmic density in his guitar strumming. This Lost Meter first occurs between the *b* and *c* lines (Figure 4.5). The initial triple meter proceeds until the would-be downbeat in m. 11, but Dylan accelerates the tempo from around 150 bpm to 200 bpm and increases his strumming density so that meter is Lost at the quarter- and dotted-half-note levels. I show the metric uncertainty of this measure with a question mark in the upper number of the time signature. I illustrate the gradually Lost Meter with dots of increasing transparency in m. 11.[13] By the most transparent dot in the quarter-note pulse level midway through m. 11, there is a sensation that the Regular Meter of the opening phrase is lost. If hierarchic meter is to be regained, it must be restored through a sudden or gradual emergence of organized metric cues: stresses and durations that create a pulse that can be organized hierarchically. This would offer the sensation of regained stability after a passage of ambiguous performance timings.

Dylan proceeds with such a restoration of Regular Meter. Anacrustic gestures in the voice and guitar in the second half of m. 11 provide the stresses and duration lengths that help to reorient meter. The vocal onset of the indefinite article "a" (at the start of the phrase "A handle hid out in the dark") signals more text to follow in the vocal line. The onset of the word "handle" arrives and becomes the downbeat of the re-gained meter. While singing the word "a," Dylan plays the D2 to C♯2 gesture on the last two quarter notes of m. 11, and these stressed events create salient durations that help

---

[13] All other annotations modify those included for the Reinterpreted Meter in the previous chapter. For example, the larger dotted-line circle in m. 11 indicates where a hyperbeat could have occurred in triple meter, whereas in the examples from Chapter 3, I include an empty solid-line circle to indicate an expected beat or hyperbeat. The dotted-line circle in Figure 4.5 modifies the reinterpretation symbol to indicate a loosening of that expectation in this flexibly timed passage.

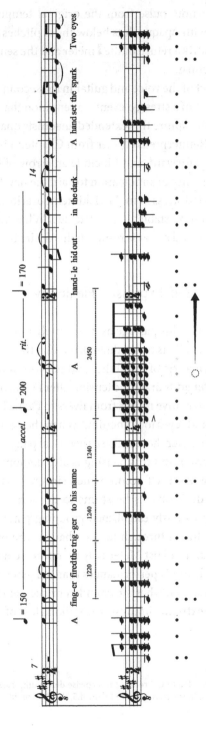

Figure 4.5 Dylan, "Only a Pawn in their Game," *b* and *c*1 lines (0:07–0:17)

94 TIMES A-CHANGIN'

to regain the quarter-note pulse from the original tempo. I illustrate this regained pulse level with opaque dots below those pitches in a dot diagram at that level.[14] This shows a return of the $\frac{3}{4}$ meter and the sensation of stability that occurs with its return.

The combined effect of the voice and guitar in the second half of m. 11 is an increasing anticipation of a stressed event—a sensation that is satisfied by the downbeat of m. 12. To capture this extended anacrusis quality, I have modified the symbols for Reinterpreted Meter from Chapter 3 in which an arrow indicated beats shifted forward, and I include an arrow of increasing size to illustrate the growing sense of anticipation toward the new beat location. His withholding an expected stress in m. 11 yields temporarily Lost Meter and an increased desire for a new, stabilizing metric cue. When this cue occurs on the downbeat of m. 12, and meter is restored, this desire is satisfied.

Self-Expressive Flexibility

I read Dylan's timings in this passage as deliberately unpredictable. It is not that I interpret these details as premeditated, but that the increasingly imperfect meter is itself a rhetoric of instability and tension in this performance. The initially Lost Meter adds dramatic tension after Dylan describes a trigger being pulled and the narrative moves from Evers to De La Beckwith—whose "hand set the spark" and "eyes took the aim." When the performance timings disengage briefly with meter there is also a rhetorical pause, allowing time for Evers's murder to register. But this pausing is also demonstrative of Dylan's performance persona. As a self-accompanied singer, he is free to make in-the-moment timing decisions, as he seems to do here. He strums a little faster, disregarding previously established grouping patterns, for a general sense of variety and drama through tempo change. The motivation for his shifts between Regular and Lost Meter may therefore be more connected to the improvisatory style of his performances than a deliberate attempt at text painting. But I propose that whether intended or accidental, the sensations associated with these extreme timings—the striking loss of salience and swift

---

[14] This descending stepwise D2 to C#2 recalls the stepwise descending bass gesture from m. 5 of Figure 4.4 (D2–C#2–B1–A2). In the passage from Figure 4.5, the B1 is omitted, and the C#2 leads directly to the A1 in m. 12.

SELF-EXPRESSIVE INNOVATIONS: LOST METER   95

restoration of meter—reflect the meaning of important passages in his original, dramatic lyrical narrative.

Later Verses

This dramatization of the lyrics through metric flexibility is repeated in the subsequent verses. The passage between the *b* and *c*1 lines in all of the verses features Lost Meter and an anticipation of eventually regained metric hierarchy. The most intense example is saved for the final verse, shown in Figure 4.6. The meter of this phrase begins similarly to the passage in Figure 4.5 but with one notable difference: Dylan's timings in m. 133 elongate the word "him," which increases the measure to four beats rather than three.[15] This stately 𝄴 continues for another two bars before the increased tempo and strumming density in m. 137 gradually disrupt the hierarchic salience. I have illustrated this gradual metric loss with dots of increasing transparency in the dot diagram. Dylan's strumming does not provide a stressed event in m. 137, as I indicate with the dotted-line circle, and the withholding of this stress marks the onset of increased anticipation toward the next stress cue.

The faster guitar strumming of verse 1 is taken to extremes in this final verse: it has a faster tempo around 250 bpm and an increased density of guitar strumming, which amplifies and lengthens the dramatic effect. For comparison, the equivalent moment in verse 1 lasted 2450 ms, and this passage spans 3450 ms. The verse 5 passage has the effect of suspended momentum, and a dramatic increase in anticipation of the next downbeat. I show this anticipation in the transcription using a longer arrow of increasing size, indicating that Dylan's more dramatic timings intensify this verse's metric trajectory. When meter emerges at the end of the phrase, his timings do not initially regain the 𝄴 meter. The anacrustic gesture in the guitar in m. 138 repeats that of the first verse, leading to the next stressed event, but this time it leads to a bar of 𝄴 before the 𝄴 meter returns in m. 139.

The metrical reinterpretation of this passage highlights the increased drama of the lyrics, which describe Evers being buried. The stately 𝄴 accompanies text about Evers's memorial, in which he was lowered down and revered "as a king." Metric emphasis withheld from the word "king"

---

[15] It is also possible to hold onto the Regular Meter longer and hear a hemiola that eventually dissolves.

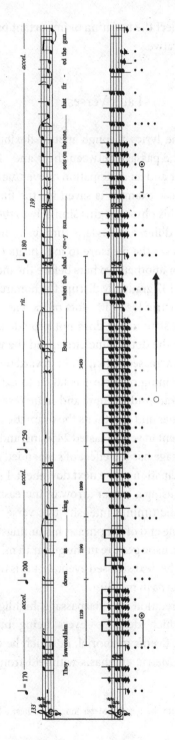

Figure 4.6 Dylan, "Only a Pawn in their Game," final verse *b* and *c*1 lines (2:58–3:10)

SELF-EXPRESSIVE INNOVATIONS: LOST METER   97

weakens the arrival of his posthumous title in comparison to the "pawn" who fired the gun. The initial change to $\frac{4}{4}$ evokes a funeral march (albeit a fast one) as the lyrics depict the burial. When salience is lost between the b and $c1$ lines in this verse, Dylan's timings create a moment of reflection—whether intentional or happenstance—to commemorate Evers's death. The subsequent delay in returning to $\frac{3}{4}$ highlights the lyrics that follow, which suggest that when De La Beckwith dies, his gravestone will be marked, or at least *should* be marked, with his status as a "pawn in their game." This reading of Dylan's performance timings using flexible meter offers a hermeneutic interpretation of the metric trajectory of the b to $c1$ lines. By attending to these metric details, we are brought in closer connection to how Dylan's timing choices influence the emotional impact of his lyrics.

Performance Frequency

With its rhetorical importance in this period both in message and timing, "Only a Pawn" has a surprisingly limited run in Dylan's performance career. Other than the studio recording, he reportedly performed the song only ten times.[16] One reason for this is that like other topical protest songs it addresses issues of cultural import to 1960s listeners and was thus too temporally specific to have staying power.[17] Instead, songs with more enigmatic lyrics, like those in "The Times They Are A-Changin'" and "Blowin' in the Wind," are more easily interpreted to suit a variety of cultural contexts and therefore have a longer life on Dylan's setlists. The specificity of the lyrics for "Only a Pawn" does, however, encourage attention from his 1960s audiences. Performing the song for farmers in Mississippi, civil-rights activists in Washington, and audiences of (mostly white) folk music community members, these audiences would have been interested in the message this young, up-and-coming, next-generation Woody Guthrie had to offer. In attending to Dylan's lyrics *for* their message, these listeners were likely to follow the fluctuations in his timing, with attention drawn (consciously or not) to changes in tempo and moments of dramatic rhetorical pause. The broader timing choices in

---

[16] The list from Dylan's official website contains eight performances but does not include the *Times* studio recording or the television performance (for which no video apparently exists) on *Songs of Freedom* (2003); Dylan, *50th Anniversary Collection 1963*.

[17] One exception to this is "The Lonesome Death of Hattie Carroll," the verses of which reference a specific event in the 1960s, but which is performed nearly 300 times, thanks in part to the song's

98   TIMES A-CHANGIN'

Dylan's dramatic protest-song performance practice affect the pacing of lyrical delivery, thereby impacting how his audiences may have interpreted narrative meaning.

The Impression of Spontaneity

Dylan's topical-song performances also offered him unique opportunities for seemingly improvised self-expression. He positioned himself as a radical, shambolic storyteller, offering an urgent and unique perspective on social situations. But there is some evidence to suggest structural foresight in his dramatic performance timings. His flexible formal structure for "Only a Pawn" seems spontaneous, as if responding to in-the-moment expressive urges, but, as I mention earlier, all available performances of the song feature the same formal structure.[18] His Lost Meter between the b and $c1$ lines of his verses also have an improvisatory quality. The strumming patterns themselves do not seem pre-planned, but their location within the verses signals evidence of a predetermined metric trajectory. That the intensity peaks in the fifth verse demonstrates Dylan's awareness of the fast-approaching ending to the song. He saved the most extreme manifestations of timing flexibility for his final statements about Evers's murder.

Spontaneous or planned, the parallel metric paths of each verse, with passages of Lost Meter, necessitate the more flexible theoretical methodology offered in this study. The anticipations and eventual restorations of meter, too, test the limits of conceptualization within Regular Meter. In challenging regular metric structures, Dylan's performance of "Only a Pawn" demonstrates several important features of his performance practice in his early 1960s songwriting. His original perspective and urgent lyrical message are delivered in a flexible and unpredictable performance context, with the dual impact on potentially mobilizing his audiences for political action alongside reflecting his cultivated shambolic persona. The metric flexibility demonstrated in his "Only a Pawn" studio-recording performance invites readings at the local narrative and broader rhetorical levels. Doing so

general, widely applicable refrain: "But you who philosophize disgrace and criticize all fears/Take the rag away from your face/Now ain't the time for your tears."

[18] Dylan's official website lists eight performances. To that list, I add three others: his performance on Silas Magee's farm, the *Times* studio recording, and his performance on the *Songs of Freedom* television program; Pennebaker (2011), Dylan (1964a), and Dylan (2013). It is possible that this structure is consistent across all performances, but many recordings are unavailable.

uncovers how Dylan's timing choices affect the pacing of his lyrical delivery and therefore impact how the narrative import may have been understood by his 1960s audiences.

Cat Stevens's "Time"

In topical-protest songs, audiences were attentive to commentary in the lyrics about specific cultural events, looking for "truth" from singer-songwriters during the turbulence of the 1960s. However, in the late 1960s and early 1970s, the second wave of the singer-songwriter style emerged. Lyrics in this period shifted away from topical, political issues to focus instead on the individual, with personal, "confessional" lyrics offering semblances of autobiographical connection.[19] Listeners attending to lyrical meaning now gained access to the personal details these singer-songwriters "reveal" in their lyrics.[20] It was during this period that Cat Stevens underwent a musical transformation from being a teenage pop star, touring with Jimi Hendrix and Engelbert Humperdinck, to becoming an introspective songwriter.[21] Stevens cites the year-long hospital convalescence following his tuberculosis diagnosis in 1968 as yielding a musical transformation that resulted in a new sound, one that "was more stripped-down and intimate" with lyrics gaining "subtlety and an intuitive edge."[22] This was fortunate timing for Stevens, since these are the precise musical features that were emerging as stylistically relevant for the confessional singer-songwriter style.[23] Alongside these changes

[19] As Everett (2008, 281) notes, this confessional songwriting is associated with the "aura of authenticity" surrounding the singer-songwriter. As discussed in Chapter 1, Frith (1988, 118) suggests that folk singers wishing to project such authenticity would perform as if the lyrics were biographical, even if the narrative is fictional.

[20] Oliver (1994, 79–80) describes a similar trend in free-verse poetry, which acted as "candid and revelatory documents" for authors, especially "women writers, Afro-American writers, and Native American writers" for whom poems were "eloquent and powerful disclosures of gender or ethnic truths." However, in some cases, it is the appearance of revelation that is most important to this rhetoric. In songs like "Winter Boy" by Buffy Sainte-Marie, she sings about the father of a child leaving in a way that *seems* autobiographical but is actually a fictional first-person narrative—Sainte-Marie had no children of her own until ten years after the song's release. For more on techniques of self-expression in "Winter Boy," see Murphy (2019).

[21] Stevens went by the name Yusuf Islam for several decades beginning in the late 1970s; he recently changed this to Yusuf and now includes Cat Stevens in his moniker—including "Yusuf/Cat Stevens" in his tours. For more on Stevens's recent career, see Fishman (2017). I will refer to him throughout this study as Cat Stevens, which is the name on his 1960s and 1970s recordings.

[22] Stevens documents his biography on his official website Stevens (2020) and in his autobiography, ·Islam (2014).

[23] His second album, *New Masters* (1967), was not a commercial success in comparison to his first; a return to the music industry for a third album would necessitate stylistic change. His move

100 TIMES A-CHANGIN'

in lyrics, Stevens added more solo performances to his repertoire, which supplemented his ensemble-based tracks and allowed him to experiment with the timing flexibilities afforded by this self-expressive performance practice.[24]

Meaning of "Time"

Stevens's song "Time" is a meeting point of his new songwriting trends: it is an introspective narrative expressed through flexible meter. Released on *Mona Bone Jakon* in 1970, "Time" was among the songs reportedly written during his tuberculosis treatment, a year in which his days were measured not by folk rock concert performance schedules but by long spans of time waiting for recovery. Its lyrical themes explore temporality—the rising and falling of time—and tackle the overall impact of what time leaves us.

I read his performance of "Time" as exploring this temporality through rhetorical metric flexibility. The song has clear rhythms articulated by his guitar strumming, but Stevens's performance timings, stress patterns, and harmony changes encourage shifts among duple, triple, and quadruple groupings. The effect is that the song is not really *in* a single meter. This is highly atypical for popular song performances even for a singer-songwriter, and it demonstrates some of the rhetorical timing possibilities for the solo-performing singer-songwriter. I position the metric flexibility of "Time" as a bridge between Reinterpreted Meter and the need for process-based meter to account for Lost and Ambiguous Meter. As a result, I interpret the song in two ways. First, I show a bottom-up interpretation of the metric hierarchy, counting strumming patterns and grouping them as Reinterpreted measures based on stress patterns and harmony changes. Second, I offer a top-down analysis, which explores larger-scale metric projections between harmony changes and then examines their irregular rhythmic subdivisions. Both options illustrate the different ways that Stevens engages flexible meter as a self-expressive illustration of temporality.

---

to introspective lyric writing might also be read as a strategic shift to capitalize on emerging songwriting trends.

[24] The song "Portobello Road" from his debut album *Matthew and Son* (1967) hints at the metric flexibility to come on Stevens's early 1970s albums. His studio-recording performance features several metrical reinterpretations including ones that reflect irony within the lyrics. For a brief analysis of this song, see Murphy (2015).

Irregular Hierarchy

In the 1970 studio recording of "Time," Stevens's vocal stresses, guitar strumming, and harmony changes create metric cues. For the first two verses, his guitar has a subdominant A2 pedal, with E minor tonic chords above. His chord changes add pitches to this Em/A harmony, creating harmonic tension through seconds, fourths, and sevenths that release when he returns to tonic over the subdominant pedal. This oscillation between dissonance and resolution suggests a sense of expansive timelessness, a sense of both motion and stasis.[25] With these harmonies anchored over an A2 pedal, Stevens expresses this suspended time with rootedness to a particular location.

Looking for metric cues at the musical surface, Stevens's guitar accompaniment provides the prominent stresses in this song. His strumming for verses 1 and 2 offers a beat level that I interpret as a quarter-note tactus in my transcription (Figure 4.7). For chords that Stevens accents in his performance, usually at harmony changes, I position each stressed event as a metric downbeat, but I leave out time signatures since no single meter is prominent. Following Stevens's groupings this way yields unequal measures, with the number of guitar strums in each group never persisting for more than a few bars at a time. For example, the first two measures of the introduction in Figure 4.7 suggest a possible ¾ meter, but this is interrupted when the return to E minor harmony over the A2 pedal in m. 4 encourages a metrical reinterpretation.[26]

Positioning that stressed event as the m. 4 downbeat results in a two-beat bar for m. 3; but this meter is also not sustained. In m. 5, the stressed Em^{add2}/A guitar chord does not occur until three beats after the downbeat of m. 4, yielding another ¾ bar. Similar shifts are needed in the remainder of this excerpt, in which grouping changes prevent any regular metric patterns. So, it would be inaccurate to claim that the song has Reinterpreted Meter because there is no governing meter, and changes do not occur in sectional and predictable ways.[27] This opening passage has the effect of temporal disorientation, reflecting one type of the "time" in the song's title.

---

[25] Malawey (2010) finds a similar technique of timelessness expressed through harmonic oscillation in several songs by Björk.

[26] It is also conceivable that the introduction be in ⅞ with various duple and triple subgroupings. As discussed in Chapter 2, in transcribing I place stressed events as metric downbeats—preferring simple over compound meters—wherever possible unless there is clear syncopation. So, I have chosen here to represent, for example, the first eight quarter-note beats as three measures rather than a single measure of ⅞ with 3 + 3 + 2 grouping.

[27] Biamonte (2014) explores changing meter in several songs, proposing categories for how metric dissonance functions in relation to song form. Though she acknowledges that metric dissonance can

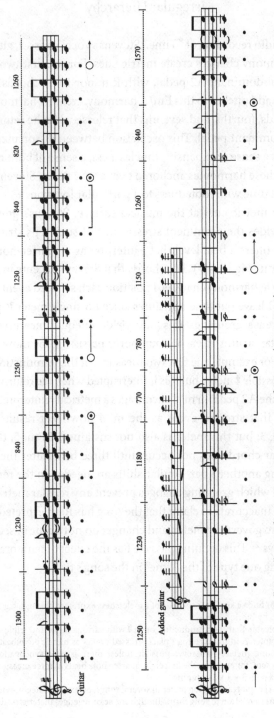

Figure 4.7 Stevens, "Time," introduction as a Reinterpreted Meter (0:00–0:19)

SELF-EXPRESSIVE INNOVATIONS: LOST METER   103

The entry of the voice provides an additional layer of stressed events, with potential to regularize the meter. However, these stresses serve to reinforce guitar accents, clarifying only a possible lyric-expressive motivation for the changes in meter. For instance, as Stevens sings the word "rise" (see Figure 4.8), he adds an extra guitar strum, and m. 19 is lengthened into a bar of $\frac{4}{4}$. By contrast, at the end of the system, at the word "falls," durations between accents are shortened, and a series of simple duple measures emerge. These shorter measure lengths give the sensation of time passing too quickly, slipping away from the narrator's control. For this passage from mm. 23–26 Stevens accents every other guitar strum without changing the Em^7/A harmony, adding a sensation of time suspended. Later, the metric shifts in the second system serve to express the "nothing" that "time leaves" him.

The Limits of Reinterpreted Meter

Stevens's performance, by avoiding Regular Meter in this way, also pushes the boundaries of Reinterpreted Meter. The resulting groupings pose the analytic question: how is meter interpreted or reinterpreted if it is never established? Though I hear a consistent tactus, I classify "Time" as lying somewhere beyond the boundaries of Reinterpreted Meter for two reasons: (1) Regular Meter, with established and consistent rhythmic groupings, is never achieved, and (2) meter cannot simply be Reinterpreted if there is no context of regularity. Because this song entirely *lacks* metric regularity, it is not so simply categorized as Reinterpreted Meter. And this seems to be the very point of Stevens's performance timings: they prevent orientation to a single, conceptually isochronous musical time, thereby creating an overall sense of temporal uncertainty. This uncertainty and unpredictability reflects the song's introspective lyrical theme and the flexible rhetoric of Stevens's singer-songwriter performance practice.

One drawback to analyzing this song as a series of metrical reinterpretations is that the beat counting is cumbersome. I find it unlikely that a casual listener, or even an attentive listener, would count beats the way I have for these

play an "expressive role in heightening tension," her study focuses on form without attention to the text-expressive role of changing meter and grouping. The one exception is her suggestion that conflicting metric layers in Led Zeppelin's "Kashmir" paint "the lyrics of the first verse ('a traveler of both time and space'), and, more generally, the dissociative state and likely drug use ('I've been flying') of the narrator."

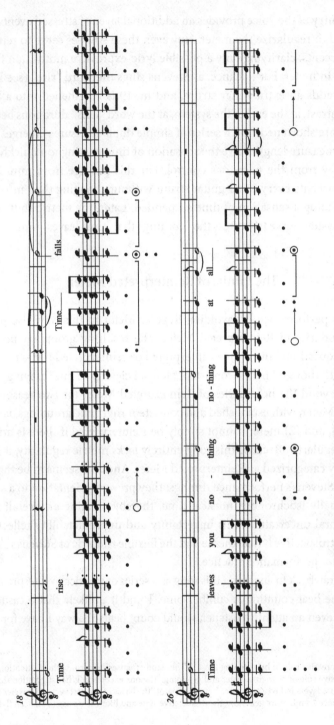

Figure 4.8 Stevens, "Time," first vocal phrases as a Reinterpreted Meter (0:19–0:36)

SELF-EXPRESSIVE INNOVATIONS: LOST METER   105

transcriptions.[28] I think it much more likely that attention would be drawn to harmony changes and vocal stresses that I have notated as downbeats. To account for this listening experience of "Time," I use a process-based approach to follow the durations between notated downbeats and how those durations fluctuate throughout Stevens's performance. As we shall see, this approach offers a different interpretation of temporality than attempting to analyze this song as Reinterpreted Meter.

Loose Metric Process

This process-based approach uses the same metric cues but attends more closely to the durations between stressed events. In Figure 4.9, I show an interpretation of durations in the first vocal phrase of "Time" as projection symbols. (For ease of comparison, I have added these symbols below the dot diagram from Figure 4.8.) This combined reading suggests that the foremost sensations are of stressed events (notated downbeats) arriving late or early according to the length of the previous duration. I represent these sensations as *rit.* for a longer duration than expected and *accel.* for a shorter duration.[29] For example, I label the duration between the m. 18 and m. 19 downbeats as a 1250 ms Q duration with a solid-line arrow.[30] Q' is shown with the dotted curved line to represent a plausible reproduction of this timespan, but Stevens's timing yields a slightly longer duration here (1570 ms). The longer curved line and *rit.* symbol show this lengthened duration and the sensation that the stressed event at m. 20 that I have notated as the downbeat arrives later than expected.[31] When durations are shorter, the reverse occurs. For

[28] I imagine three possible "close listening" scenarios in which a listener would count beats. The first is one in which the goal is to illustrate the performance as a descriptive transcription, as I have done for these figures. A second type engages closely with the recording to gather instructions on how to reproduce the sounding events in performance. With this motivation, a fan might count the number of strums to know how many to play in a metrically precise cover version of Stevens's studio recording. And a third type counts the strumming as a way to analyze the physical gestures required for Stevens to produce this performance. All three types necessitate a close listening to the exact number of quarter-note beats Stevens produces, but I would not classify any of these as a "casual" listening experience of this song.

[29] Hasty (1997, 87–88) prefers *rallentando* for durations that are longer than the previous duration. He places such symbols (both *accel.* and *rall.*) below his curved arrows.

[30] For my summary of the relevant Hasty projection symbols, see Chapter 2.

[31] In the previous analysis, I quantified this duration as a half note lengthened by a quarter-note beat. This created a bar of ⁴—a different metric unit than the ⁴ of the previous measure. In this process-based analysis, Q' is conceptually the same as Q, just longer. Without a dot diagram and timings included, it is visually obvious that the Q' curved line is slightly longer than the Q'

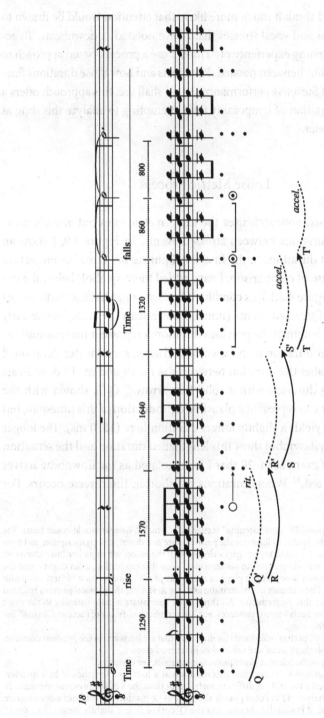

Figure 4.9 Stevens, "Time," first vocal phrase with metric projections (0:19–0:27)

example, the S duration is followed by a slightly shorter S' duration, which denotes that the downbeat of m. 22 arrives slightly earlier than expected.[32] The flexibility of this approach affords that these two quantitatively different timings are understood as conceptually the same. The detailed strumming count from Figure 4.8 does quantify the exact number of beats that gives rise to these shorter and longer groupings, but the appeal of the process-based approach is that such quantifying of precisely "how late" or "how early" is not necessary. The focus is instead on the sensations of "late" or "early," which aligns with the more plausible listening experience of flexible temporality— of time expanding and contracting—in this song.

The projective reading of this passage illustrates a more flexible way to follow Stevens's stress patterns. It allows a conception of these larger-scale durations as isochronous but flexibly timed, the same way *rubato* and *accelerando* are accommodated in performances of metrically regular passages. In some ways, this approach is preferable because it avoids a meticulous beat counting and focuses instead on the sensations of comparing duration lengths—durations that are conceptually equivalent but made longer or shorter in support of local lyrical meaning. But this metric reading represents only one conception of temporality during this transformative period of Stevens's life. These larger durations, as musical representations of lived experiences of temporal spans (the hours or days of his convalescence), are underscored by the ever-present beat articulations that offer shorter subdivisions of time. These faster articulations may account for minutes or seconds, the ticking of a clock between larger events. It is easy to imagine Stevens conceptualizing time both through an immediate moment-to-moment experience and through larger spans between events. It is important to consider both the quantification of the metrical reinterpretations and the flexibility of the process-based approach to add nuance to both conceptualizations of temporality in interpreting the meaning of "Time."

---

curved arrow. In the process-based analyses that follow in this chapter and Chapter 6, I always include IOI values for all durations for ease of comparing precise timings. But it would also be possible to illustrate a process-based metric analysis using only the sensations of durations as perceptually equivalent to, shorter than, or longer than the previous duration, without quantifying exact measurements. It is that kind of measuring (based on the quality rather than quantity of a duration) that I propose best represents a casual listening experience of this flexibly timed music.

[32] In my analysis, I quantify this as an omitted quarter-note beat.

108   TIMES A-CHANGIN'

Synthesized Flexible Meter

A synthetic approach to these two conceptions of time is also possible. For this, I propose that the harmony change and vocal stress cues for process-based meter represent a highly flexible hypermeter. Observing this possibility in the passage from Figure 4.9, each of the notated downbeats represents a hyperbeat, but the span between hyperbeats is flexible and has a varying number of subdivisions.[33] If we can accept, as the process-based analysis suggests, that the notated measures are conceptually equivalent but flexibly timed, then the quarter-note beat layer can be considered consistent but with irregularly grouped subdivisions. I propose this synthetic approach as a method of holding the dual interpretations of "Time" simultaneously. This way the precision of metric regularity and flexibility of projection analysis can be combined into a single meter: a flexible hypermeter with changing subdivisions, which reflects the dual interpretation of the temporal themes.

Metrically Regular Ending

The expressive impact of the song relies on the two types of flexible temporalities and how these flexibilities contrast with the regularity of the final section. The song's ending sets the malleable verses into relief. Stevens's lyrics in this passage address "going back," which marks the end of his isolation, his return to good health, and his eventual re-entry into society. Stevens stresses the first appearance of the word "back" m. 57 in Figure 4.10, and his strumming pattern quickly organizes into a ⁴₄ meter that persists for the remainder of the song. This is a moment of metric clarity in which the previous conflict between duple and triple groupings is suddenly organized as a consistent quadruple. The flexible timing of the previous sections, representing the types of time Stevens experienced in his year-long hospitalization, snaps into order with his recovery and re-entry into the temporal world.

---

[33] As explored in Chapter 2, there is some conceptual precedents for flexible subdivisions in theories of metric regularity, which allows for irregular tactus subdivisions as long as the tactus beats are evenly subdivided. Lerdahl and Jackendoff (1983, 72) propose this as a revision to their MWFR 4, stating that the tactus may be "subdivided into threes at one point and twos at another, as long as particular beats of the tactus are evenly subdivided."

SELF-EXPRESSIVE INNOVATIONS: LOST METER 109

Figure 4.10 Stevens, "Time," return to 4/4 meter (0:44–1:06)

Introspective Temporalities

Stevens's "Time," therefore, offers multiple explorations of temporality. His listeners would hear the ambiguity of the song's verses and feel the disorienting effects of his timing flexibility. The stability of the song's conclusion is marked for attention in its contrast to the previously ambiguous content. Though it is not explicit in its connection to his autobiography, it is possible to read that the different types of time explored in Stevens's song have meaningful ties to his experiences with long-term illness and recovery around the time he wrote the song. Attention to the timing details of his performance through the lens of flexible meter helps to illustrate the types of

110 TIMES A-CHANGIN'

temporality engaged and their self-expressive implications within Stevens's newfound confessional songwriting style. The varying types of meter high- light his introspective lyrics and the freedoms of expression possible in the rhetoric of his 1970s singer-songwriter performance practice.

Joni Mitchell's "Blue"

This theme of introspection is an important feature of 1970s singer-songwriter music, and it is associated in particular with Joni Mitchell's output. Starting with her first album *Song to a Seagull* in 1968, she developed her folk-influenced musical aesthetic of self-expression through her storytelling lyrics.[34] But in the early years of the 1970s, Mitchell's self-expressive rhetoric became personal and introspective. Her 1971 album, *Blue*, is lauded as the zenith of confessional songwriting, with her lyrics acting as intimate, personal, autobiographical documents, and songs like "River," "All I Want," and "A Case of You" offering introspective accounts of her desire for love and personal autonomy.[35]

As Mitchell's lyrics shift to a personal perspective, her performance prac- tice engages more self-expressive metric flexibility. In Chapter 3, I explored the ways that Mitchell's timing creates rhetorically important metrical reinterpretations. In this chapter, I analyze the studio recording of her song "Blue" and propose that the vacillations between Regular and Lost Meter are critical features of her self-expression in this performance. When Mitchell shifts between various flexible metric types, she signals moments of signif- icance in her personal lyrics and reinforces broader themes of freedom and non-conformity in her singer-songwriter performance practice.

Central Relationship

On the album's titular track, Mitchell sings of a lost love, whom she nicknames Blue, and explores seafaring metaphors for her conflicting desires: further in- timacy (to be anchored in closeness) or freedom (to "sail away"). In Lloyd

[34] Whitesell (2008, 12) points to an early "acoustic folk aesthetic" and "various explorations into in- tricate poetic structure, rhapsodic expression and idiosyncratic instrumentation" as features her first period (1966–1972).
[35] "Little Green" is an exception to the use of the first-person pronoun. Instead of stating "I" like other songs on this album, she instead states "you" to describe actions undertaken by the narrator.

Whitesell's insightful analysis of "Blue," he proposes that Mitchell's harmonic progressions reflect this unresolved central relationship, which is "poised between anchored commitment and undone moorings."[36] To his observations, I would add that Mitchell's flexible performance timings are also critically important for understanding the song's expressive impact and its connection to her broader self-expressive performance practice. I explore the central relationship between the ties of commitment and unmoored freedom of the song "Blue" as expressed through vacillations between different types of flexible meter: between "anchored" Regular Meter and moments of metric loss, when meter is "unmoored" and comes undone.[37] The passages of Lost Meter in this song are moments of rhapsodic self-expression that signal Mitchell's perspective on the relationship, on the harmful activities it contained, and on her ultimate freedom from the situation. The flexible performance timings on the studio recording of "Blue" express an ideological tension between intimacy and freedom, connected to broader liberties in Mitchell's performance practice: her rhapsodic expression, her working as her own producer, and her creative license as a solo artist.

Lyrics and Accompaniment

The song's lyrics address Blue as a central character, the presumed love interest of Mitchell's narrator.[38] The lyrical imagery ranges from descriptions of tattoos ("Ink on a pin/Underneath the skin"), to drug references ("Acid, booze, and ass/Needles, guns, and grass"), and to various nautical images ("You know I've been to sea before," "Or let me sail away," "You can make it through these waves," and "here is a shell for you").[39] The outcome of the failed romance narrative is clarified in the final line ("There is your song from me"), which acts as her parting statement to Blue.

---

[36] In a reference to Mitchell's work as a painter, Whitesell (2008, 137) calls this her "harmonic palette."

[37] Following the precedent I set with "Time," I analyze metric regularity and reinterpretation from the lens of metric hierarchy and explore the loss of meter using projective theory.

[38] Whitesell (2008, 44–47) classifies this song as having a "lyric" voice, in which Mitchell is conveying personal sentiments directed to her lover, which the audience overhears. This contrasts with a "dramatic" voice in which the audience is a group of spectators to fictional character dialogues, "narrative" in which the singer is a storyteller speaking directly to the audience, and "political" when the singer is appealing to an audience about a particular issue.

[39] In a few lines, the boundary is less clear between the tattoo imagery and drugs. For example, the text "An empty space to fill in" can be read both ways: as a description of empty skin soon to be filled with ink or as an emotional emptiness that Blue fills with the temporary distractions of "acid, booze, and ass."

112 TIMES A-CHANGIN'

The song has a piano accompaniment that was typical of Mitchell's songwriting since her arrival in Laurel Canyon.[40] "Blue" is one of several keyboard-based songs on her 1971 album. Her piano accompaniment features a steady stream of eighth notes in the left hand, arpeggiating tones of a given harmony, with triadic figures in the right hand that most often align with half-note beats.[41] The prevailing context is one of Regular Meter with occasional syncopation. But in some passages, Mitchell's accompaniment seems to follow the rhapsodic impulses of her vocal line and obscures meter-sustaining rhythms, which subverts the $\frac{4}{4}$ meter established in the introduction and results in expressive use of Lost Meter.

Reinterpreted Meter: Narrative Space

In certain cases, the song's metric flexibility results in similar metrical reinterpretations to those found in Chapter 3. Figures 4.11 and 4.12 demonstrate two moments in which Mitchell adds an extra fifth bar to a four-bar hypermetric unit. This causes a metric shift at the level of the hypermeter and illustrates imagery of space and freedom in the lyrics. In Figure 4.11, this extra measure (m. 13) occurs as Mitchell proclaims she wants to "sail away" if Blue is unable to "crown and anchor" her. In Figure 4.12, the extra bar in m. 22 occurs as she sings about "an empty space to fill in," which locally addresses a tattooing process but metaphorically signals an emotional emptiness left by the conclusion of this relationship. These metric shifts are local details that stylistically create musical space to reflect the thematic lyrical meaning and give listeners time to absorb the narrative import.

Expressively Lost Meter

In other passages of the song, Mitchell's rhetorical timing flexibility results in a loss of meter. The most dramatic examples of this arise at critical

---

[40] For Whitesell (2008, 19), the instrument choice—in its size and lack of portability—reflects a stability in Mitchell's personal life starting in 1969, when the instrument was readily available in a new home in Laurel Canyon with Graham Nash.

[41] Whitesell (2008, 19) and Sonenberg (2003, 72) observe that Mitchell's harmonies between the hands in her typical piano technique often result in extended harmonic structures.

Figure 4.11 Mitchell, "Blue," expressive extension on "sail away" (0:32–0:45)

structural moments in the song and heighten their expressive impact. This occurs in three locations: within the initial vocal phrase at the first statement of "Blue" (0:12–0:32), when she recounts the drug use and "lots of laughs" in the relationship (1:12–1:29), and in her final reflection about having sung the "foggy lullaby" to Blue (2:16–2:32). Repeated content in the song's formal structures ensures that each of these three passages of ambiguity can be compared to a parallel moment elsewhere in the song that features Regular Meter.

To contextualize these passages of metric loss within the formal structure, I categorize two vocal phrase types—*a* and *b*—according to similarities of

Figure 4.12 Mitchell, "Blue," expressive extension on "space to fill in" (0:53–1:06)

pitch and lyrical content.[42] Figure 4.13 outlines the formal layout of the song including vocal phrases and instrumental framing and interludes.[43] To show parallelisms between similar phrase types, in Figure 4.14 I illustrate the melodic profile of the two phrase types using $a1$ and $b1$ acting as prototypes. This diagram shows similar melody notes with open note heads, with a beam connecting melodic lines.[44] I include changes of harmony below the staff,

---

[42] This classification method is modeled on Whitesell (2008, 135).
[43] Similar form charts can be found in de Clercq (2012).
[44] I have assigned closed note heads to pitches either not shared by all parallel lines or to those with clear non-chord-tone function. For the b line, I transcribe the initial repeated descending melody with open note heads and subsequent repetition of the melodic descent with closed note heads.

SELF-EXPRESSIVE INNOVATIONS: LOST METER 115

SECTION	TIMINGS
Introduction	0:00–0:12
a1	0:12–0:44
a2	0:44–1:05
b1	1:05–1:14
b2	1:14–1:32
Interlude	1:32–1:37
b3	1:37–1:47
a3	1:47–1:59
Interlude	1:59–2:06
a4	2:06–2:42
Outro	2:42–3:05

Figure 4.13 Mitchell, "Blue," formal structure and timings

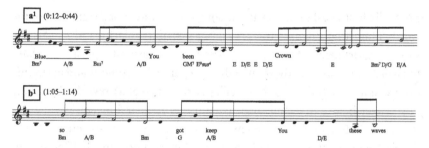

Figure 4.14 Mitchell, "Blue," prototype *a* and *b* phrases with similar motives and contour

which typically occurs on every half-note beat in most transcriptions.[45] The subsequent *a* and *b* lines follow a similar melodic contour to these prototypes.

Mitchell's flexible meter in her performance creates dramatic contrast between parallel melodic lines. The first passage of metric ambiguity occurs in the *a* phrase at the first statement of the word "Blue," which is juxtaposed with each subsequent repetition of the *a* melody line with more salient Regular Meter. And the same is true for other parallel moments. When Lost Meter occurs at the end of *a*4, the hiatus is more dramatic in comparison to the Regular Meter of the parallel passages in *a*1 and *a*2 at "Crown and anchor me" and "An empty space to fill in," respectively. Similarly, Mitchell's

---

[45] The harmonic progressions for my transcriptions of "Blue" were made in reference to those available on jonimitchell.com—particularly Finch and Blackburn (2023)—as well as studies by Whitesell (2002, 181; 2008, 135). The vocal transcriptions, including those combined with information from available piano transcriptions, are entirely my own. I have not included rhythm and meter in this diagram. I explore the timing details of her performance in a notated meter in the analyses that follow.

116   TIMES A-CHANGIN'

recollection of "Acid, booze, and ass" in *b*2 dissolves into metric ambiguity where a parallel moment in *b*1 features metric regularity. This intensifies the dramatic impact of Mitchell's vacillation from regularity to ambiguity.

To study these techniques of metric flexibility more closely, I examine each section of Lost Meter in the examples that follow, to appreciate the nuances of Mitchell's metric rhetoric in this song and her broader self-expressive performance aesthetic.

First Statement of "Blue"

Mitchell's first vocal utterance in the song is a flexibly timed statement of the word "Blue" that disrupts the prevailing metric regularity and signals the word's importance in the narrative. The first and second *a* phrases declaim the word "Blue" differently, though they are parallel in contour and harmonic progression. The timings of Mitchell's performance of *a*1 reveals an initially Lost Meter before the song snaps back into a regular $\frac{4}{4}$ meter. My analysis in Figure 4.15 demonstrates a few ways of hearing these structures. I represent the piano chords as half notes and illustrate how this half-note layer slows and eventually disappears with wider spacing in the proportional transcription. Mitchell's accompaniment takes a secondary role here, responding to the rhapsodic vocal timings, and this reflects an available freedom of Mitchell's solo performance practice.[46] As the Regular Meter dissolves in m. 5, I include projective arrows below the staff to illustrate possible metric readings of the more flexible timings.[47] Reading (a) considers only the half-note chords for metric cues. The Q duration spans the right hand's Bm^7 chord to the subsequent A/B chord. Since there is no third event for the span of 7580 ms, the Q' projection is not realized.[48] By including a hiatus symbol (||), I denote an interruption of these projections when it is clear that the possible third event does not arrive. The (b) reading includes the voice in a search for metric cues.[49] This gets slightly further with R–R' realized and

---

[46] A similar subservient accompaniment role can be found in other piano songwriting examples like "The Arrangement" (from *Ladies of the Canyon,* 1970) in which the "piano takes a supporting role with little melodic interest" once the voice enters; see Whitesell (2008, 19).

[47] I do not assign rhythmic values in Figure 4.15 for Mitchell's vocal line in mm. 5–6 and instead use proportional spacing for m. 5 and return to notated rhythms in m. 7 once the $\frac{4}{4}$ meter is re-established

[48] The longer Q' dotted curved line indicates an attempt to hear a *rit.* for this duration, but even with this modification, no event occurs to confirm it.

[49] Here, R is the same duration as Q but the vocal articulation on F♯3 realizes the R' projection.

SELF-EXPRESSIVE INNOVATIONS: LOST METER 117

Figure 4.15 Mitchell, "Blue," *a*1 phrase (0:12–0:32)

S–S' projected, but there is again a hiatus when no third event confirms the S' projection. The IOI between the voice's F♯3 and the next vocal onset on F♯4 is 5240 ms, which is too long to consider as a reproduction of the 2340 ms S duration.[50] So a hiatus occurs, giving the impression of Lost Meter. In either reading, the metric cues suggest stress and duration, with a pulse nearly emerging in reading (b), but sensations of Regular Meter are eventually lost. The effect is one of vocal-led metric flexibility at the statement of the song's subject. Mitchell's expressive pause at the first mention of the name "Blue" suspends and disorients metrical time to illustrate the impact of her nostalgic recollection of this failed romance. Metrical space in this passage of

---

[50] London's (2012, 46) range for entrainment posits an upper limit of 5 or 6 seconds, so the 5240 ms duration is already nearing the boundary. But the main issue is that 5240 ms is more than twice as long as 2340 ms, and so it is unlikely to be heard as a conceptually equal duration.

118   TIMES A-CHANGIN'

ambiguity reflects the physical and emotional space following the end of her relationship.

Restored Regularity

After this statement of "Blue," Mitchell's performance timings begin to restore the meter. The same two piano chords from m. 5 return in m. 6, and the voice begins to reorient to Regular Meter. This time, the T duration between the two chords is realized, and the stressed events on the downbeat of m. 7 complete T'. (This also creates the whole note U duration that is reproduced as U' when' the tempo accelerates to the downbeat of m. 8.) Using projection symbols in my analysis of m. 6, I illustrate a process parallel to that of m. 5, but this time with metric cues that eventually yield a pulse and a subsequent restoration of the $\frac{4}{4}$ meter. By m. 6, the pulse groups into patterns of strong and weak beats, re-establishing the metric hierarchy and restoring emotional stability.

The timing Mitchell gives to her singing of the word "Blue" is no surprise, given its centrality in the song, but it also clarifies the word's meaning in the lyrical syntax. On first reading, the lyrics "Blue songs are like tattoos" might suggest grouping "Blue songs" together, but the performance's loss of metric salience, which yields a hiatus in either metric reading, breaks the syntactical continuity between these two words in the lyrics, separating out the name Blue from "songs are like tattoos." The subsequent renewed projections in m. 6 vividly portray the narrator pulling herself out of the reverie of her past relationship and back to observing her song's subject at an emotional distance.

Reinterpreted Then Lost Meter

The next passage of Lost Meter occurs in the $b2$ line, which contrasts the metrically regular $b1$ that precedes it. The b lines all feature descending melodic motives, with the third b phrase transposed down a perfect fourth. In $b2$, a metrical reinterpretation occurs to accommodate the groupings of Mitchell's emphatic declamation of "Acid, booze, and ass/Needles, guns, and grass." In this passage (Figure 4.16), the $\frac{4}{4}$ meter of m. 26 is interrupted in m. 27 with the stress on the word "Needles" a beat earlier than expected. The

Figure 4.16 Mitchell, "Blue," *b*2 phrase (1:12–1:29)

omitted beat causes a metrical reinterpretation at the half-note level.[51] The half-note beat that occurs on the word "ass" continues the previous pattern, and the next beat on the first syllable of "Needles" arrives a quarter note early, resulting in metrical reinterpretations at the half- and whole-note levels. The effect is of Mitchell rushing through this list of vices, hoping to find a more pleasant memory.

Following this change of meter, the timings slow for Mitchell's declamation of the subsequent lyrics ("Lots of laughs"), which are repeated twice. At the first statement, I can hear Mitchell associating the pleasures of laughter with the aforementioned drug use. But then her pausing on the word "laughs" seems to send her into a recollection of other similar occurrences of drug use or laughter. The metric ambiguity of m. 30 illustrates the pausing for this recollection, which creates a hiatus in the metric structure. In m. 29,

---

[51] It might also be possible to accommodate these groupings as a hemiola in a ⁴₄ meter. But this grouping and the one I offer in Figure 4.17 all result in a loss of metric salience in m. 30.

120 TIMES A-CHANGIN'

the increasingly transparent dots illustrate how the quarter-note beat layer is lost as Mitchell's tempo slows across the measure. This creates a more ambiguous metric structure that recalls the loose, opening declamation of "Blue." Her piano's Em^{11} chord on the downbeat of m. 30 seems like it may mark a return to the typical half-note durations of the right-hand accompaniment, and the Q duration spans the onset of this chord to her E^{7sus} chord that follows. Reproducing this 1540 ms duration as Q', however, fails because the 2980 ms IOI between that chord and the A^{sus} chord in m. 31 is too long in comparison. It is not that the Q' duration cannot be spanned conceptually but that the 2980 ms duration is almost twice as long as the 1540 ms Q duration and unlikely to be heard as the same duration reproduced. The result is a hiatus and Lost Meter in m. 29 that evokes the narrator's reverie. Her recollection of these laughs with Blue are pleasant memories that are now temporally distant, unmooring the metric structure. To pull herself back to the narrative present, Mitchell eventually moves from ambiguity to salience. By m. 31, the whole-note durations represented as R and R' in Figure 4.16 are becoming salient again. The second half of m. 31 (not shown) illustrates a flexibly timed $\frac{4}{4}$ meter before returning in m. 32 to the more consistent timing of the song's introduction. The passage of metric flexibility signals a moment of self-expressive, rhetorical pause in this performance. The overall effect is of Mitchell making in-the-moment performance decisions that follow her sentiments as she recollects this purportedly autobiographical narrative.

An Expressive Ending

Mitchell's final passage of self-expressive pause is in the final *a* phrase (*a*4), shown as Figure 4.17. Mitchell revisits the melody of *a*1 and *a*2 but alters the rhythm to highlight the text "A foggy lullaby" in a similar manner to the initial statements of "Blue" and "Lots of laughs." The Q and Q' arrows below the staff span the half-note durations created by the stressed right-hand chords in m. 51. These chords recall the accompaniment from the passages setting the text "sail away" and "empty space to fill in" from the earlier *a* phrase endings from Figures 4.11 and 4.12. In this passage, Mitchell's Lost Meter reflects the disorienting effects of the increasing "fog" of her lullaby and the distance this represents between her and Blue. The space between half notes grows in m. 52, which in turn increases the measure lengths, as shown with the *rit.* for

SELF-EXPRESSIVE INNOVATIONS: LOST METER   121

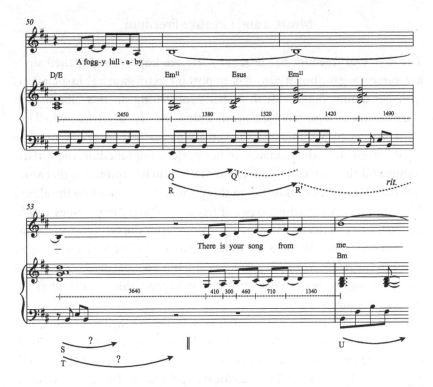

Figure 4.17 Mitchell, "Blue," second half of *a*4 (2:16–2:32)

the R' duration. In m. 53, the half-note layer disappears as if obscured by the fog, and a hiatus occurs when the T duration is left unrealized. This allows for one final moment of musical space for reflection before Mitchell sings her final line "There is your song from me" as a summary of her distance from the relationship. She has, indeed, sailed away.

In analyzing the flexible meter of these passages in "Blue," I uncover the details of how Mitchell's timing choices highlight the song's central relationship: the conflict between her desire for romantic stability and her longing for freedom. She vacillates between passages of "anchored" Regular Meter and passages in which the meter becomes "unmoored," and regularity gives way to the perception of Lost Meter. The moments of metric loss, especially when considered alongside parallel moments of regularity, are marked for attention in her performance and reflect the broader ideological tension between freedom and confinement.

122   TIMES A-CHANGIN'

Musical and Creative Freedom

The theme of freedom has broader narrative import for Mitchell since her career began, but it also has important extra-musical associations with her album *Blue*.[52] Much of her songwriting on this album took place during a hiatus from the music industry in 1970, after Mitchell became exhausted by fame and the success of her first three albums. She freed herself from the demands of her performing schedule and artistic responsibilities, as well as from the limitations to her autonomy that arose from her romantic relationship in this period.[53] The tracks on the album *Blue* are a nexus of various types of freedom: illustrating themes within her lyrics, and reflecting her independence from the typical restrictions on her gender both in romance and in the music industry, all encouraged by a brief reprieve from the pressures of fame. Her flexible meter on the title track showcases how her timing can express this important sentiment in her songwriting.

In vacillating between Regular and Lost Meter, Mitchell is signaling that flexible meter is an important feature of her self-expressive rhetoric, both in this song and in her performance practice. Her timing freedom as a self-accompanied performer illustrates local import in her lyrics and points to broader liberties in her musical production. Mitchell's presence as a solo, female artist, cited as a producer on all but one of her albums, is a creative freedom secured by her record contract, which allowed her complete control over her music and its production.[54] Mitchell's autonomy allowed for rhapsodic self-expression of her personal narratives, both free from the limitations of a producer's input. The inclusion of lyrics about her ideologies,

---

[52] For example, her titular track on her first album, *Song to a Seagull* (1968), includes lyrics like "My dreams with the seagulls fly/Out of reach."

[53] O'Brien (2001, 129) notes that Mitchell had accepted a proposal from her then-boyfriend Graham Nash, who she claims "wanted a stay-at-home wife to raise his children"; later realizing she could not commit to this role, Mitchell ended her relationship with Nash in 1970 while she was away in Europe. She sent him a telegram from Crete to break off her engagement, stating, "If you hold sand too tightly in your hand, it will run through your fingers."

[54] This was a sticking point for her and her manager, Elliot Roberts, in initially signing a contract with Reprise, a subsidiary of Warner Brothers. O'Brien (2012, 68) notes that after several failed attempts at securing artistic freedom, Roberts managed to negotiate an "almost unprecedented concession, particularly for a new artist; his client was given complete artistic control over her albums ranging from the cover art to sleeve notes and musical content . . ." *Song to a Seagull* (1968) lists David Crosby as producer. In McKenna (2017, 152) Mitchell explains that Crosby agreed to produce her first album as a means of preventing producers from interfering with her recording process.

SELF-EXPRESSIVE INNOVATIONS: LOST METER   123

particularly her modern, countercultural approach to romance and independence, was a choice available to Mitchell in part because of her artistic autonomy.[55]

As a result, her 1971 album redefines the kind of self-expressive freedom associated with an "authentic" 1970s singer-songwriter performance practice. For *Blue*, this freedom allowed Mitchell to include personal, confessional songwriting that became an essential feature of singer-songwriter music.[56] On the album, her audiences can find messages assumed to be autobiographical: about Mitchell's romantic relationships (to which the media paid particular attention) and her general ideas about romance, loss, and various manifestations of personal and creative independence.[57] Mitchell's work gains cultural capital through its signs of authenticity, made manifest most clearly in its personal lyrics and self-expressive timing flexibility. Both act as equally important markers of her creative freedom and self-governance in musical production.

***

As I illustrate in my analyses in this chapter of "Only a Pawn in Their Game," "Time," and "Blue," a loss of meter expressively illustrates the meaning of personal lyrics, both political and introspective. These songs demonstrate how dramatic timing flexibility can result in losing the sensations of metric regularity. The theory of flexible meter illustrates the process through which meter is established, lost, and then regained and how this metric trajectory impacts performance-based self-expression. When metric structures loosen, the focus shifts to metric cues and to the potential for these cues to regularize and restore meter. Both occurrences, the loss and restoration of meter, have noticeable sensations for listeners, whose attention is drawn to the moments when the meter vacillates between regularity and hiatus. Because these

---

[55] Sonenberg (2003, 83) sees her artistic and personal independence as giving her work "particular relevance to its historical moment." He argues that Mitchell's label (Warner-Reprise) nurtured her creative flexibility and non-conformity, which, alongside support from peers like David Crosby, helped to foster her original musical style.

[56] In her explanation of why *Blue* became more autobiographical, Mitchell states that she began to demand a "greater honesty and revelation" in her work in part as a response to the "kind of weird worship" she was receiving from audiences. Yaffe (2017, 136) includes references to Mitchell, feeling the confinement and pressures of fame, offering the album as an invitation into her psyche because, as she argues, listeners "should know who they were worshipping."

[57] Whitesell (2008, 199) sees this theme of freedom extending back to her first album, *Song of a Seagull* (1968), listing the central themes of that album as heartbreak, "people's relation to their natural surroundings (alienated or nurturing), and the struggle between personal ideals of domesticity and freedom." Sonenberg (2003, 83) suggests that her performance freedom echoes broader liberties particularly for her gender of "individualism and non-conformity" in the period of personal growth transforming American culture and counterculture in the 1960s and 1970s.

124   TIMES A-CHANGIN'

vacillations occur at moments of lyrical significance, this reinforces the role of metric flexibility for narrative expression in performance.

These timings also have important broader implications for the self-expressive rhetoric of these singer-songwriters. For Dylan, timings help convey his dramatic topical narratives, his original perspective, and his unpredictable, imperfect performing style. For Stevens, temporality is closely connected to personal experiences with time. And for Mitchell, varying types of flexible meter express a tension between stability and freedom in life, romance, and her musical career. The broader role of flexible meter as self-expression in their 1960s and 1970s performances positions it as an essential feature of singer-songwriter self-expression. This self-expressive rhetoric helps to shape style, persona, and notions of authenticity in the singer-songwriter performance practice.

5

Intensifying "Imperfection":
Ambiguous Meter

The examples of lost meter in Chapter 4 pointed to some methods of metric ambiguity available to the 1960s and 1970s singer-songwriters in this study. These primarily solo artists could include spur-of-the-moment timing choices or plan flexible structures into their performances. Seemingly spontaneous timing decisions help to develop a performance practice that, unlike other popular music genres, is free from the expectations of Regular Meter.[1] In this chapter, I explore how the inclusion of more extreme Ambiguous Meter in singer-songwriter music signals a network of flexible, "imperfect" timing possibilities available for this self-expressive performance practice. Locally, this Ambiguous Meter acts to illustrate narrative meaning. More broadly this more extreme timing is a marker of stylistic inclusion for individual personas in the singer-songwriter genre.

Ambiguous Meter does not necessarily mean that a situation is ametric. Indeed, metric cues are still present in passages of extreme flexibility in singer-songwriter performances. There is, therefore, always *potential* for metric regularity to emerge.[2] The term *emerging meter* captures the process by which metric cues (stresses, pulse levels, and alternating strong and weak beats) gradually or swiftly organize into more regular levels of meter.[3] The process of metric emergence is a more dramatic version of the regained

---

[1] As discussed in Chapter 1, ensemble music featuring the prototypical guitar, bass, and drums of a rock band more often than not demonstrates regular meter throughout. But there are many notable exceptions like the Beatles, Radiohead, The Police, and metal bands like Meshuggah and The Dillinger Escape Plan that include sometimes frequent changes of meter or irregularities in grouping. These are ensemble-specific expectations—in the case of progressive rock and metal, genre-specific exceptions. All of these bands maintain a tactus or a sub-tactus level throughout changes to meter and grouping. For some examples of ensemble-based irregularities, see Biamonte (2014), Pieslak (2007), Lucas (2018), Osborn (2011), Everett (2009).

[2] As established in the early chapters, a truly ametric scenario would be entirely devoid of metric cues and therefore lack metric potential. This situation does not occur in singer-songwriter music.

[3] For more on "metrical emergence," see Horlacher (2000/2001, 271).

Times A-Changin'. Nancy Murphy, Oxford University Press. © Oxford University Press 2023.
DOI: 10.1093/oso/9780197635216.003.0005

126 TIMES A-CHANGIN'

meter explored after passages of metric loss in Chapter 4.[4] Emerging meter represents a generative effort to establish regularity, which has a striking effect in contexts that were initially ambiguous. In other words, stresses and durations in Ambiguous Meter have metric potential, and metric emergence engages that potential. Listening to these extreme manifestations of flexible meter in performance allows an observation of timings that either remain ambiguous or fulfill metric potential and move from Ambiguous to Regular Meter. The sensations of following these metric cues are critical for understanding the techniques of self-expression in this flexibly timed singer-songwriter repertoire.

I begin this chapter with an investigation of metric ambiguity in two Bob Dylan songs: "Down the Highway" and "Restless Farewell." In these songs, flexible meter illustrates Dylan's relationship to source material and argues that Ambiguous metric structures are essential features of his original 1960s singer-songwriter music. In my analysis of "Down the Highway," I position Dylan's adapted blues style as bridging the divide between metric regularity and ambiguity. Then I explore how "Restless Farewell" illustrates Dylan taking the expressive timing of traditional source material to extremes including Unrealized Durations, Ambiguous Meter, and emerging meter within his early, formative period of persona-fashioning through songwriting and performance.

In the final two examples of this chapter, I explore Ambiguous Meter in songs by Joni Mitchell and Buffy Sainte-Marie. I revisit Mitchell's "The Fiddle and the Drum" and show how its metric fluctuations are central to Mitchell's self-expressive rhetoric. The flexible meter signals her important lyrical meaning, with her "protest song" perspective as a Canadian outsider to America's military involvement. Flexible meter positions the song as part of Mitchell's broader experimentations as a singer-songwriter. In my final analysis, I propose a way of hearing the flexible meter in Sainte-Marie's folk song adaptation "Sir Patrick Spens" as an example of the most extreme ambiguity in this singer-songwriter repertoire. Her performance includes both Unrealized Durations and Ungrouped Beats and signals a connection between her self-expressive metric techniques and the folk-influenced singer-songwriter movement. Together, the four analyses in this chapter demonstrate how the most malleable extremes of Ambiguous Meter are

---

[4] This is because emerging meter encompasses passages of salience evolving from previously Ambiguous metric contexts, whereas regained meter represents an achievement of "back to normal."

INTENSIFYING "IMPERFECTION": AMBIGUOUS METER   127

an important rhetorical marker of self-expression in the 1960s and 1970s singer-songwriter performance practice.

Bob Dylan's "Down the Highway"

Bob Dylan's "Down the Highway" from his 1963 album *The Freewheelin' Bob Dylan* illustrates a meeting point of Regular and Ambiguous Meter. This song showcases how Dylan absorbed metric influence from the Delta blues into his own original blues style and it positions flexible meter as a critical feature of his self-expression in this genre. Dylan was familiar with many blues artists, particularly Delta blues singers whose recordings from the 1920s and 1930s were re-released in the 1960s. His blues songs feature some important features relating to the self-expressive performance practice of the Delta blues: an *aab* lyric structure, a narrative of personal struggle, and a malleable manifestation of the twelve-bar blues harmonic template.

Dylan's studio-recording performance of "Down the Highway" features a flexible meter that situates it alongside some of the most extreme Delta blues performances.[5] While his other blues songs feature a regular and consistent tactus beat level, "Down the Highway" includes highly flexible tactus strumming patterns that are at times missing (not articulated by the voice or guitar) or obscured through syncopation and misalignment.[6] The larger-scale grouping of these tactus beats is also unpredictable and irregular, yielding mostly groups of three beats with several groupings of twos or fours. This extreme, stylistic metric imperfection is taken further in Dylan's avoiding a depth of meter beyond the two levels of these tactus beats and their groupings. His guitar strumming occasionally includes faster rhythms that subdivide tactus beats, but these are not maintained enough to be understood as metric layers. That is, they do not provide a consistent additional level of meter. At most there are two metric layers in his strumming patterns, one that is highly flexible and the other, irregular.

---

[5] There are many examples of this in the Delta blues repertoire. Songs like Muddy Waters's "My Captain" and passages from his "Cold Weather Blues" and "Feel Like Going Home" (all from his 1964 album *The Folk Singer*) have flexible tactus beats similar to Dylan's "Down the Highway." Ford (1998) explores some metric flexibility in Robert Johnson performances; many of these feature a consistent tactus but include irregular hypermetric groupings and some include omitted harmonic zones.

[6] There are several possibilities for this analysis, some of which place this highly flexible beat level as tactus, and some of which view this as a highly flexible hypermetric level. It is possible to hear both. But for this analysis, I have chosen to interpret it as a tactus beat level to analyze it in dialogue with the typical regular tactus beat levels of songs in a Delta blues style. This reading positions "Down the Highway" in closer alignment with the generic expectations of the Delta blues.

128 TIMES A-CHANGIN'

a	Well I'm walking down the highway/With my suitcase in my hand
a	Yes I'm walking down the highway/With my suitcase in my hand
b	Lord, I really miss my baby/She's in some foreign land

Figure 5.1 Dylan, "Down the Highway," first stanza

Indeed, Dylan's performance avoids the depth of meter found in the regular passages from the examples in Chapters 3 and 4. With its inconsistent rhythms, Dylan's studio-recording performance of "Down the Highway" is situated between the categories of Regular and Ambiguous Meter.[7] In the analysis that follows, I examine the techniques through which Dylan creates and obscures metric regularity in this performance, resulting in a metric structure that aligns with his broader "imperfect" performance aesthetic.[8] My analysis offers a way of hearing flexible meter in this more ambiguous metric context and a method for conceptualizing metric flexibility as Dylan's self-positioning within the blues genre. To attend to the particularities of meter in this performance illuminates the techniques by which Dylan defies Regular Meter and showcases the self-expressive rhetoric of his original blues.

The Blues Model

Dylan's lyrics borrow the model from the blues in content and *aab* organization.[9] The lyrics for "Down the Highway" are the "most directly autobiographical" of his blues compositions.[10] The first stanza (Figure 5.1) explains that Dylan misses his "baby," presumably his then-girlfriend Suze Rotolo, who he states in the fifth verse has gone away to Italy. Around the time Dylan wrote this original blues song, Rotolo was studying abroad, with a six-month absence that affected him enough to be referenced in several songs during

---

[7] In his brief examination of "Down the Highway," Harvey (2001, 26) notes the lack of any "clear meter" and prevalence of speech-like vocal rhythms in the song. He cites Tommy McClennan's 1940 recording of "New Highway No. 51" as one of several possible inspirations for Dylan's original blues "Down the Highway." McClennan's song contains a steady pulse amid some standard timing flexibilities.

[8] As mentioned in Chapter 1, Rings (2013, [3]) cites several scholars who define an "aesthetic of imperfection" surrounding Dylan's performance practice, which is often "lauded by fans as a marker of authenticity" in his rhetoric.

[9] Gioia (2009, 14) sees the repeated first line in the Delta blues as connected to call-and-response group singing.

[10] Heylin (2001, 99).

> Well I'm **walk**ing down the **high**way
> With my **suit**case in my **hand**
> Yes, I'm **walk**ing down the **high**way
> With my **suit**case in my **hand**
> Lord I **really** miss my **baby**
> She's in **some** foreign **land**

Figure 5.2 Dylan, "Down the Highway," performed dynamic accents in stanza 1

this period.[11] That such personal information is included in his lyrics for "Down the Highway" suggests an awareness on Dylan's part of how autobiographical details could elevate his blues rhetoric and capitalize on the popularity of self-expressive blues storytelling.[12] This first stanza also shows some ways these lyrics set him apart from Delta blues performers, who frequently sang of traveling and highways, but rarely referenced foreign lands.[13]

Stressed Events

With these personal lyrics, Dylan also mimics the structure of the blues vocal stress patterns in this performance. He stresses two accented syllables per line, as shown in Figure 5.2, with stressed syllables in boldface.[14] It is possible to read the lyrics alone as having a series of simple trochees, four per line with the occasional monosyllable in the place of a trochee. The regularity of these twelve stresses could conceivably align with downbeats in a twelve-bar blues. But Dylan's setting omits harmonic zones and guitar strums and sometimes obscures vocal stresses by not aligning them with meter-orienting gestures in the guitar.[15] In doing so, he disrupts the metric potential of these lyrics with his unpredictable performance practice.

[11] Rotolo (2008, 169) cites June 9, 1962 as the date of her departure from New York for Italy; Dylan recorded the song on July 9. For more on other Dylan "come-on" songs and a discussion of Dylan "attempting to write something as archetypal as 'Crossroad Blues'" with "Down the Highway," see Heylin (2009, 85–86). Harvey (2001, 26) suggests that "Down the Highway" is one of several songs Dylan wrote during his separation from Rotolo; see also Scorsese (2005).

[12] In a more generous interpretation, the blues allowed him a genuine opportunity for introspection to work through his feelings about Rotolo's absence through his experimentations with blues style.

[13] Many thanks to Steven Rings for this observation.

[14] Vocal stresses transcribed from Dylan (1963). It may also be possible to hear a stress on the second syllable of "highway," following Bickford's (2007, 449) interpretation. Bickford also hears the second syllable of "suitcase" emphasized instead of the first syllable. In the final line, I hear emphasis on the words "some" and "land" in this phrase, so I have put those in boldface. But Dylan also adds a dynamic accent on the first syllable of "foreign," which confuses the stress pattern in his performance.

[15] For reference, and though there are many variants, the blues harmonic prototype is typically: I (4 bars), IV (2 bars), I (2 bars), V (1 bar), IV (1 bar), I (2 bars).

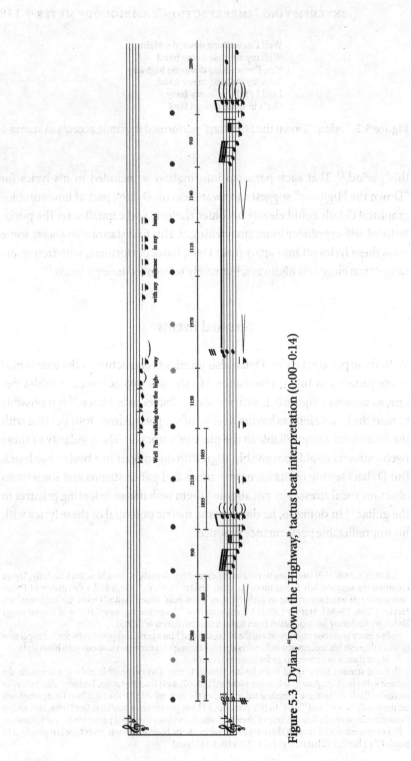

Figure 5.3 Dylan, "Down the Highway," tactus beat interpretation (0:00–0:14)

Flexible First Line

His guitar introduction and first vocal line introduce the metric cues of this performance: a guitar tremolo and descending arpeggiation leading to tonic arrival and a weak-to-strong pattern in the voice. These cues yield a flexible but consistent tactus in his voice and guitar strumming patterns. Some of the cues in this passage (0:00–0:14, included as Figure 5.3) retain their initial metric function on the same strong or weak beat, and some are transformed on subsequent appearances amid the varying timings of Dylan's performance. The first stressed event occurs when he initiates a tremolo figure in the guitar on a minor seventh chord with an omitted third. Dylan's fast strumming subdivides the tremolo's duration, notated as a dotted-half-note beat, into thirty-second notes. I interpret this as a quarter-note tactus around 860 ms indicated with the IOI values above the lower staff. The black dot above the IOI values indicates this clear tactus beat at the onset of the tremolo. Grey dots denote the less salient but still possible beat articulations from grouping Dylan's strumming subdivisions.

Metric Orientation

After the tremolo, Dylan includes a descending figure and subsequently arrives on a G tonic pitch. Together these two figures (the descending arpeggiation and tonic arrival) are a meter-orienting gesture that articulates an anacrusis-to-downbeat metric pattern. The subsequent iterations of this gesture, like that at the end of the system in Figure 5.3, retain the initial metric function of leading to a downbeat. By contrast, the tremolo figure onset never regains its initial downbeat function in subsequent occurrences. Its arrival in the remaining lines of this verse occurs on other beats in the measure or not synchronized with a tactus beat, thus destabilizing its potential as a meter-orienting cue. These are signals of ambiguity in Dylan's guitar accompaniment that reinforce the effects of metric disorientation in this performance.

Once the voice begins, there is some regularity to its stresses. Dylan's two-beat vocal fragments project a clear arrangement of weak leading to strong, the latter of which I interpret as a downbeat. And yet even with this clear weak-to-strong beat pattern, which Dylan borrows from the Delta blues,

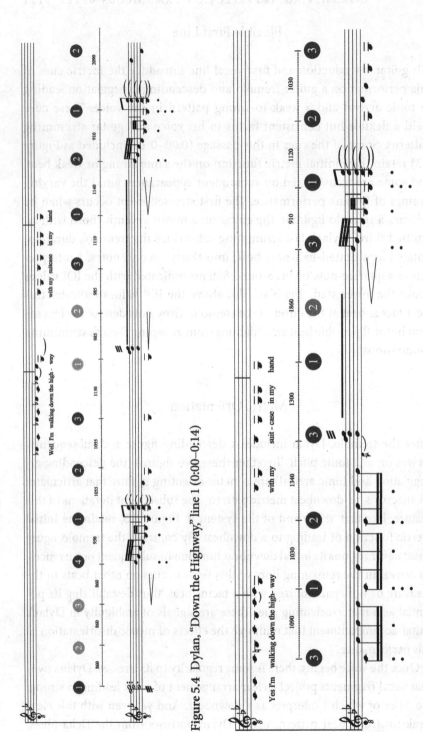

Figure 5.4 Dylan, "Down the Highway," line 1 (0:00–0:14)

Figure 5.5 Dylan, "Down the Highway," line 2 (0:14–0:24)

INTENSIFYING "IMPERFECTION": AMBIGUOUS METER 133

Dylan obscures the first vocal stress by syncopating the first syllable of "highway" and offsetting his guitar's plucked tonic pitch and tremolo onset.[16] The stress on "highway" arrives earlier than expected, and the guitar's events sound later than expected. It is not until the first syllable of "suitcase" that the tactus beat is clearly articulated again, indicated by the black dot between the staves after two inferred tactus beats shown as grey dots. The overall impression is of an imperfect meter, as befits the style.

Loose Metric Structure

There is some resemblance between the meter of this line and a Delta blues prototype. In Figure 5.4, I illustrate a possible metric grouping of the tactus beats that results in five downbeats for this line: (1) at the initial tremolo introduction, (2) articulated by the first meter-orienting gesture's tonic arrival, (3) inferred from the obscured first vocal downbeat, (4) at the arrival on the word "hand," and (5) at the downbeat on the next meter-orienting gesture.[17] The resulting measure lengths are 4, 3, 3, 2, and 3 beats (the last beat of which I do not include in this diagram), all on tonic harmony in the first line of this three-line blues construction. Dylan's self-expressive performance has thus far offered some metric framework but obscured it in ways that put this song in a context of stylistic metric flexibility leaning toward Ambiguous Meter more than of predictable metric regularity.

Second Line

The stylistic metric imperfection is continued in the rest of the first stanza. In line 2 (Figure 5.5), Dylan's strumming subdivides the tactus beats in a way that recalls the guitar introduction's tremolo subdivisions. These sixteenth-note beats on subdominant harmony add an additional metric layer to the rhythmic organization, shown with the dot diagram below the staff. But he does not maintain this depth of metric salience. And the

---

[16] To show this syncopation, I place the downbeat symbol after my notated bar line. The number "1" is enclosed in a starred grey circle to denote that this downbeat is inferred, since neither the vocal onset nor the guitar's tonic pitch aligns with it.

[17] For each meter-orienting gesture, I show how its more salient rhythms and subdivisions offer instances of further depth to the possible metric hierarchy of Dylan's performance.

following strumming obscures his previously established meter. Dylan's shifts to tonic at the articulation of "suitcase," which occurs earlier than expected following a blues prototype and aligns the stress on the first syllable of "suitcase" with a tremolo in the guitar that is no longer a reliable metric cue. It could be possible to shift the meter here, to position "suitcase" on an unexpected downbeat, but the subsequent stronger stress on "hand" confirms that the weak-to-strong beat arrangement of vocal stresses is still an active downbeat orientation. The subsequent tactus beat on beat 2 must be imagined amid the tremolo articulations until the meter-orienting gesture confirms the next downbeat. While this line offers some depth of meter at its onset, Dylan includes enough ambiguity to keep his performance from engaging a clear, multi-leveled metric hierarchy. The impression is one of the performer thwarting expectations within an already unpredictable performing style.

Third Line

The final line of the stanza continues to thwart predictability and distinguishes Dylan from his Delta blues precedents with its mention of "foreign land." His third line (Figure 5.6) signals a shift to the dominant, which is expected from the blues harmonic prototype. Again, Dylan includes some subdivisions of the tactus in his accompaniment, but this time they are short-lived, as if when he sings the word "baby" (the reason for his blues) he is caught up in his sentiments and forgets to keep the subdivisions active in his guitar. As a result, the second beat of this line must be imagined amid pairs of pitches picked in his guitar. The final downbeat on "land," too, is undercut by Dylan's stresses on "some" and "foreign," the latter of which aligns with a fast-strummed tremolo onset. Despite some regularity in the tactus, and a predictable weak-to-strong arrangement of the vocal stresses, Dylan's performance prevents Regular Meter from emerging, undercutting expectations in ways that are both stylistic and original.

Flexible Blues

The resulting harmonic structure of Dylan's performance offers a loose version of the blues prototype. Figure 5.7a summarizes a possible twelve-bar

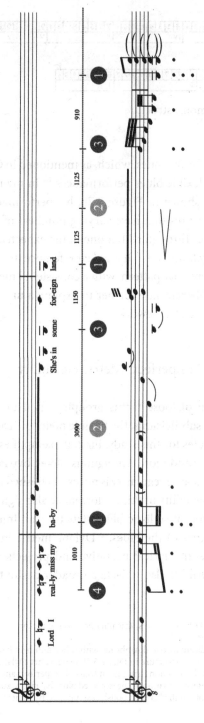

Figure 5.6 Dylan, "Down the Highway," line 3 (0:24–0:34)

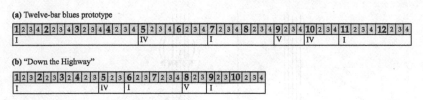

Figure 5.7 Blues harmonic structure

harmonic trajectory for the blues, which, as mentioned in Chapter 1, is commonly thwarted by flexible blues performances.[18] In my reading of Dylan's harmonic structure, shown in Figure 5.7b, his performance yields a blues pattern with ten measures that have varying numbers of tactus beats. And his progression moves through all but one of the expected harmonic zones, skipping the final subdominant.[19] It is a clear reference to the blues in which a complete regular twelve-bar pattern, with a consistent $\frac{4}{4}$ meter, is far from the norm, but also a deliberate step further to explore a unique compositional voice within this stylistic framework.

"Imperfect" Metric Flexibility

In its demonstration of loose tactus groupings and unclear, inconsistent strumming of tactus subdivisions, the flexible meter of "Down the Highway" fills two important roles for this study. First, it exemplifies a bridge between a loose Regular Meter and more Ambiguous Meter, bypassing sensations of Lost Meter entirely because regularity is never established enough to feel lost. Second, the metric flexibility of this performance also signals both a connection to and subversion of stylistic blues structure, an imperfect meter that itself is a prized feature of the blues.[20] Dylan's metric imperfection serves to express an "authentic" lyrical narrative and projects an imperfect performance persona. And it also reflects a broader desire to incorporate the

---

[18] For example, as Ford (1998) explores, this phenomenon of metric irregularity occurs often in Robert Johnson's recordings.

[19] Boldface numbers indicate metric downbeats, with other numbers indicating the tactus beats in each bar. The harmonic zone structure in Figure 5.7b begins after Dylan's introduction, with the onset of his vocal line. This is a common structure in Delta blues performances, in which a metrically loose introduction precedes the initiation of the expected blues harmonic zones.

[20] Gioia (2009, 242) points to the "lack of polish" exemplified by imperfect meter as an essential feature of the Delta blues.

INTENSIFYING "IMPERFECTION": AMBIGUOUS METER   137

coveted features of blues self-expression. Dylan engaged self-expressive features of the blues in his personal lyrics about heartache in a flexible metric structure to fashion himself as a bluesman. If these features are markers of "real" blues expression, "Down the Highway" is Dylan's attempt to capitalize on these trends and position himself as a possible successor to the blues tradition. Yet with this as his most original Delta blues song, it stands as the apex of his stylistic explorations in this genre; this song is a culmination and conclusion of his attempts at fashioning his persona as a bluesman.[21]

Bob Dylan's "Restless Farewell"

Alongside Dylan's blues influences, his early style was also immersed in folk music. On his debut album, *Bob Dylan* (1962), all but two songs are folk standards.[22] By his third album, *The Times They Are A-Changin'* (1964a), Dylan's original songwriting style was more clearly emerging amid his influences. All the tracks on the album are listed as original, but two of these have clear source material: "With God on Our Side" is developed from Dominic Behan's "The Patriot Game," and "Restless Farewell" is adapted from the Scottish folk song "The Parting Glass," which Dylan learned from his folk-revival contemporaries The Clancy Brothers.[23] "The Parting Glass" is a sentimental song about leaving, typically sung at the end of a night of drinking.[24] "Restless Farewell" has a similar departure theme, with Dylan exploring a release from his enigmatic, initial (and disputed) identity.[25]

[21] Indeed, Harvey (2001, 26) argues that "Down the Highway" is Dylan's "most creative work in the [blues] genre."

[22] The album's two original songs have clear sources: his "Song to Woody" is dedicated to Woody Guthrie, and "Talkin' New York" mimics Guthrie's talking blues style.

[23] Harvey (2001) explores seventy Dylan songs from his early albums as connected to pre-existing sources, including "With God on Our Side" and "Restless Farewell." Dominic Behan claims the melody and lyrics from "The Patriot Game" and Dylan's "With God on Our Side" as his own. But Harvey (2001, 122–23) cites several possible influences on "The Patriot Game," which include the Appalachian Mountain song "The Merry Month of May" and "The Bold Grenadier." For a detailed study of expressive timing and transcription as analysis in different performances of "With God on Our Side," see Murphy (2020).

[24] The Clancy Brothers (1963) often used this song as a finale for their live performances. "The Parting Glass" is the final song on their 1968 live album with Tommy Makem, *In Person at Carnegie Hall.*

[25] This is one instance of Dylan exploring various personas in his songwriting. Harvey sees Dylan searching for and shifting identity manifest itself in two particular songs: "Bob Dylan's Dream" in which the singer laments a lost identity, and "Restless Farewell" in which Dylan releases himself from a current identity. Harvey (2001, xxiv–xxv) claims that "Bob Dylan's Dream" also features metric flexibility, though it has a steady tactus throughout. The song features hypermetric shifts, with Dylan regularly omitting measures in his instrumental interludes. It also includes examples of performed-out fermatas, explored in Murphy (2018).

138 TIMES A-CHANGIN'

My analysis of "Restless Farewell" positions the song's flexible meter as a reflection of Dylan exploring personas, identities, and original songwriting through his folk revivalist song adaptations. (This is particularly true of the Ambiguous Meter of his studio-recording performance.) His reworking of the source material into a more metrically flexible, personal version shows Dylan engaging the trends of adapted songwriting of the Greenwich Village folk scene. The flexible meter in "Restless Farewell" marks it as original and signals that metric flexibility is an essential feature of Dylan's folk-influenced singer-songwriter performances.

The flexibility of Dylan's performance results to some degree from inconsistent coordination between voice and guitar strumming. Brief moments of coordination offer passages of regularity with one line showcasing metric emergence, but the overall effect is of Ambiguous Meter with brief moments of regularity. With his restless timing, Dylan echoes the struggle with parting found in the source material but adds layers of meaning in his flexible meter that mirror an evasive identity and a performance persona that resulted in challenges to his authenticity.

Influence from "The Parting Glass"

In his repurposing material from "The Parting Glass," Dylan's version maintains the harmonic structure and sentiment found in The Clancy Brothers' interpretation, adapting the melody, text, and timing for "Restless Farewell."[26] His accompaniment lacks the fast guitar strumming of many of Dylan's other folk-influenced songs like "Talkin' New York" and his other identity-themed song "Bob Dylan's Dream," instead mimicking the style of The Clancy Brothers' version.

The Clancy Brothers' performance signals a possible template for the lyrical stress pattern of Dylan's adaptation. Their phrase units in their 1959 recording of "The Parting Glass" demonstrate the "arrival point" folk singing style: there are four stressed events per line (shown in Figure 5.8) reinforced by coordinated vocal accents and harmony changes in the guitar.[27]

---

[26] Of Dylan's seventy songs between 1961 and 1963, Harvey (2001, xxi–xxii) cites only a third as original to Dylan containing only a phrase or two from an earlier source. The remaining two-thirds of his melodies were borrowed from the traditional song repertoire, and Dylan "changed rhythms to fit the new text he had composed, sometimes extending phrases, often changing accented pitches and flattening the melodic contour."

[27] Similar stress diagrams can be found in Rings (2013) and Murphy (2015, 175).

INTENSIFYING "IMPERFECTION": AMBIGUOUS METER 139

	1	2	3	4
Of	**all** the	**mon**-ey that	**e'er** I	**spent**
I	**spent** it	**in** good	**comp**-an-y	——
And	**all** the	**harm** that I	**ev**- er	**did**
A-	**-las** it	**was** to	**none** but	**me**
And	**all** I've	**done** for	**want** of	**wit**
To	**mem**-'ry	**now** I	**can't** re-	**-call**
So	**fill** to	**me** the	**part**-ing	**glass**
Good	**night** and	**joy** be	**with** you	**all**

Figure 5.8 The Clancy Brothers, "The Parting Glass" (*Come Fill Your Glass with Us*, 1959), lyrics and four-beat metric structure (verse 1)

The Clancy Brothers' performances on *Come Fill Your Glass with Us* (1959) and *In Person at Carnegie Hall* (1963) both include tempo fluctuations, but none so flexible as to obscure the expectation of beat arrivals, as Dylan's performance does. Their vocal line provides the most salient metric cues, with the accompaniment supporting the vocal stresses. This performance demonstrates the stylistic timing flexibility associated with ensemble folk music, which avoids the extremes of metric ambiguity found in singer-songwriter performances.

Stressed Events

Dylan's "Restless Farewell" has ties to the four-beat units of "The Parting Glass," but he obscures this structure through more extreme timing flexibility. Dylan's original text does offer some four-beat stress patterns: the chart in Figure 5.9 illustrates this possible quadruple reading of the vocal stresses for his first verse.[28] But Dylan's timings in the studio recording obscure this

---

[28] There are some notable similarities here to "The Parting Glass": most lines begin with an anacrusis, and all lines either have four vocal stresses or fill in a fourth stress with time in the performance. The first word of Dylan's lyrics is likely "Of" to match The Clancy Brothers' version. I have included "Oh" in this diagram to match the lyrics published on Dylan's official website.

140 TIMES A-CHANGIN'

	1	2	3	4
Oh	all the	mon-ey that in my	whole life I did	spend
	Be it mine	right or	wrong-ful-ly	——
I	let it slip	glad-ly	to my	friends
To	tie up the	time most	force-ful-ly	——
But the	bot-tles are	done We've	killed each	one
And the	tab-le's	full and	o-ver-	flowed
And the	cor-ner	sign says it's	clos-ing	time
So I'll	bid fare-	well and be	down the	road

Figure 5.9 Dylan, "Restless Farewell," lyrics and possible four-beat metric structure (verse 1)

four-beat reading. Rather than reinforcing the possible regular stress pattern, his guitar strumming challenges the voice for prominence, adds additional beats between phrases, and creates surprising asynchronies with the vocal line.[29] Together, the voice and guitar create a flexible meter that expresses the restlessness of the song's subject. Dylan's unpredictable timings highlight the originality of his version of this song and how it resists the metric regularity of his source material.

Opening Line

Dylan's first vocal fragments shown in Figure 5.10 introduce his rebellious approach to structuring the possible four-beat stress pattern of the lyrics. His stress on the word "all" marks the first beat.[30] The strummed E/B chord in the guitar could have aligned with the voice to reinforce this first stress as it does in "The Parting Glass," but instead his chord is slightly delayed from the vocal arrival. His initial asynchrony hints that this misalignment between voice and guitar is an important signal of restlessness in this performance.

[29] I see Dylan's use of asynchrony connected to the "expressive asynchrony" developed for performance analysis in studies of expressive timing in piano works between 1775 and 1850; see Dodson (2011) and Yorgason (2009). For application of expressive asynchrony, and the analysis of Buffy Sainte-Marie songs, see Murphy (2019).

[30] His initial guitar strum shown at the beginning of Figure 5.10 sounds introductory and key-orienting, so I have not included it in my metric analysis. In "The Parting Glass," the guitar does not strum until the voice arrives on the word "all."

INTENSIFYING "IMPERFECTION": AMBIGUOUS METER   141

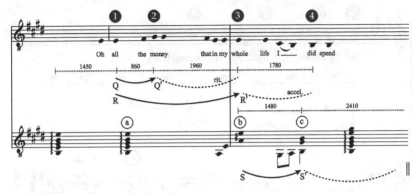

Figure 5.10 Dylan, "Restless Farewell," phrase 1 (0:00–0:08)

The opening line also illustrates that obscuring or avoiding vocal stress patterns is an important technique of metric ambiguity in this performance. This is achieved through withholding of guitar-strumming support for a stressed event in the voice or through a surprising accent in the guitar instead of his vocal line. As an example of the former, Dylan's stress on the first syllable of "money" articulates the second beat but does so without support from the accompaniment. Restoring predictability briefly, his stress on the word "whole" aligns with an A–E strummed dyad in the guitar at (b). But then he illustrates the latter technique of ambiguity by avoiding a possible stress on the word "spend," and shifting the stressed event to the structural B2 dominant in the guitar at (c). As a result, it is possible to hear multiple words as the fourth stress of this line—"I," "did," or "spend"—all of which are asynchronous with the stress at (c) in the guitar. I show his emphasis on the word "did" taking aural precedence because it has the closest proximity to the guitar strum only 2 ms later. By obscuring an expected stress on "spend" and avoiding coordination between voice and accompaniment, Dylan is establishing the context of Ambiguous Meter of the majority of the verse.

Attending to the durations between each pair of stressed events in this phrase illustrates some additional challenges to hearing Regular Meter in Dylan's performance. The Q duration that spans his first two stresses creates an 860 ms duration; to reproduce this as Q' I must wait until the third stress. But this results in a Q' IOI of 1960 ms, more than twice as long as Q. It is tempting to subdivide this longer duration; instead I prefer a dramatic *ritardando* for the Q' duration because I hear the voice as such a strong stress determinant in this passage. The regularity of the vocal stresses between "all" and "money," alongside a syntactical

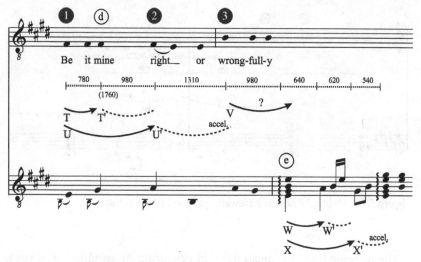

Figure 5.11 Dylan, "Restless Farewell," phrase 2 (0:08–1:15)

and semantic need for resolution (what about the money?), encourages attention toward the next stressed event. Within this passage, the metric cues of stress and duration are active, and some of these durations are realized, but a strong pulse does not emerge. The primary sensation is of metric ambiguity reflecting a broader self-expressive unpredictability in Dylan's performance.

Second Line

The song's second phrase (Figure 5.11) does little to resolve the ambiguity of the first. Dylan adds vocal stresses that obscure the regularity of his melodic line. After articulating the first stress on the word "Be," Dylan adds an unexpected stress on "mine" at (d) that creates a possible new faster pulse layer, reinforced by the guitar's grace note figures on E3, G#3, and A3. This increased rhythmic density mimics the structure of the third line of "The Parting Glass," but the effect in Dylan's version is different.[31] In The Clancy Brothers' song, the metric structure is so regular it can withstand flexible timing, so an increase in strumming density emerges as a subdivision of the established slow pulse level. In "Restless Farewell," the meter is already so Ambiguous that an emerging pulse layer

---

[31] In "The Parting Glass," this happens in the line "Alas it was to none but me" (0:17–0:22). Guitar strums reinforce a pulse layer on the second syllable of "Alas," and the words "it" and "was." This creates a pulse layer that subdivides the prevailing metric structure, which is twice as slow.

INTENSIFYING "IMPERFECTION": AMBIGUOUS METER   143

becomes the primary pulse layer by default, even if it is plausibly a subdivision. The realized T–T' durational projections in Figure 5.11 show that this faster pulse is a passage of emergent salience that seems metric within this Ambiguous metric context. It challenges the sense of loose four-beat meter as the structural background for the performance, confusing rather than clarifying the meter. This pulse layer is then lost toward the end of the phrase, and a new series of durations emerges in the guitar, beginning at (h).[32] The way this phrase moves in and out of engagement with meter reinforces the sensations of restlessness through the metric ambiguity heard so far in the song.

Third and Fourth Lines

The third and fourth phrases engage similar techniques of ambiguity to the first two, with Dylan saving metric emergence for the fifth phrase. In phrase 3, shown in the upper system of Figure 5.12, the vocal stress on the word "let" is asynchronous from the guitar articulation, this time with the guitar articulating an E3 and the voice arriving slightly later. A further asynchrony occurs on the third beat, when the guitar's arpeggiated chord at (h) articulates a stress confirming the Q' and R durations that is followed by the expected vocal stress on the word "to." The fourth beat of this phrase has support from the E/B guitar chord but has a surprising vocal stress. I expected a stress on the word "friends" because it would rhyme with "spend" from phrase 1 and has syntactic importance to the song's message. But Dylan instead aligns the word "my" with the guitar chord at (i).[33] The asynchronies in this phrase reinforce the unpredictable disconnect between voice and guitar.

The fourth phrase (the second system of Figure 5.12) mostly parallels the structure of the second, but the meter becomes more regular to "tie up the time" in preparation for the metric emergence in the fifth phrase.[34] The first vocal stress is asynchronous with the guitar's F♯3, but Dylan coordinates the subsequent events on the second and third hyperbeats. A fourth hyperbeat

[32] It may be possible to relate the 980 ms V duration to the identical IOI for T' (between "mine" and "right"), but I would argue that the 1310 ms U' duration obscures this connection and that the guitar chord at (e) sounds like it arrives too early.

[33] This structure parallels the end of phrase 1, when the vocal arrival on B3 occurred "too early" and added stress to the word "did" instead of "spend."

[34] Starting with this figure—and then again for Figure 5.13—I restart my lettering at Q for projection labels. I do this to avoid progressing to the beginning of the alphabet and the confusion that might create with pitch names and/or formal labeling.

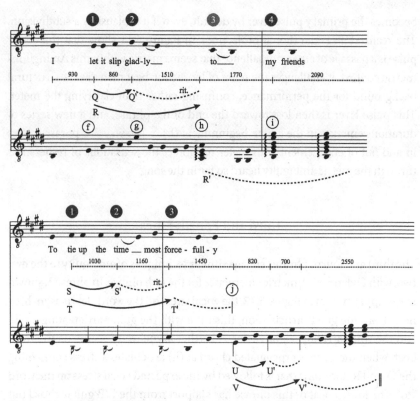

Figure 5.12 Dylan, "Restless Farewell," phrases 3 and 4 (0:15–0:29)

is missing from the voice, and the guitar's tonic pitch at (j) serves to articulate a fourth stress. This time, the fourth stress sounds as if it interrupts the longer T' projection, which could have replicated the 2190 ms T duration. The realized S–S' durations initiate a regular pulse that signals a tightening of the metric structure to follow. If the narrator is indeed singing "Restless Farewell" at the end of a social gathering, or as a farewell to a former identity, then Dylan's preceding ambiguity reflects the restlessness that resists the gathering's natural conclusion: an effort to "tie up the time most forcefully," as phrase 4 would have it. This flexible meter evokes Dylan's sentiments and also sets up a contrast for the regularity that follows.

Fifth Line

In the fifth phrase, Regular Meter emerges first with a clear pulse layer and then with hierarchic meter. The phrase opens with a pair of two-beat

INTENSIFYING "IMPERFECTION": AMBIGUOUS METER   145

Figure 5.13 Dylan, "Restless Farewell," phrases 5 and 6 (0:29–0:41)

hypermetric units, following the structure of the poetry. But Dylan's timing separates these units by two beats of a newly emerged quarter-note pulse layer. His stresses on the first syllable of "bottles" and the word "done" (as shown in Figure 5.13) are subdivided into quarter-note beats, reinforced by the rhythms of the guitar strumming. This pulse layer recalls the faster pulse that emerged in phrase 2. This time, however, the pulse layer continues. The Q–Q' layer I show between the staves illustrates the half-note pulse articulated by vocal stresses and features a hiatus when the stress on "killed" is delayed. But the accompaniment spans this duration. Here there is a sensation of strong and weak stress organization, with quarter- and half-note pulse levels spanning the first two vocal stresses and the arrival on B3 at (k). The meter has only two levels but is Regular for the first time in the song at the moment when Dylan emphasizes that the bottles "are done."

146 TIMES A-CHANGIN'

The second vocal fragment of this line reinforces the meter even further, with Dylan's stress on "killed" initiating regularity. To parallel the first hypermetric unit, I give the subsequent two-beat unit, at "We've killed each one," the same metric structure. The stressed "killed" marks the first hyperbeat, with the second articulated by the word "one." I then show a new hypermeasure beginning, with "table's" initiating the next hyperdownbeat. A four-beat hypermeasure follows with beats on "table," "full," a syncopated vocal arrival with the guitar accent at (l), and a stress on the final syllable of "overflowed." Beginning with the hyperdownbeat on "killed," there is a large-scale four-beat hypermetric structure reinforced by a salient $\frac{4}{4}$ meter.

Flexible Effects

The effect of this emergent meter is notable, especially given where it occurs in the verse. Once it is realized that the "bottles are done," there is a growing awareness that it is the end of the evening and the gathering must conclude. The increase in cues for Regular Meter can be read to reflect this awareness, as Dylan sings about noticing the full table of "killed" bottles.[35] In the context of the song's lyrics, this fifth phrase is a process of gradually stilling the restlessness brought out by the previous phrases. The emerging meter of phrase 5 sets into relief how ambiguous Dylan's timings were for the opening phrases, especially in comparison to his source material. The regularity is unexpected, based on the initially Ambiguous context, and is therefore a dramatic shift in Dylan's level of engagement with meter to bring out the lyrics at this moment.

Self-Presentation and "Authenticity"

This metric emergence can also be read as illustrating a rhetorical strength of Dylan's message about his own authenticity. Dylan wrote "Restless Farewell" around the time an article was released in *Newsweek* in 1963 that accuses the singer of embellishing his personal history.[36] The piece suggests that Dylan "shrouds his past in contradictions" but that he actually grew up in "a

[35] Looking ahead, the final two phrases of this verse return to the more ambiguous meter of the opening lines, with the lyrics reinforcing the "closing time" and necessity of bidding "farewell."
[36] See Harvey (2001, 95) and Coleman (2016).

conventional home and went to conventional schools."[37] Specific lines of the lyrics in "Restless Farewell" can be read as direct responses to the *Newsweek* article. His comments about "the dirt of gossip" and "dust of rumors" directed at him seem to reference the content of the *Newsweek* publication. His final lines offer his ultimate response, stating that he will make his stand, remain as he is, and "bid farewell and not give a damn."[38] From this lens, his song can be seen as an attempt to move past the rumors and gossip through his explorations of a more authentic persona.

Restless Metric Imperfection

The lyrical meaning, both as a general farewell at the end of a night of drinking and as Dylan departing from earlier, experimental personas, is set into relief by the contrast built into his choice of song title. His inclusion of the word "restless" suggests an unwillingness to depart, a desire to not move forward, but also a desire not to remain. This may reflect Dylan's reluctance to pin down a single identity, since experimentation is so central to his performance aesthetic. But as I argue throughout the preceding analysis, I also see this restlessness having metaphorical correspondence with the timing choices in his studio recording, with Ambiguous Meter signaling agitated sentiments. His source material ties him as an insider to the folk revivalists, while his lyrical commentary and loose engagement with meter mark the song as original and set him apart as a singer-songwriter. Dylan's use of flexible meter keeps him in his favored position of outsider and renegade, rebelling against regularity and signaling a broader "aesthetic of imperfection" with his Ambiguous Meter.[39]

In preserving the sentiment of "The Parting Glass" but taking the timing flexibility to new extremes, Dylan marks his own version as connected to but distinct from his source material. For Dylan, this "restless" timing is both a rhetorical device expressing specific lyrics and general narrative import as well as a reflection of his song adaptations. "Restless Farewell" helps to illustrate his poetics of self-expression in modifying source material.

---

[37] Coleman (2016). The *Newsweek* article's most inflammatory statement is an accusation that Dylan purchased the rights to his song "Blowin' in the Wind" from a high-school student, which evidently caused Dylan to "[explode] with anger" and go "underground" for several weeks after reading the article.

[38] Full lyrics can be found in Dylan (2004).

[39] Rings (2013, [3]).

148   TIMES A-CHANGIN'

But it also situates his performance aesthetic and his position as a slippery figure, exploring various public personas and evading a singular identity. His Ambiguous and emerging meter reflects his avoidance of predictability, locally in the song structure and more broadly in his performance persona.

Joni Mitchell's "The Fiddle and the Drum"

While Dylan's songs show how meter can move toward ambiguity, other singer-songwriter music includes more distinctly Ambiguous Meter. With its unaccompanied performance, Joni Mitchell's "The Fiddle and the Drum" is a provocative example of metric ambiguity and metric emergence. I explore how the flexible meter of her studio-recording performance and similar timings from her live television performance signal Mitchell's exploration of a self-expressive political rhetoric within her otherwise introspective 1960s output.

The initially Ambiguous Meter of "The Fiddle and the Drum" reflects several features of Mitchell's early performance aesthetic. In one sense, it indicates a reluctance to state her political opinions in this antiwar song, which contrasts the storytelling trends in the rest of her repertoire.[40] Originally titled "Song for America," her lyrics pointedly question the soldier, Johnny, who traded his fiddle for a military drum.[41] Mitchell's narrative position is as a female outsider, a Canadian woman offering commentary on the actions of insider, American men. Her timidity in performance, alongside her initially Ambiguous metric structure, suggest a lack of confidence in delivering this potentially provocative message.[42] But as the performance unfolds, and Ambiguous Meter eventually gives way to an emerging Regular Meter, Mitchell's rhetorical voice strengthens. The contrast between these two metric states—one of ambiguity and one of increased regularity—locally highlights this rhetorical shift and signals a broader conviction in Mitchell's

---

[40] "The Fiddle and the Drum" is one of only two examples of political "protest" songwriting on her early-period albums. The other, which is perhaps one of her most well-known songs, is the environmental protest song "Big Yellow Taxi," from *Ladies of the Canyon* (1970).

[41] By the final verse, she is broadly questioning America's military participation.

[42] Whitesell (2008, 91–92) suggests that Mitchell's critical judgement, dialectic thought, and reluctance to belong to any groups offered her perceptual distance. He sees this as relating to her expatriate status in the United States "as a female songwriter of formidable intelligence and talent in a male-dominated industry." He also notes details in her biography, including a hospitalization in her childhood for polio, that suggest her status as an outsider was well-established since her youth, gradually becoming a personality trait.

INTENSIFYING "IMPERFECTION": AMBIGUOUS METER   149

self-expression in performance. It is from this place of confidence that some of her boldest, most intimate songwriting emerges on her subsequent albums. Examining the details of Mitchell's studio-recording performance of "The Fiddle and the Drum" uncovers the techniques by which she initially obscures and then gradually reveals metric regularity.

First Vocal Fragment

The loose performance timings of her song's first phrases offer a succession of textual and musical stresses of varying weights, exhibiting only some of the metric cues that when tightened create Regular Meter. Figure 5.14 is my transcription from her studio recording of the metrically ambiguous first vocal fragments that feature Unrealized Durations. Mitchell's timing obscures specific rhythms, so the melody notes are spaced proportionally to their sounding duration, with IOI values above the staff. In these first two vocal fragments, stresses and durations are the only clear cues for meter. As I explored in Chapter 1, each pair of stressed events in her voice has the potential to engage a pulse. The dynamic and durational accents on D4 and F4 result in a two-stress structure between the words "so" and the second syllable of "again," creating the Q duration. If a third stressed event occurred after "again," a pulse could emerge with Q' reproducing Q. But no such third event occurs and there is a hiatus. So far, this passage has some metric cues but no sustained metric regularity.[43] Its ambiguity is as metrically timid as Mitchell's rhetorical voice.

Second Fragment

In the second fragment ("My dear Johnny my dear friend" in Figure 5.14) Mitchell's timings repeat this ambiguous metric structure. Her subsequent vocal lines, with the lyrics "And so once again" and "You are fighting us all,"

---

[43] There is a radical reading of this passage that infers a stress after "again" to span the two vocal fragments in Figure 5.14. In fact, it is possible to interpret the first verse as a four-beat metric structure, with the most accented events as hyperdownbeats. However, the result is that only half of those beats would align with vocal cues and the result would need to be inferred. Since my approach relies on performance-based cues and infers beats very rarely, I do not prefer these interpretations. But I will note that when Mitchell's timings snap into a meter and therefore fewer beats would need to be inferred, the expressive effect is similar to the analysis I have shown here.

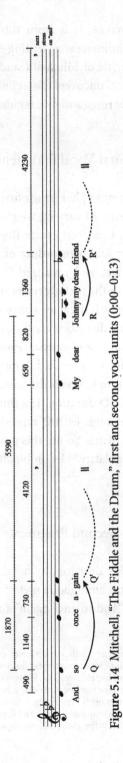

Figure 5.14 Mitchell, "The Fiddle and the Drum," first and second vocal units (0:00–0:13)

INTENSIFYING "IMPERFECTION": AMBIGUOUS METER   151

repeat this pattern of metric cues. Each time she sings, a pulse layer has the potential to emerge, but Mitchell's rhetorical pauses demonstrate a reluctance to engage that potential; the space between fragments interrupts possible regularity. Her "and so once again" statements serve as a commentary about her continual attempts to communicate with Johnny and locally reflect her attempts at the rhetoric that Regular Meter would give to a confident personal voice.

Metric Emergence

As the song progresses, a possible performance-expressive rationale for her initial metric ambiguity is made clear. The fifth vocal fragment (included as the first half of Figure 5.15) begins as if it will parallel the structure of the opening melodic units. Mitchell's stress on the word "when" is followed by a similar stress on the word "why," and this seems to reproduce the two-stress trajectory of the previous vocal fragments.[44] However, unlike those passages, the 2160 ms timespan between "why" and the word "raise" is shorter than the timespan between previous fragments. This offers the structural possibility to infer or imagine a stressed event between "why" and "raise," as indicated with the arrow in Figure 5.15. The inferred stress divides the timespan into conceptually equivalent durations, allowing a pulse to emerge.[45] Counting in this way anticipates the regularity that follows. I have shown this pulse level as dots at the half-note level, below the words "when" and "why" and the imagined stresses that are carried into the sixth fragment (the second half of the figure).[46] Mitchell's vocal emphasis on the words "raise," "sticks," "cry," "I," and "Oh" generate a quarter-note pulse level that subdivides the previously established half-note pulse. This increased regularity of the stress and duration metric cues yields multiple pulse layers that organize hierarchically for the first time in the song.[47]

---

[44] It may also be possible to hear the stress on "why" as anticipating a subsequent downbeat that itself is not articulated; this would move the imagined stress slightly later.

[45] I have chosen that this occur at the halfway point between "why" and "raise," which results in two 1080 ms durations. But it is possible for this imagined stress to occur at various points between these stressed events so long as the two durations are conceptually isochronous.

[46] It is because of this regularity continuing into the next stress, and the fact that only one stress needs to be inferred to do so, that I am comfortable imagining stresses in this line where I was not for previous lines.

[47] There are a few other possibilities for the meter in this passage, one of which places the strongest stress on "fall," followed by a strong downbeat on "friend."

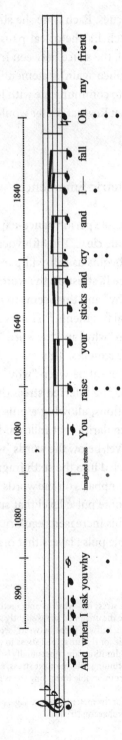

Figure 5.15 Mitchell, "The Fiddle and the Drum," fifth and sixth vocal units (0:23–0:31)

Expressive Emergence

This achieved Regular Meter is the culmination of efforts of the previous vocal fragments and is made especially significant when considered in contrast with the initially Ambiguous Meter. When the lyrics address general tendencies toward violence in America, lyrical imagery builds on contrasts between peace and war. Mitchell uses degrees of engagement with meter in her performance timings to highlight this contrast. In the first four units, her timings hint at potential to create metric regularity, but moments of expressive hiatus halt that progress. Meter only emerges as Mitchell describes raising weapons and marching into war. It is as if the vivid imagery of soldiers marching has snapped the reluctance of her ambiguous timings into rhetorical and metric order. We lose the ability to hear her meter in multiple ways because the meter is finally clear. As she sings "You raise your sticks and cry," the music fits a simple duple meter, with marching dotted rhythms illustrating Johnny's trading his fiddle for the military drum.[48] Mitchell's choices highlight the contrast between sections: one metrically Ambiguous, repeating the lyrics "and so once again" in fragmented pleas to the soldier, and one Regular, as he marches into war. When she follows a similar metric trajectory in the second verse as she sings "Can I help you find the peace and the star," the metric emergence illustrates her desire to help Johnny escape military action, and for military participation in general to end.[49]

Self-Presentation and Flexible Meter

The shift from Ambiguous to Regular Meter is an essential feature in Mitchell's performances of "The Fiddle and the Drum." The timings of her studio recording are mostly replicated in her 1969 television performance of the song on the Dick Cavett Show, in which her initial timidity visibly

---

[48] Mitchell's choices here engage the network of military topical associations; see Monelle (2006, 81). The parallel moments in the second and fourth verse have the line "Can we help you find the peace and the star/Oh my friend," which is less directly connected with marching, but offers "peace" as an alternative to war.

[49] The final two stanzas repeat the lyrics of the first two, changing the address from the specific "Johnny" to "America" more generally. Though the timings are less flexible in these stanzas, the climactic lines—"You raise your sticks and cry" and "Can I help you find the peace and the star"— feature the most salient meter in each verse.

154 TIMES A-CHANGIN'

reinforces her auditory cues. On television, Mitchell's quiet voice and submissive body language reinforce the reluctance of her performance's metric ambiguity. Before she begins, she introduces the song with her hands clasped behind her back, where they remain for the duration of the performance; she reminds her audience of her position as an outsider, introducing the song by explaining that she wrote it "for America as a Canadian living in this country." She is undercutting the political message through her self-distancing, her physical attempts to take up less space, and her ambiguous metric structure, to lessen her provocation of the audience.[50]

These physical signs of timidity are also reflected in how the Cavett Show performance mirrors the studio recording's flexible meter.[51] The initial ambiguity signals a reluctance to engage the strong rhetoric of Regular Meter. But when her timings become more Regular, it reflects her increasing rhetorical strength and comfort in her performance as she delivers her important lyrical message. Locally, the specific moments of metric emergence in her performances also express calls to action in her narrative. "The Fiddle and the Drum," therefore, captures a moment of vulnerability in Mitchell's exploration of political subject matter and her process of generating rhetorical strength through self-expressive meter in performance.

Buffy Sainte-Marie's "Sir Patrick Spens"

My final example in this chapter is among the most metrically ambiguous performance from this 1960s and 1970s songwriting period: Buffy Sainte-Marie's "Sir Patrick Spens." Like Dylan, Sainte-Marie was influenced by folk sources in her development as a songwriter in the 1960s.[52] Her traditional

---

[50] Ironically, her song's lyrics are likely not harsh enough to provoke: she does not admonish the soldier, instead asking him to justify his participation in the war and then gently offering to help him "find the peace."

[51] The metric trajectory of the television performance matches the *Clouds* version, but the former features a slightly faster tempo and a different key. It is possible that the faster timings of the Cavett Show performance are a reflection of nervousness during live performance, in which Mitchell performs more quickly to reduce the amount of time she has to be on stage. I explore this possibility of faster timings reflecting a desire to leave the stage in an early Bob Dylan TV performance of "With God on Our Side" in Murphy (2020).

[52] She cites influences including chanteuse Édith Piaf, rock, and other genres including folk, traditional music, and the blues. See Warner (2018, 9–53).

INTENSIFYING "IMPERFECTION": AMBIGUOUS METER   155

song adaptations on her early albums with Vanguard Records show the clearest ties in her songwriting to the trends in the Greenwich Village folk revival.[53] But it is her flexible meter on these adaptations that positions her alongside artists like Dylan and Mitchell as a contributor to the rhetoric of singer-songwriter self-expression.

In 1966, on her third album *Little Wheel Spin and Spin*, Sainte-Marie included "Sir Patrick Spens" among three other traditional song adaptations.[54] Her studio-recording performance of "Sir Patrick Spens" is significant in that it demonstrates some of the most flexible and Ambiguous Meter of any singer-songwriter example in this study. The performance has two instruments that provide stress and duration cues without a clear pulse level: Sainte-Marie's mouthbow and a double bass.[55] These structures demonstrate Ungrouped Beats, which are illustrated by the faster pulse level of Sainte-Marie's mouthbow, and Unrealized Durations, which occur between the slower, spaced-apart onsets in the double bass. When her vocals enter, the meter is more salient, with increasing isochrony in the double bass oriented around stressed events in the voice, but these timings never become metric in the way that the previous examples in this chapter do. "Sir Patrick Spens" is an extreme case of Ambiguous Meter in this repertoire that vacillates only slightly toward metric emergence with several detached passages of metric regularity. In other words, the song is never entirely in Regular Meter. Sainte-Marie's studio-recording performance uses flexible meter to express the sentiments of the seafaring source narrative in a folksong adaptation that blends her traditional influences and idiosyncratic instrumentation.

---

[53] Sainte-Marie recorded three traditional songs on her first studio album, *It's My Way* (1964): "Ananias," "Cripple Creek," and "You're Gonna Need Somebody on Your Bond." The album also includes "Mayoo Sto Hoon," Sainte-Marie's version of the Hindi song "Maaus to hoon vade se tere" from the movie *Barsaat Ki Raat*. On her second album, *Many a Mile* (1965), she includes adaptations of six traditional songs, a version of Delta bluesman Bukka White's "Fixin' to Die," and an adaptation of "Many a Mile" by the Irish and Native American folk singer (and Greenwich Village figure) Patrick Sky. Sainte-Marie adapted songs by traditional sources or those of her singer-songwriter contemporaries on nearly every album between her 1964 debut and her 1974 album *Buffy*. Starting in 1975, she composed the majority of her recorded tracks, with a few exceptions, mostly citing songwriting collaborators. There is the ten-year period, then, between 1964 and 1974 in which her music draws from other sources within the folk revival.

[54] The other three are "The House Carpenter," which Dylan also recorded in the 1960s, "Waly Waly," and "Lady Margaret."

[55] The liner notes to *Little Wheel Spin and Spin* (1966) credit Russ Savakus on bass. To my knowledge, the studio-recording performance is the only recorded performance of this song.

156 TIMES A-CHANGIN'

Ballad Narrative

Sainte-Marie based "Sir Patrick Spens" on a popular Scottish Child ballad of the same name.[56] The song's text describes the demise of Sir Patrick Spens, a renowned, likely fictional, sailor ordered by the king of Scotland to undertake a tragic sea voyage to Norway in a winter storm. Spens must either disobey the king or follow orders and face certain death at sea.[57] Sainte-Marie's version of these lyrics reflects the growing tension of the original story. From a third-person narrative, she recounts the king's decision to enlist Spens (stanzas 1 and 2) and the sailor's receipt of and reaction to the fatal assignment (stanzas 3 and 4). She then describes the intended location and purpose of Sir Patrick's sea voyage (stanza 5). She shifts to a first-person perspective in the climactic sixth stanza to depict "an awful dream" she has of "shipwreck and storm and hum." The final stanza portrays the ladies "waiting for their good Scot sailors" who will not return home.

Instrumentation

Though the original ballad was likely unaccompanied, Sainte-Marie includes mouthbow and double bass in her 1966 studio recording, each of which has broader stylistic signification.[58] The mouthbow is a traditional instrument with a string attached to either end of a wooden stick, in the shape of a hand-made hunting bow. When she plays it, Sainte-Marie holds one end of the wooden stick in her mouth, strums on the string with a guitar pick (in alternating up-down duple strummed patterns), and changes the pitch through different shapes of her mouth.[59] The mouthbow signals possible connections to Sainte-Marie's heritage as an Indigenous Canadian of Cree background; the double bass is a more typical folk music cue.[60] But the use of the double

[56] Child Ballads were standards in the 1960s folk scene; the collection includes 305 traditional English and Scottish songs anthologized in the nineteenth century by Francis James Child. "Sir Patrick Spens" is no. 58; see Child (1904, 103–5).

[57] Three published versions follow a similar narrative, containing up to seventeen stanzas. See Child (1904, 103–5).

[58] Sainte-Marie's Indigenous heritage is the likely source of her introduction to the mouthbow. She includes an explanation on her website for her educational platform The Cradleboard Teaching Project (2021a), explaining the instrument, how to play it, and where to buy one.

[59] Sainte-Marie introduced the instrument to Sesame Street (1976) audiences during her tenure on the show. She also performed with mouthbow on Pete Seeger's Rainbow Quest (1966).

[60] The performer, Russ Savakus, was a figure in the 1960s folk and jazz scene. Unterberger (2003, 205) notes that Savakus played on Sainte-Marie's 1965 album Many a Mile and Dylan's Highway 61 Revisited (1965). Sainte-Marie cites American folk music as an early influence on

INTENSIFYING "IMPERFECTION": AMBIGUOUS METER 157

bass as a drone is less typical of 1960s American folk music and can be read as signaling a pastoral, seafaring, Scottish folk style.

Stressed Events

The two instruments offer several cues for meter, but their timings challenge metric grouping in ways that connect to the song's turbulent narrative. Her mouthbow strumming pattern presents a fast duple structure, indicated by the upward and downward wrist motion in her strum pattern, as indicated by symbols above the staff in Figure 5.16 at (b) above the staff. The double bass articulates single notes or open fifths, usually on D2 and A2. It begins with two onsets of an A1 pitch at (a) leading to an open fifth that presents a possible first downbeat shown by the circled 1. There is a clear sense of weak-to-strong beat pattern with this gesture, as indicated by the anacrusis symbol at (a).[61] And the fast articulations of the mouthbow have promise as subdivisions of these longer double-bass articulations. But my attempt to count them as generative of larger durations is thwarted, firstly because there are no consistent accentual cues in the mouthbow, and secondly because there are simply not enough stressed events in the double bass to support such a reading.[62] While I can hear a duration from the first beat to a possible second, shown as the Q duration, I am forced to abandon the tedious counting of strums when no third beat occurs and the projected Q' duration fails. In the material that follows (c), several accentual cues emerge, but none are able to activate their metric potential into a Regular Meter.[63] Therefore, this passage from the beginning of the song demonstrates Ambiguous Meter, with Ungrouped Beats evoking an uncertain outcome for the subsequent meter and the overall narrative.

---

her songwriting, finding models in the "true folk songs that have lasted hundreds of years"; see Stonechild (2012, 10–44).

[61] I borrow this anacrusis symbol from Hasty (1997) and its applications in Attas (2015) and Butterfield (2006).

[62] With much effort, I can count the strumming between the events at the first downbeat to a possible second beat shown with the circled 2 and a question mark, which yields 24 mouthbow onsets. Her strumming pattern encourages duple groupings, so that could be 12 pairs of strong and weak beats. But nothing happens to encourage further groupings. To try to maintain this pattern fails when no onset occurs at (c), which is 24 strums after the stress on the possible second beat.

[63] There is an accented strum at (d) that offers a possible metric stress cue, potentially in relation to the onset of R at the next downbeat. But by (e), when no other stressed event has occurred, it is clear that no meter has emerged.

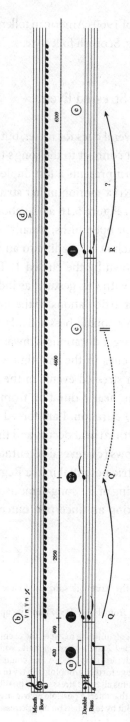

Figure 5.16 Sainte-Marie, "Sir Patrick Spens," introduction (0:00–0:17)

INTENSIFYING "IMPERFECTION": AMBIGUOUS METER   159

There are two layers of metric activity: one has a fast-duple pattern and the other that has longer durations. But neither of these layers is able to generate a multi-leveled meter. Sainte-Marie's timings create metric ambiguity that reflects Sir Patrick Spens's conflict in choosing his fate from two unappealing options. Her mouthbow gives rhythmic activity and a pitch—similar to various types of drumrolls—but no real metric information. It is as if this instrument is trying to mimic the drone effect of the double bass but must do so as a series of ungrouped strumming patterns since the instrument cannot sustain a pitch. The metric uncertainty of this introduction foreshadows the story's tragic outcome.

This marks the first of many examples in this song of this type of Unrealized Durations, which occur when a clear stressed event initiates a duration's onset but no second event occurs to confirm a timespan.[64] These events have metric potential but offer no durations from which a pulse can be generated. This illustrates the second method of Ambiguous engaged in this introductory passage, further expressing the foreboding nautical conditions that will cause Sir Patrick's death and reinforcing Sainte-Marie's use of rhetorical flexibility.

Vocal Entry and Narrator Authority

When the voice enters and Sainte-Marie begins the tragic narrative, more metric regularity seems like it might emerge. Figure 5.17 begins at the double-bass dyad that precedes her vocal entry. The stressed event has potential as a downbeat, as I have indicated by the circled (1), but the V projection fails when no event confirms its duration. Sainte-Marie's first vocal stress on the word "in" aligns with the D–A double-bass dyad, marking the most accented moment in the song since the first downbeat. The dyad repetitions at (g) sound like an anacrusis group to the next long dyad at (2), repeated between the second and third beats. Since the durations are realized in this passage, I hear a slow, three-beat pulse emerging, as represented by the circled numbers 1, 2, and 3 above the staff. Sainte-Marie creates a pattern here that encourages a strong-weak grouping of these beats: a coordination of the bass and voice, a solo double-bass dyad, followed by another coordination. My

---

[64] This corresponds to scenario 6 from the metric projection summary in Chapter 2. It differs from the type of unrealized duration found with S–S' in Figure 5.16, when an initial duration occurs between two stressed events, but its projection fails when a third event does not arrive.

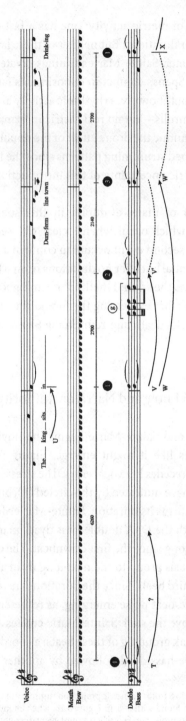

Figure 5.17 Sainte-Marie, "Sir Patrick Spens," first vocal phrase (0:20–0:35)

attempt to continue this duple pattern, however, is thwarted by the moment of coordination at the first syllable of "drinking." I had expected a bass dyad by itself at this moment, following the previous pattern, but instead there is a point of coordination that sounds like a downbeat and initiates the next vocal phrase.[65] This interruption signals that ambiguity will prevail in the song's metric structure. Similar moments of minimal metric emergence and interruption occur throughout the rest of the song, with the timings just barely achieving a strong and weak organization before giving way to Ambiguous Meter again. With the mouthbow articulations demonstrating Ungrouped Beats, Unrealized Durations prevent metric emergence that would stabilize the meter and signal a positive outcome for the narrative.

There are signals of metric emergence in this passage, with a slow three-beat pulse and near establishment of a strong and weak beat pattern. These are noteworthy especially in contrast with the highly Ambiguous introduction and point to a more stable role for the narrator, who sees the perspectives of the king, Sir Patrick, and dreams of the awful storms that will come. The passages of increased regularity have the effect of organizing the storytelling, giving agency to the narrator. But the lack of hierarchy and subsequent return to ambiguity signal that this narrator has no control over the outcome. In adapting this traditional song, Sainte-Marie's flexible timings and original instrumentation help to express the song's tragic narrative. Her use of flexible meter points to a connection with the broader poetics of self-expression in singer-songwriter performance practice. Though she is often overlooked in studies of singer-songwriter music, her engagement with flexible meter signals that she is an important figure in this period.

Folk Song Adaptations

That this self-expression is so closely tied to folk songs in Sainte-Marie's repertoire is somewhat surprising, given her apparent critiques of the "vanilla" folk music trends of the 1960s.[66] The inclusion of folk songs like "Sir Patrick Spens" on her early albums signals some possible pressure to conform to Greenwich Village trends. This may have been motivated by her contract with the Vanguard label, which also released Joan Baez's records of

---

[65] The Y' duration is therefore interrupted, and a new projection (Z) begins.

[66] Warner (2018, 41).

162 TIMES A-CHANGIN'

adapted folk songs and may have wanted the same from Sainte-Marie.[67] Or Sainte-Marie may have chosen to participate in this practice of song adaptation alongside her inclusion of flexible meter in some performances as a way to keep herself connected to other 1960s songwriters and maintain her coffeehouse gigs. There are other possible readings, too. It could be an effort to demonstrate her appreciation for musical precedents or simply to adapt folk source material as a compositional experiment. Or she is adapting the song to transform Sir Patrick Spens's tragic choices—obey the king's order and die at sea or disobey him and face a fatal punishment—into an allegory of the Native American experience: adapt to the culture of colonizers and witness the death of your own culture or defend your heritage and die at the hands of the colonizers.[68] Regardless of intent, Sainte-Marie's flexible timing demonstrates an expressive technique of her 1960s performance practice, and the instrument choices reflect her engagement with traditional folk sources and her Indigenous heritage. Though not one of her most famous songs, "Sir Patrick Spens" ties Sainte-Marie to the trends of adapting traditional songwriting in the 1960s and illustrates her use of flexible meter for self-expression within this singer-songwriter period.

***

The examples in this chapter illustrate the extremes of timing flexibility available to 1960s and 1970s singer-songwriters as part of their poetics of self-expression. In exploring how these artists bridge Regular and Ambiguous Meter, include Ambiguous Meter through techniques like Unrealized Durations, and employ emerging meter, I illustrate the expressive effects of timing choices in these songs and how these are connected to rhetorical techniques of self-expression for each artist. Flexible meter is a method by which these singer-songwriters explore lyrical meaning and persona, and

---

[67] By Sainte-Marie's account, Vanguard's sole focus on selling her as an "Indian folk singer" limited her creative vision; Warner (2018, 115). This is one reason for the fraught relationship between the singer and her label during their seven-year contract. In 1971, Vanguard planned to release *The Best of Buffy Sainte-Marie, Vol. 2*, to capitalize on the success of "Soldier Blue" and "I'm Gonna Be a Country Girl Again" in the United Kingdom. Sainte-Marie desired neither the album nor the image the label chose for its cover, which Warner describes "looks like a literal red-washing of Sainte-Marie's face ... her smile doesn't quite reach her eyes ... It looks like the punishment Sainte-Marie says it was" (Warner 2018, 120). After fulfilling her contract and allowing the release of the compilation—"the blackmail album"—Sainte-Marie did not re-sign with the label.

[68] Sainte-Marie is an outspoken activist, promoting messages against military violence and oppression of Native Americans. As I explored in Chapter 1, many of her most popular songs from the 1960s and 1970s protest the Vietnam War and mistreatment of Native Americans both historically and in the twentieth century. For more on Sainte-Marie's activism, from the 1960s to present, see Warner (2018).

develop the broader expressive trends of this songwriting period. As I have shown, these trends are closely connected to traditional source materials, especially precedents in folk music and the Delta blues, and to political, protest, and topical songwriting in the 1960s and the later development of confessional, introspective songwriting in the 1970s. Investigating specific techniques of self-expressive timing through the lens of flexible meter allows for close attention to the details of this performance practice. The effect of these timing details—at the local and broader stylistic levels—gives insight into the self-expressive practices of each of the artists that make up the poetics of singer-songwriter performances in this period.

6

What Happens Next to Self-Expressive Flexible Meter?

In the previous chapters, I explore how Bob Dylan, Buffy Sainte-Marie, Paul Simon, Cat Stevens, and Joni Mitchell use the various types of flexible meter as techniques of self-expression in their performances between 1962 and 1972. Alongside their self-expressive features of self-presentation, lyric writing, and vocal production, flexible meter helped to shape the rhetoric of this formative singer-songwriter period. The emerging singer-songwriters in the 1960s drew on performance techniques from precedents in earlier twentieth-century popular music and developed individual expressive styles, personas, and communicative relationships with their audiences. This metrically flexible acoustic tradition culminated in the 1970s confessional singer-songwriter period. The five artists in this study stand apart from their singer-songwriter peers in their use of Reinterpreted, Lost, and Ambiguous Meter as techniques of seemingly improvised, self-expressive rhetoric in performance. Exploring the details of their self-expressive metric flexibility brings us in closer connection to the unique features of their performance rhetoric and how those features position them as innovators within the broader singer-songwriter performance practice.

Beyond 1972

The more extreme types of Reinterpreted, Lost, and Ambiguous Meter that occur in the singer-songwriter music explored in this study are in some ways the result of the texture and acoustic style of the singer-songwriter tradition. In self-accompanied performances, these artists need not plan or coordinate their metric disruptions, but instead have the option to include them as spur-of-the-moment decisions. (This is not impossible to achieve in ensemble textures of two or more performers, but it is much more easily achieved in solo contexts.) As such, there is a strong correlation between changes in

Times A-Changin'. Nancy Murphy, Oxford University Press. © Oxford University Press 2023.
DOI: 10.1093/oso/9780197635216.003.0006

WHAT HAPPENS NEXT TO SELF-EXPRESSIVE FLEXIBLE METER?   165

musical texture for these five artists and the disappearance of the more extreme types of flexible meter. As time went on, these five artists added more instruments and performers, experimenting with styles and genres outside of the intimate, acoustic singer-songwriter aesthetic. Consequently, the stylistic metric extremes explored in Chapters 4 and 5 generally do not extend into the later years of the 1970s.

Ensemble Careers

Some of these artists did not make it past the mid-1960s as soloists. Dylan had already traded in his acoustic guitar for an electric and added a band to his performances as early as the now-infamous 1965 Newport Folk Festival.[1] Mitchell included additional musicians most notably on her 1970 album *Ladies of the Canyon*, on songs like "Conversation" and "Big Yellow Taxi."[2] By 1972, Mitchell's album *For the Roses* explores more folk-rock and jazz styles that signal the genre experimentations and fusions of her later 1970s albums.[3] Stevens was already performing with a folk-rock band on some of his early singer-songwriter tracks in the 1970s and continued with an ensemble until he left the music industry in 1977 to devote himself to the study of Islam.[4] Simon is perhaps the most well known for performing in ensembles. His 1965 solo album was his only foray into the "authentic," solo, self-accompanied singer-songwriter texture, though his early duet albums with Simon and Garfunkel engaged a similar performance aesthetic and expressively Reinterpreted Meter.[5] Sainte-Marie also favored an ensemble

---

[1] For more on the electric set and reactions to it, see Heylin (2001, 206–21).

[2] Stephen Stills plays bass on "Night in the City" for Mitchell's debut album, *Song to a Seagull* (1967). But the majority of Mitchell's tracks in the 1960s and early 1970s are solo. On *Blue*, songs like "All I Want," "Carey," "California," and "A Case of You" include additional performers. For Mitchell, the inclusion of Lost or Ambiguous Meter seems to be correlated with tempo. Her faster-tempo songs are almost entirely in Regular Meter. Songs with a slower tempo are much more likely to shift into Lost or Ambiguous meter.

[3] Her 1974 album *Court and Spark* is a fusion of pop, folk, and jazz. Later albums in the 1970s, including *Hejira* (1976), *Don Juan's Reckless Daughter* (1979), and *Mingus* (1979) move toward a freer jazz fusion style.

[4] Stevens (2020) reports that he nearly drowned when swimming in the Pacific Ocean and "fearing imminent death" he "called to God pleading that should he be saved he would dedicate his life to God's service." Stevens survived this event and later in 1978, upon receiving a copy of the Koran from his brother, changed his name to Yusuf Islam and "amazed the world by walking away from fame and his career as a music star, to start a family and dedicate himself to charitable work."

[5] Two songs from this study ("April Come She Will" and "The Sound of Silence") exemplify the acoustic aesthetic and Reinterpreted Meter that occur in Simon's solo performances and his duets with Art Garfunkel. Other works are metrically regular duets with Garfunkel and then

166 TIMES A-CHANGIN'

texture in most of her solo performances beyond the 1960s.[6] And here, again, a move away from the extremes of flexible meter correlates with a shift for these singers in preferring ensemble textures. It is not that techniques of self-expression disappear in singer-songwriter music post 1972, but that flexible meter plays a less critical role in the rhetoric of that self-expression.

Future Singer-Songwriters

The successors to the singer-songwriter tradition in later decades also rarely included the extreme types of flexible meter in their performances. In singer-songwriter music after 1972, there is typically expressively timed Regular Meter and sometimes Reinterpreted Meter in connection with other features of self-expression in performance.[7] The mainstream soft-rock artists of the mid-1970s and early 1980s, the female singer-songwriters in the late 1980s and early 1990s, and the indie artists of the millennium and beyond generally include many self-expressive features to demonstrate individual expressive styles. Much could be written, for example, about the lyrics, personae, and self-expressive vocal techniques of the main stage artists at the 1997 Lilith Fair—Sarah McLachlan, Tracy Chapman, Fiona Apple, among others—as representatives of a broader sociocultural statement, originally directed at a misogynistic music industry. But the extremes of flexible meter found in the Lost and Ambiguous metric contexts of 1960s and 1970s singer-songwriter music are not generally present in repertoire by these later artists.[8] Those

---

later, after the duo split up, with larger ensembles of musicians and singers, like Ladysmith Black Mumbazo on *Graceland* (1986). For more on this album and the notion of collaboration, see Meintjes (1990).

[6] Sainte-Marie lists additional instruments on her debut album, *It's My Way!* (1964)—Patrick Sky on second guitar for "He Lived Alone in Town" and Art Davis on bass for "Now That the Buffalo's Gone." Sky also performs on her next two albums.

[7] In Kate Bush's "Wuthering Heights" (from *The Kick Inside*, 1978), for example, Reinterpreted Meter in the form of omitted beats occurs in the refrain, emphasizing the narrator Catherine's excitement in her declarations of being "home," and in her repetitions of Heathcliff's name, causing a metric disorientation that expresses the theme of bewildering Gothic romance. Losseff (1999) explores harmony and timbre as representing the duality of the "real and the Other world" in this song.

[8] Performers like Diana Krall are more likely to include more extreme expressive timing in their solo, piano-accompanied songs, likely because of their connections to the jazz traditions. The introduction to Krall's (2004) version of Elvis Costello's (1982) song "Almost Blue" sounds as close to Ambiguous Meter as anything I have found outside of the 1960s and 1970s singer-songwriter repertoire. It becomes metrically regular when the ensemble enters. As a more direct comparison: Krall's (2002) version of Joni Mitchell's "A Case of You" features metric flexibility that channels Mitchell's own Reinterpreted Meter.

WHAT HAPPENS NEXT TO SELF-EXPRESSIVE FLEXIBLE METER?   167

techniques seem to be reserved for a specific subset of singer-songwriters from a specific time period, for those wishing to create dialogue with the solo, flexibly-timed musical traditions of the early twentieth century, or even for those wishing to take self-expressive techniques to more dramatic lengths.

Buffy Sainte-Marie's "My Country 'Tis of Thy People You're Dying" (1966)

Though the more extreme timings of the 1960s and 1970s singer-songwriter tradition generally disappear in the 1970s, this self-expressive technique was always available to artists as a way to intensify self-expression in performance. A striking example of extreme types of flexible meter being resurrected in recent performances occurs with Buffy Sainte-Marie's 2017 version of her song "My Country 'Tis of Thy People You're Dying" (hereafter "My Country"). The song was first released in 1966 on *Little Wheel Spin and Spin* and was also performed on Pete Seeger's television program *Rainbow Quest* the same year. Sainte-Marie returned to the song for her 2017 album *Medicine Songs* alongside a few others from her 1960s catalogue and some from later years of her career. The song is an "anthem to decolonization," describing an "Indigenous reality that has changed remarkably little in over a half century" between the 1966 and 2017 performances.[9] Sainte-Marie's recordings of the song demonstrate the four main features of self-expression, with her self-presentation as an Indigenous singer of Cree birth, with a striking vocal timbre and vibrato as stylistic markers of her vocal production, with lyrics offering commentary on colonization and genocide in North America, and with a flexible metric profile that shifts between passages of Regular and Lost Meter. The 1966 performances showcase these features to varying degrees. The 2017 version revives and intensifies the metric profile of the original, drawing out contrasts between fast sections and those that threaten to permanently derail the song's metric regularity. In the remainder of this chapter, I offer brief analyses of different self-expressive features in her three performances of this song: her 1966 studio recording, her performance on Pete Seeger's *Rainbow Quest* from 1966, and her 2017 studio recording. I propose that flexible meter is both an expressive technique in Sainte-Marie's performances and a critical

---

[9] Ogg (2021) also notes that the song is "a master class in Indigenous awareness."

168 TIMES A-CHANGIN'

site of expressive communication between the messages of the 1966 and 2017 recordings and their respective historical contexts.

Self-Presentation

In her emergence in the singer-songwriter scene in the 1960s, Buffy Sainte-Marie was performing her own acoustic songs, influenced by personal experiences, musical interests, and cultural background. Sainte-Marie was born on the Piapot Cree First Nations reserve in the Canadian province of Saskatchewan and adopted by an American family, who raised her in Maine and Massachusetts. With her songwriting, Sainte-Marie sought to create music about the human condition that "would be meaningful in all kinds of different countries in all kinds of different generations."[10] Her songs, like those of her singer-songwriter peers, followed contemporary trends in poetry in which passages of free verse acted as "candid and revelatory documents," as methods for authors to speak about their lives from personal and community-based perspectives.[11]

Sainte-Marie's singer-songwriter music used her musical platform for social activism on behalf of marginalized and underrepresented social groups. On Pete Seeger's *Rainbow Quest*, for example, she performed songs about immigrants ("Welcome, Welcome Emigrante") and farmers ("Men of the Fields"), offering the lyrics as tools for educating her audiences. She is known best as an activist for Indigenous people, particularly Native Americans, who she argues were not accurately represented (or represented at all) in American history and media.[12] Sainte-Marie's protest songs act as vehicles to educate her mostly white audiences about Indigenous life and history.[13]

---

[10] Stonechild (2012, 43–44).

[11] Oliver (1994, 79–80). Warner (2018, 89) describes Sainte-Marie's debut album *It's My Way!* as a "powerful work made by a Cree woman who thoroughly and proudly centered Indigenous identity at its core, whose voice rattled the moon and the status quo, and who refused to capitulate to popular stereotypes and clichés of Indigeneity. With each record that followed, Sainte-Marie expanded her message, increasing awareness, and making the invisible visible."

[12] Though born in Canada, Sainte-Marie was raised in the United States, so many of her songs specifically address the history of Native American people. In interviews and commentary, she often refers to herself as an Indian woman. Throughout this discussion, I use the word Indigenous to refer to the first inhabitants of lands that were later colonized by white settlers. When specifically speaking of Indigenous people in the United States, I use the term Native American. When referring to Canadian Indigenous populations, I sometimes use the term First Nations, since this term encompasses Sainte-Marie's Cree heritage.

[13] Sainte-Marie often criticized the lack of Indigenous history in American schools (as she references in "My Country"). Her activism in education led to the creation of an Indigenous curriculum for schools called the Cradleboard Teaching Project, teaching science, art, and other subjects

WHAT HAPPENS NEXT TO SELF-EXPRESSIVE FLEXIBLE METER? 169

Her first widely popular Native American protest song was "Now That the Buffalo's Gone," lyrics of which "object to the hypocrisy of Americans who lamented the nation's past injustices while allowing current ones." Sainte-Marie mentions specific events in the 1960s like the building of the Kinzua Dam in upstate New York, which displaced many Native Americans.[14]

Activist Music

This activism shaped Sainte-Marie's self-presentation as a solo, female, Canadian, American, Cree songwriter, and it influenced much of her 1960s song lyrics. Her Native American protest songs were powerful and important contributions from an Indigenous voice to the civil-rights movements in the 1960s and 1970s.[15] Her visibility as a Cree woman in live performances (both at concerts like the Newport Folk Festival and on Pete Seeger's *Rainbow Quest*) established the aura of authenticity surrounding her work. As a representative from the larger group she sings about, she gives the impression that the messages she delivers to her audiences are truthful, intended to raise awareness, educate people, and motivate their actions.[16]

Lyrics

The lyrics in her 1966 version of "My Country" are, as Sainte-Marie describes, "Indian 101" for the majority of Americans who have "been denied the real history of how Indigenous people in North America got to be in the tragic state of affairs most suffer today: poor health, domestic insecurity and

---

from an Indigenous perspective. She also used her tenure as a regular on *Sesame Street* to educate children about Native Americans. For more on Sainte-Marie's life and activism, see Warner (2018).

[14] Stonechild (2012, 11).

[15] The American Indian Movement (AIM) was founded in Minneapolis in 1968 and staged several public protests in the early years of the 1970s. For more on AIM, see King (2013, 144–54).

[16] Sainte-Marie's self-presentation contrasts that of heavily produced singers like Mary Travers from Peter, Paul, and Mary, who was chosen for the group by producer Albert Grossman and encouraged to stay as pale as possible to retain her Nordic image. In Scorsese (2005), it is revealed that Grossman kept Travers away from the beach on a trip to Florida because he did not want her to get a tan. Singers like Sainte-Marie and Joni Mitchell had more autonomy over their own images.

170   TIMES A-CHANGIN'

poverty."[17] She wrote the song in the 1960s "before people used the word genocide" or even acknowledged what she calls the Indigenous "holocaust of the Americas."[18] Sainte-Marie conveys the deep patriotism she has as an Indigenous woman alongside her strong desire to express bitterness at the loss of land, the forced removal of children from their homes to residential schools, and the inaccurate, distorted, and one-sided history of the United States that is taught in schools.[19] Sainte-Marie argues that she would "very much like to see the history books corrected . . . so that there's a justified amount of space given to the true history of the American Indians" and offers "My Country" as a way of giving voice to the silenced parts of that history.[20]

She begins the song by asking several questions to her audience, hoping for a dawning realization in them that a population of people called "colorful, noble and proud" are reduced in American cultural thought to the villains in cowboy movies.[21] In the verses, Sainte-Marie describes children being sent away from their families to schools where children were forced "to despise their traditions," were forbidden from speaking their languages, and then were taught the version of American history that begins when "Columbus set sail out of Europe." To answer her questions, Sainte-Marie offers a comment as the refrain to each verse by way of reference to the American patriotic song "My Country 'Tis of Thee."[22] Borrowing the melody, she sings on behalf of Native Americans with the refrain "My country 'tis of thy people you're dying." It is a pointed refrain that asks her listeners to interrogate the word "my" in both this song and its "patriotic" source.

---

[17] Sainte-Marie (2021b). For more on the relationship between Indigenous people and white settlers in North America, see King (2013).

[18] Sainte-Marie (2021b). The singer also released the song "Suffer the Little Children" in the 1960s to command attention to the issue of residential schools.

[19] This commentary is taken from Sainte-Marie's interview with Pete Seeger on *Rainbow Quest* (1966). For a timeline of residential schools in Canada, see Jeganathan and Lucchetta (2021).

[20] *Rainbow Quest* (1966).

[21] Contemporary portrayals of Native Americans were very much on her mind when Sainte-Marie was cast in a 1968 episode of the NBC series *The Virginian* as an Indigenous woman. Warner (2018, 99–100) suggests that Sainte-Marie agreed to appear on the show with two demands: first, that Indigenous actors be cast for the Indigenous roles, and second, that "the writers had to give her character more complexity, elevating her beyond that of a one-note, Hollywood cliché." Three years later Italian-American actor Iron Eyes Cody was cast in the "Crying Indian" advertisement for the anti-litter organization *Keep America Beautiful*. For more on how this advertisement capitalized on 1970s countercultural embraces of "authentic" Native American culture, see Dunaway (2017).

[22] Of course, this song also uses the melody of the British anthem "God Save the King," only further highlighting its European colonial associations.

Vocal Production

In her performances of "My Country," Sainte-Marie showcases her characteristically striking vocal timbre, with its tight vibrato and timbre that at times reaches a rasp and growl.[23] In other songs from 1966's *Little Wheel Spin and Spin*, like "Men of the Country," she demonstrates a folk song style with a relatively unmarked vocal production that shows some of her characteristic vibrato but without much timbral contrast. Songs like "Rolling Log Blues" show off more of Sainte-Marie's range of vocal techniques. But her most striking vocal resources are reserved for "My Country," the album's fifth track. Here Sainte-Marie takes the role of educator, not so much singing a melody as reporting her lyrical information to a tune, with limited melodic and harmonic resources, alternating two simple lines in a repeating strophic form.

The pitch materials of the song have the potential, like many strophic folk-song precedents, to tire a listener with their simplicity. But this limited palette is enriched by the features of Sainte-Marie's vocal production. The few long-held vowel sounds in the song are mostly overpowered by clipped vowels that give more prominence to the subsequent nasal consonants.[24] (She lingers particularly on "n" sounds, like the "ng" ending of the word "dying" at the end of each of her refrains.[25]) Her vibrato and raspy vocal timbre are characteristic of her style in general; I interpret her vocal techniques broadly as both a stylistic and self-expressive feature of many of her performances. But when considered alongside the content of the lyrics of "My Country," her vocal production choices, specifically at moments of intensity in her narrative, read as in-the-moment self-expressive performance decisions.

---

[23] Rings's (2015, 668) analysis of Sainte-Marie's song "Cod'ine" describes her voice as having a "focused intensity, manifested in part by her tight vibrato and her extraordinary timbral resources." For a detailed study of analyzing the popular singing voice, see Malawey (2020). For other research on the expressive vocal production, see Heidemann (2016), Milius (2021), Nobile (2022), and Hardman (2022).

[24] Rings (2015, 668) notes a similar contrast in vowel sound in "Cod'ine," with some sustained pitches giving "way to three alarmingly abrupt short syllables, with upward-swooping contours and a jarringly exaggerated change in vowel format."

[25] Another example is the word "send" just after the one-minute mark, as part of the phrase "You force us to send our toddlers away," in which she clips the vowel and allows her vibrato to linger on the "-nd" word ending.

172 TIMES A-CHANGIN'

Flexible Meter

To further intensify her performance on the 1966 studio album, Sainte-Marie includes a metrically flexible opening stanza for "My Country" that gives way to mostly Regular Meter in the remainder of the song. For several passages in this first verse, her timings result in hiatus and a sense of Lost Meter that breaks up possible metric regularity. The diagram in Figure 6.1 illustrates some of the fluctuations in timing between stressed syllables in Sainte-Marie's vocal line.[26] There are four stressed events per line as I have numbered above the lyrics; some of these vocal stresses are asynchronized from the guitar-accompaniment strumming.[27] Subdivisions of these four beats from Sainte-Marie's guitar strumming or even her vocal stresses are sparse and unreliable, so I have not included them in this diagram.[28]

For each line, I have included IOI values to quantify the timings between vocal stresses. I include projection symbols below these to interpret this data. As the diagram indicates, for the most part, I can accommodate Sainte-Marie's timing fluctuations as lengthened or sped up versions of the previous duration, maintaining an expressively timed Regular Meter.[29] But at certain moments, hiatus occurs and I lose this sense of malleable regularity. In some cases, a duration is so long that even with a *rit.*, my conception of "the duration" is broken and meter is Lost.[30] (One example is at the end of line 1, when the S' duration is too long to reproduce S.) The effect of this amount of contrast is that of Sainte-Marie rushing through her statement of the word "finally" as if she has been patiently awaiting her audience's realization, then pauses after "opened" to leave time for the awakening to occur.

---

[26] Transcriptions of the song are in ⅜ meter, which is eventually confirmed by Sainte-Marie's timings and accompaniment strumming in verse 2.

[27] I include a circled number to the left of each group of four vocal stresses for ease of discussion. On Sainte-Marie's official website (2021b), she breaks line 6 into two, two-stress fragments. I have retained that formatting here but conceptualize these with my numbers above the lyrics as a group of four stresses, spaced apart.

[28] I have also left out the pitches of her melody to focus on the timing and for ease of comparison between this diagram and the 2017 version seen in Figure 6.2.

[29] I hear durations either repeating the previous duration (as in line 1, when the initial Q duration is repeated identically, or line 3, where Q' is nearly the same as the previous duration), shortening through an *accel.* (as in R' in line 1) or lengthening through a *rit.* (as occurs with the S' duration in line 1).

[30] The reverse type of event also occurs, corresponding to scenario 4 from Figure 2.8 (from Chapter 2). I hear the 740 ms B' duration as so fast that Sainte-Marie's stress on the word "real" interrupts the possible reproduction of the 2090 ms B duration. The vertical line indicates this interruption. This 740 ms C duration then projects forward only to result in a hiatus at the end of the line.

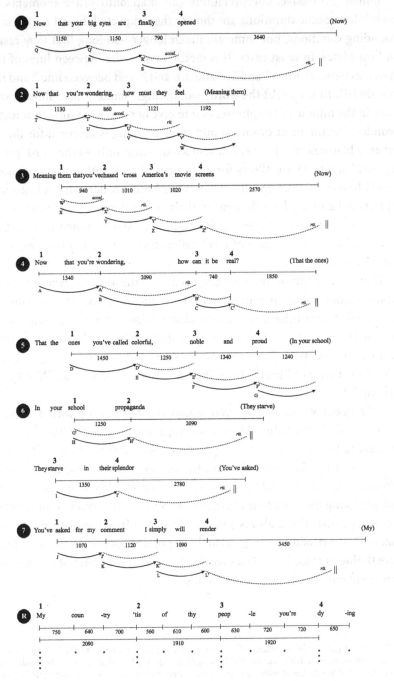

Figure 6.1 Sainte-Marie, "My Country" (*Little Wheel Spin and Spin*, 1966) (0:00–0:54)

174 TIMES A-CHANGIN'

Similar expressive interpretations can map onto other moments of metric loss. Some durations are shorter than expected, based on the surrounding durations, but some are much longer—so long that they result in Lost Meter. In most cases, this metric loss occurs between lines of the lyrics, as between lines 1 and 2, 3 and 4, 6 and 7, and between line 7 and the refrain (R). In Line 4, at the word "wondering," Sainte-Marie allows extra time in the middle of the phrase, as if to give her audience time to actually wonder. But the most dramatic mid-phrase timing is reserved for line 6, where a hiatus occurs in the middle of a four-stress unit. At the word "propaganda," Sainte-Marie allows for a moment of recognition that textbooks might have a colonist agenda, positioning Native Americans as historical objects to be revered, while some of their contemporaries face poor living conditions. The Lost Meter in Sainte-Marie's self-accompanied performance allows her moments of acceleration and pause to reinforce her narrative import.

The most dramatic tempo shift occurs in the refrain, where Sainte-Marie's timings dramatically snap into fast and clear vocal stress patterns and quicker chord changes that articulate a Regular $\frac{3}{4}$ meter. As she recalls a melody familiar to her listeners, the shift from Lost to Regular meter is a call to attention: Sainte-Marie is urging her listeners to recall lyrics like "Sweet land of liberty" from the melody's source and ask "liberty for whom?"[31]

Subsequent verses of the 1966 studio recording settle into a $\frac{3}{4}$ meter more clearly, with Sainte-Marie's accompaniment subdividing the vocal durations. In a few passages, like the lines "Now that the pride of the sires receives charity/Now that we're harmless and safe behind laws," Sainte-Marie slows her timing to recall the opening verse. This timing adds variety to the strophic song form, with its alternating two lines that would eventually become repetitive. But it also is a signal of Sainte-Marie highlighting specific lines of her text, adding emphasis to the importance of her lyrics. Her expressive timing in these later verses recalls the nearly Lost Meter of the opening verse and reinforces the song's meaning.

---

[31] In Frank (2017), Sainte-Marie talks about not feeling like an insider to the "Woody Guthrie crowd" whose activism felt "quite vanilla." In King (2017) she explains that she was asked to do a performance on *Rainbow Quest* with a group of singers performing "This Land Is Your Land," and she claims she could not do it because the singers "had no consciousness how that would affect the Native American people watching."

WHAT HAPPENS NEXT TO SELF-EXPRESSIVE FLEXIBLE METER? 175

"My Country" (1966, *Rainbow Quest*)

This self-expressive manipulation of vocal production is even more noteworthy in her 1966 performance of "My Country" on Pete Seeger's *Rainbow Quest*. For this performance, Sainte-Marie restrains some of the flexible meter of her studio recording and instead showcases techniques of vocal production and self-presentation. She offers the song to Seeger and his audience as a different perspective on American history than the inaccurate version offered in schools. The cameras quickly cut to a dramatic close-up of Sainte-Marie's face, with its expression of combined empathy and devastation as she sings "They starve in their splendor." I get the impression that the show's producers were signaled by Sainte-Marie's vocal production and timing that this was a moment of emotional declaration, and chose to offer this dramatic framing of her face.[32] Her performance here echoes the timing of her 1966 studio recording to allow space between the lines "In your school propaganda" and "They starve in their splendor," which I interpret as a moment of respite, a brief pause to collect herself.

Expressive Voice

While her meter is initially less flexible in the *Rainbow Quest* performance, her techniques of vocal production are amplified. Here again Sainte-Marie lingers on "n" consonants, allowing her vibrato to resonate as a nasal sound rather than the typical open-throat production.[33] Yet Sainte-Marie's voice reaches more dramatic peaks with this performance of "My Country" than on her studio recording. Her voice trembles as she sings about "the nation of leeches that conquered this land." She emphasizes the words "thud" and "mud" when metaphorically suggesting that the Liberty bell "rang with a thud over Kinzua mud," as if she is shouting them. She slows her timings as she sings the resonant line "Now that my life's to be known as your heritage." And she nearly shouts the line "Choke on your blue white and scarlet

---

[32] The choice for a close up shot at this moment may indeed have been a recognition that the singer might cry during this performance and they would want to have visuals of this event, should it occur.

[33] This can be heard in her first two lines, with words like "opened" and "wondering" (in the phrases "Now that your big eyes are finally opened" and "Now that you're wondering how must they feel") ending with sustained nasal sounds on the final syllables.

176 TIMES A-CHANGIN'

hypocrisy." It is a powerful performance that signifies through techniques of self-expression that Sainte-Marie is experiencing raw and "authentic" emotions through the song's performance. Even Pete Seeger is briefly shown on camera to be enraptured by Sainte-Marie's song. This is exactly the kind of performance for which he designed the *Rainbow Quest* television program— one that demonstrates the significance folk-influenced singer-songwriter music can have for its listeners.

"My Country" (2017, *Medicine Songs*)

The 2017 recording of "My Country" (for the album *Medicine Songs*) is in dialogue with the self-expressive features of the 1966 versions, particularly with the flexible meter of the 1966 studio recording. For this 2017 album, Sainte-Marie re-recorded several of songs from her previous catalogue and released them alongside some new tracks. For four songs from her 1960s output, she revives her singer-songwriter voice-and-guitar texture: "Little Wheel Spin and Spin," "Universal Soldier," "My Country," and "Now That the Buffalo's Gone."[34] For "My Country" she also recalls the flexible metric setting of her 1966 studio recording.

The lyrics for the 2017 version of "My Country" are modified from the original to offer a Canadian perspective on colonization, this time directly targeting the country of Sainte-Marie's birth. In this version, she sings about the acts of genocide against First Nations people in Canada, coming at a time of increased public interest and scrutiny of actions undertaken by the Canadian government against Indigenous people, which were the subject of the Truth and Reconciliation Commission.[35] For example, for the lyrics

---

[34] The final song on the album ("The War Racket") is also an acoustic self-accompanied performance. In it she sings about the military industrial complex, offering a variety of timbral techniques to highlight her fairly static vocal line. Her short vocal phrases and speech-like vocal production in this song are strongly reminiscent of Dylan's 1960s protest songs. For an investigation of the effects of mimicking Bob Dylan in Joan Baez performances, see Haddon (2021).

[35] As Attas (2020, [8]) explains, the Truth and Reconciliation Commission (TRC) was "a government-appointed commission that was one component of a class action settlement regarding the Indian Residential Schools system, a government-supported and mostly church-run boarding school program that was most active from the 1880s to the 1980s." Indigenous children who were sent to these schools were "taken from their families and brought to distant schools where physical, emotional, and sexual abuse was rampant and legitimate education minimal." The residential school system, as Attas argues, "is widely recognized as the most egregious example of Canada's colonialism via institutionalized 'cultural genocide.'" For the official TRC documents, see Truth and Reconciliation Commission of Canada (2015).

WHAT HAPPENS NEXT TO SELF-EXPRESSIVE FLEXIBLE METER? 177

that in 1966 state "Choke on your blue, white, and scarlet hypocrisy," Sainte-Marie changes the colors to represent the Canadian flag ("true white and scarlet") and the country's similar history of colonization.

Sainte-Marie's 2017 performance offers a multitude of self-expressive features as a dialogue to her previous recordings of the song. The pitch is slightly lower, and her vocal timbre reveals the raspier quality of her aged voice.[36] Her vocal production leans more into growl sounds and continues her 1960s practice of rushing through vowels to linger on the vibrato of her voiced consonants. The self-expressive qualities of her vocal production are highlighted by the performance's looser metric structure, which intensifies the metric profile of the original. Her relatively fast durations are faster, creating greater contrast with longer durations at the ends of her vocal lines. The overall effect is a disorienting sense of flexible meter, with passages of clearly Lost Meter contrasted with unsettled regularity.

Figure 6.2 shows my interpretation of the timings in Sainte-Marie's 2017 recording, which, when compared to those in the 1966 version in Figure 6.1, offers a much less regular opening line. Sainte-Marie's initial Q duration is followed by two accelerated realized durations before giving way to an S' duration that is over four times as long as S duration, resulting in a hiatus and Lost Meter. This is a shorter S' duration than the equivalent moment in Figure 6.1, but it is proportionally longer and therefore feels longer, making the opening line feel metrically unsettled. The faster tempo in general gives a strange metric uncertainty to this more recent performance. This entire first verse continues this effect of barely sustained Regular Meter occasionally giving way to Lost Meter. Sainte-Marie's refrain, again, snaps dramatically into Regular Meter, drawing attention to the import of this line and its associations with colonial, North American "patriotism." This metric profile amplifies the effects of the 1966 meter, expressing the lyrics more urgently.

In verse 2, Sainte-Marie's meter becomes slightly more regular, with durations that are conceptually equal, but still with more contrast in duration length than the 1966 version. Her vocal production, too, is enhanced by the age of Sainte-Marie's voice, and the growling, almost shouting, effects

---

[36] Malawey (2020, 19) cites age among the characteristics that combine in vocal performance to create a person's identity, alongside gender identity, sexuality, race, ethnicity, etc. Sainte-Marie was 76 when *Medicine Songs* was released; she was 25 when *Little Wheel Spin and Spin* came out in 1966. The change in vocal timbre here reminds me of the striking timbral contrast between Joni Mitchell's 1966 recording of "Both Sides Now" in comparison to her 2000 recording on the album of the same title, the latter of which reveals a lower contralto voice that contrasts to the soprano ingénue of the 1960s version.

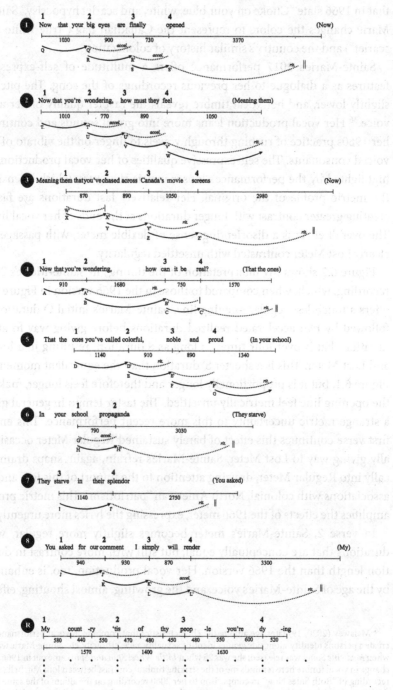

Figure 6.2 Sainte-Marie, "My Country" (*Medicine Songs*, 2017) (0:00–0:44)

WHAT HAPPENS NEXT TO SELF-EXPRESSIVE FLEXIBLE METER? 179

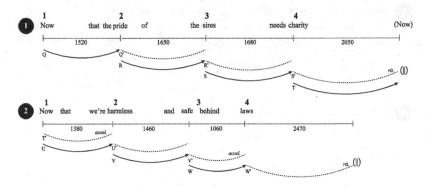

Figure 6.3 Sainte-Marie, "My Country" (*Medicine Songs*, 2017) (3:50–3:56)

she gives certain words. In verse 5, for example, she returns to the more extreme profile of the first verse, with Regular Meter giving way to Lost Meter by the end of certain lines. (This occurs in line 1, shown in Figure 6.3, where the longer T duration is long enough to potentially result in a hiatus, but also not so long as to necessarily do so.[37]) Sainte-Marie emphasizes the word "charity" with nearly a shout and removes vibrato for this word, creating contrast with the nasal vibrato sound of the previous vocal stresses on "Now," "pride," and "sires." There's a similar self-expressive emphasis with her vocal production on the word "choke" at the beginning of line 7 (shown in Figure 6.4). It is very nearly an onomatopoeic effect, as Sainte-Marie seems to choke on the word's delivery, with an expressive break in her voice. Then she rushes through the rest of the line, accelerating each duration to the word "hypocrisy" where she leaves a longer (W') duration (around two and a half times as long as the W duration) at the end of the line that threatens metric loss, giving Sainte-Marie a moment to recover and her listeners time to register the meaning of "true white and scarlet hypocrisy."[38] It is a striking self-expressive moment, especially when considered in comparison to the American version.

---

[37] Some listeners might be able to hear S' as conceptually equivalent to S; I capture this possibility by putting the hiatus symbol in parentheses, for both lines 1 and 2 in Figure 6.3

[38] A similar effect occurs around the two-minute mark, when the flexible meter of this song shifts into the fastest metric profile of any recording as Sainte-Marie asks "And where does it tell of the starvation hell/As the children were herded and raped and converted/And how do we comfort the missing and murdered."

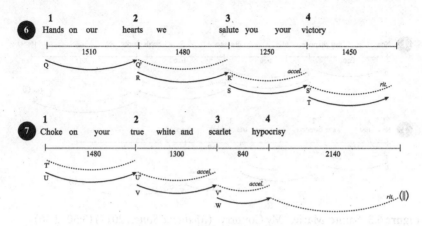

Figure 6.4 Sainte-Marie, "My Country" (*Medicine Songs*, 2017) (4:24–4:33)

Self-Expressive Impact

The self-expressive features of Sainte-Marie's 2017 performance of this song have two important impacts for me as a listener. First, these features make an obvious connection to her 1966 recordings. Sainte-Marie is still an Indigenous woman and an activist; she employs a unique vocal production and a flexible meter that highlight her song's message and link it to the tradition of protest songs from her and her 1960s and 1970s peers. Second, the revival and intensification of the flexible meter of her 1966 performance for the most recent version of "My Country" reinforces the import of the song's message fifty years after its release. In 2017, Sainte-Marie's audience is still in need of an education about Indigenous people in America and Canada. There are still issues with curriculum in schools that at best misrepresent and at worst erase acts of colonization that underlie typical conceptions of history in these two countries, not to mention the present-day inequities facing many Indigenous people throughout North America. The 2017 recording's faster durations signal a rush to deliver this message, an urgency to educate her audiences and enact any meaningful change she still can. Sainte-Marie is, fifty years later, still offering the same lesson. In returning to and amplifying the flexible metric rhetoric of her original performance, she reinforces the import of her timeless message, highlighting how much change still needs to happen and how little has been accomplished in the last half century. As a voice for Indigenous people in North

America, Sainte-Marie's contemporary activist song performances continue the traditions of the early 1960s protest singer-songwriters, offering messages to listeners through features of song performance that signify authentic self-expression.

Conclusion: Flexible Meter as Self-Expression

That Sainte-Marie returns to more extreme types of flexible meter for her 2017 performance of "My Country" suggests that flexible meter is a critically important feature of her self-expressive singer-songwriter performance practice. The techniques of self-expression used by artists like Sainte-Marie, Dylan, Mitchell, Simon, and Stevens were useful for performers in the 1960s and 1970s and are still options available to contemporary artists. As explored in this study, various techniques of self-expression can be amplified at different moments to varying degrees in a single performance or between performances. For singer-songwriter performances that give the impression of unmediated and perceptually authentic self-expression, flexible meter is a critical component of the rhetoric of self-expression that shapes the dialogue between performer and audience.

While this study is grounded in singer-songwriter music of the 1960s and 1970s, the metric theory it offers can be used much more widely. Similar types of flexible meter can be found in unaccompanied performances like plainchant and folk song, and accompanied, soloist-led examples of *rubato* in genres like jazz and opera. In some of these scenarios, the relationship between meter and performance timings are informed by score notations. But the theory of flexible meter offered in this study allows for a consideration of how the metric cues in performance can occur in dialogue with score-based representations of meter and rhythm.[39] It permits Ambiguous Meter to be considered metric and meter to vacillate between different types. This option for meter to be flexible opens up new considerations of metric malleability encompassing a wider variety of timing patterns as metric.

---

[39] Lawrence (2019), for example, explores how rubato impacts the perception of rhythm in Italian opera, offering that timing is "made expressive by the ascription of agency" rather than deviation from written note values.

In singer-songwriter music, flexible meter is an act of self-expression, in dialogue with other self-expressive techniques in performance. In other repertoires, this flexible meter may occur as an act of expression moving beyond the self to broader considerations like genre, history, narrative, and plot, entering into a larger network of expressive musical acts. This study thus both deepens our understanding of an important singer-songwriter tradition and gives us a tool for the analysis of meter more broadly.

Bibliography

Allcock, Phil. 2016. "Authorship and Performance in the Music of Elton John." In *The Cambridge Companion to the Singer-Songwriter*, edited by Katherine Williams and Justin A. Williams, 131–36. Cambridge: Cambridge University Press.

Attas, Robin. 2011. "Meter as Process in Groove-Based Popular Music." PhD diss., University of British Columbia.

Attas, Robin. 2015. "Form as Process: The Buildup Introduction in Popular Music." *Music Theory Spectrum* 37, no. 2: 275–96.

Attas, Robin. 2020. "Review of Dylan Robinson, *Hungry Listening: Resonant Theory for Indigenous Sound Studies* (University of Minnesota Press, 2020)." *Music Theory Online* 26, no. 4. https://mtosmt.org/issues/mto.20.26.4/mto.20.26.4.attas.html.

Benadon, Fernando. 2009. "Gridless Beats." *Perspectives of New Music* 47, no. 1: 135–64.

Benjamin, William E. 1984. "A Theory of Musical Meter." *Music Perception: An Interdisciplinary Journal* 1, no. 4: 355–413.

Bennighof, James. 1993/1994. "Fluidity in Paul Simon's 'Graceland': On Text and Music in a Popular Song." *College Music Symposium* 33/34: 212–36.

Bennighof, James. 2007. *The Words and Music of Paul Simon*. The Praeger Singer-Songwriter Collection. Westport, CT: Praeger.

Bennighof, James. 2010. *The Words and Music of Joni Mitchell*. The Praeger Singer-Songwriter Collection. Santa Barbara, CA: Praeger.

Bentley, Christa Anne. 2016a. "Forging the Singer-Songwriter at the Los Angeles Troubadour." In *The Cambridge Companion to the Singer-Songwriter*, edited by Katherine Williams and Justin A. Williams, 78–88. Cambridge: Cambridge University Press.

Bentley, Christa Anne. 2016b. "Los Angeles Troubadours: The Politics of the Singer-Songwriter Movement, 1968–1975." PhD diss., University of North Carolina at Chapel Hill.

Bernstein, Jonathan, Pat Blashill, Jon Blistein, Nathan Brackett, David Browne, Anthony DeCurtis, Matt Diehl et al. 2012. "500 Greatest Albums of All Time." *Rolling Stone*. May 31, 2012. https://www.rollingstone.com/music/music-lists/500-greatest-albums-of-all-time-156826/joni-mitchell-blue-2-168787/.

Berry, Wallace. 1976. *Structural Functions in Music*. Englewood Cliffs, NJ: Prentice Hall.

Biamonte, Nicole. 2014. "Formal Functions of Metric Dissonance in Rock Music." *Music Theory Online* 20, no. 2. https://www.mtosmt.org/issues/mto.14.20.2/mto.14.20.2.biamonte.html.

Bickford, Tyler. 2007. "Music of Poetry and Poetry of Song: Expressivity and Grammar in Vocal Performance." *Ethnomusicology* 51, no. 3: 439–76.

Blackburn, Dave. 2023. "Transcriptions: Lesson in Survival." JoniMitchell.com. Accessed March 16, 2023. https://jonimitchell.com/music/transcription.cfm?id=488.

184 BIBLIOGRAPHY

Borshuk, Michael. 2016. "The 'Professional' Singer-Songwriter in the 1970s." In *The Cambridge Companion to the Singer-Songwriter*, edited by Katherine Williams and Justin A. Williams, 89–100. Cambridge: Cambridge University Press.

Brackett, David. 1995. *Interpreting Popular Music*. New York: Cambridge University Press.

Burns, Lori. 2005. "Meaning in a Popular Song: The Representation of Masochistic Desire in Sarah McLachlan's 'Ice.'" In *Engaging Music: Essays in Music Analysis*, edited by Deborah Stein, 136–48. New York: Oxford University Press.

Burns, Lori. 2010. "Vocal Authority and Listener Engagement: Musical and Narrative Expressive Strategies in the Songs of Female Pop-Rock Artists, 1993–95." In *Sounding Out Pop: Analytical Essays in Rock Music*, edited by Mark Spicer and John Covach, 154–92. Tracking Pop. Ann Arbor: University of Michigan Press.

Burns, Lori, and Mélisse Lafrance, eds. 2001. *Disruptive Divas: Feminism, Identity, and Popular Music*. New York: Routledge.

Butler, Mark J. 2001. "Turning the Beat Around: Reinterpretation, Metrical Dissonance and Asymmetry in Electronic Dance Music." *Music Theory Online* 7, no. 6. https://www.mtosmt.org/issues/mto.01.7.6/mto.01.7.6.butler.html.

Butler, Mark J. 2006. *Unlocking the Groove*. Profiles in Popular Music. Indiana University Press.

Butterfield, Matthew. 2006. "The Power of Anacrusis: Engendered Feeling in Groove-Based Musics." *Music Theory Online* 12, no. 4. https://mtosmt.org/issues/mto.06.12.4/mto.06.12.4.butterfield.html.

Campbell, Olive Dame, and Cecil Sharp. 1917. *English Folk Songs from the Southern Appalachians*. New York: The Knickerbocker Press.

Cantwell, Robert. 1991. "Smith's Memory Theater: The Folkways Anthology of American Folk Music." *New England Review* 13, no. 3/4: 364–97.

Cantwell, Robert. 1996. *When We Were Good: The Folk Revival*. Cambridge, MA: Harvard University Press.

Charters, Samuel. 1963. *The Poetry of the Blues*. New York: Oak Publications.

Child, Francis James. 1904. *English and Scottish Popular Ballads*, edited by Kittredge George Lyman and Helen Child Sargent. Boston: Houghton Mifflin Company.

Coleman, E. 2016. "Revisit Our Infamous 1963 Profile of Bob Dylan." *Newsweek*, May 24, 2016. https://www.newsweek.com/bob-dylans-75th-birthday-revisit-our-infamous-1963-profile-462801.

Cook, Nicholas. 2012. "Introduction: Refocusing Theory." *Music Theory Online* 18, no. 1. https://mtosmt.org/issues/mto.12.18.1/mto.12.18.1.cook.html.

Cooper, Grosvenor, and Leonard B. Meyer. 1960. *The Rhythmic Structure of Music*. Chicago: University of Chicago.

Covach, John. 2010. "Leiber and Stoller, the Coasters, and the 'Dramatic AABA' Form." In *Sounding Out Pop: Analytic Essays in Rock Music*, edited by Mark Spicer and John Covach, 1–17. Ann Arbor: University of Michigan Press.

Covach, John, and Graeme Boone, eds. 1997. *Understanding Rock: Essays in Musical Analysis*. New York: Oxford University Press.

Danielsen, Anne. 2006. *Presence and Pleasure: The Funk Grooves of James Brown and Parliament*. Middletown, CT: Wesleyan University Press.

Danielsen, Anne. 2010. "Here, There and Everywhere: Three Accounts of Pulse in D'Angelo's 'Left and Right.'" In *Musical Rhythm in the Age of Digital Reproduction*, edited by Anne Danielsen, 19–35. Aldershot: Ashgate.

BIBLIOGRAPHY 185

de Clercq, Trevor. 2012. "Sections and Successions in Successful Songs: A Prototype Approach to Form in Rock Music." PhD diss., University of Rochester, Eastman School of Music.

Dodson, Alan. 2002. "Performance and Hypermetric Transformation: An Extension of the Lerdahl-Jackendoff Theory." *Music Theory Online* 8, no. 1. https://www.mtosmt. org/issues/mto.02.8.1/mto.02.8.1.dodson.html.

Dodson, Alan. 2008. "Performance, Grouping and Schenkerian Alternative Readings in Some Passages from Beethoven's 'Lebewohl' Sonata." *Music Analysis* 27, no. 1: 107–34.

Dodson, Alan. 2011. "Expressive Asynchrony in a Recording of Chopin's Prelude No. 6 in B Minor by Vladimir de Pachmann." *Music Theory Spectrum* 33, no. 1: 59–64.

Dunaway, David King, and Molly Beer. 2010. *Singing Out: An Oral History of America's Folk Music Revivalists.* New York: Oxford University Press.

Dunaway, Finis. 2017. "The 'Crying Indian' Ad that Fooled the Environmental Movement." *Chicago Tribune*, November 21, 2017. https://www.chicagotribune.com/opinion/commentary/ct-perspec-indian-crying-environment-ads-pollution-1123-20171113-story.html.

Dunn, Michael. 2023. "Transcriptions: Woodstock." JoniMitchell.com. Accessed March 16, 2023. https://jonimitchell.com/music/transcription.cfm?id=447.

Dylan, Bob. 2004a. *Chronicles: Volume One.* New York: Simon & Schuster.

Dylan, Bob. 2004b. *Lyrics: 1962–2001.* New York: Simon & Schuster.

Dylan, Bob. 2020. "Setlists That Contain 'Only a Pawn in Their Game.'" BobDylan.com. Accessed April 30, 2020. https://www.bobdylan.com/setlists/?id_song=26633.

Dylan, Bob. 2021. "Restless Farewell by Bob Dylan," BobDylan.com. Accessed February 25, 2021. www.bobdylan.com/us/songs/restless-farewell.

Dylan, Bob. 2021. "Setlists That Contain 'The Lonesome Death of Hattie Carroll.'" BobDylan.com. Accessed March 1, 2021. bobdylan.com/setlists/?id_song=26458.

Everett, Walter. 1992. "Voice Leading and Harmony as Expressive Devices in the Early Music of the Beatles, 'She Loves You.'" *College Music Symposium* 32: 19–37.

Everett, Walter. 1997. "Swallowed by a Song: Paul Simon's Crisis of Chromaticism." In *Understanding Rock: Essays in Musical Analysis*, edited by John Covach and Graeme Boone, 113–53. New York: Oxford University Press.

Everett, Walter, ed. 2000. *Expression in Pop-Rock Music: A Collection of Critical and Analytical Essays.* New York: Garland.

Everett, Walter. 2008. *The Foundations of Rock: From Blue Suede Shoes to Suite: Judy Blue Eyes.* New York: Oxford University Press.

Everett, Walter. 2009. "Any Time At All: The Beatles' Free Phrase Rhythms." In *The Cambridge Companion to the Beatles*, edited by Kenneth Womack, 183–99. New York: Cambridge University Press.

Feldman, Martha. 2015. "Why Voice Now?" *Journal of the American Musicological Society* 68, no. 3: 653–85.

Finch, Barnaby, and Dave Blackburn. 2023. "Transcriptions: Blue." JoniMitchell. com. Accessed March 16, 2023. https://jonimitchell.com/music/transcription. cfm?id=387.

Fishman, Howard. 2017. "The Unlikely Return of Cat Stevens." *The New Yorker*, September 15, 2017. https://www.newyorker.com/culture/culture-desk/the-unlikely-return-of-cat-stevens.

Ford, Charles. 1998. "Robert Johnson's Rhythms." *Popular Music* 17, no. 1: 71–93.

186 BIBLIOGRAPHY

Ford, Charles. 2012. "The Development of Bob Dylan's Rhythmic Sense: 'The Times They Were a'Changin' (1958–64)." In *Critical Musicological Reflections: Essays in Honour of Derek B. Scott*, edited by Stan Hawkins, 159–78. New York: Routledge.

Ford, Charles. 2019. "Searching for Ghosts: Fluidity and Temporal Expansion in Joni Mitchell's First Five Albums (1968–1972)." *Popular Music* 38, no. 3: 399–422.

Frank, Alex. 2017. "Protest Songs Spell Out Problems. Activist Songs Spell Out Solutions." *The Village Voice*, November 15, 2017. https://www.villagevoice.com/2017/11/15/prot est-songs-spell-out-problems-activist-songs-spell-out-solutions/.

Frith, Simon. 1988. "Why Do Songs Have Words." In *Music for Pleasure: Essays in the Sociology of Pop*, 105–28. New York: Routledge.

Frith, Simon. 1996. *Performing Rites*. New York: Oxford University Press.

Gioia, Ted. 1988. *The Imperfect Art: Reflections on Jazz and Modern Culture*. New York: Oxford University Press.

Gioia, Ted. 2008. *Delta Blues: The Life and Times of the Mississippi Masters Who Revolutionized American Music*. New York: W. W. Norton & Co.

Gracyk, Theodore. 2006. "When I Paint My Masterpiece: What Sort of Artist Is Bob Dylan?" In *Bob Dylan and Philosophy*, edited by Carl J. Porter and Peter Vernezze, 169–81. Chicago: Open Court.

Green, Mitchell S. 2007. *Self Expression*. New York: Oxford University Press.

Griffiths, Dai. 2003. "From Lyric to Anti-Lyric: Analyzing the Words in Pop Song." In *Analyzing Popular Music*, edited by Allan Moore, 39–59. New York: Cambridge University Press.

Griffiths, Dai. 2012. "Internal Rhyme in 'The Boy with a Moon and Star on His Head', Cat Stevens, 1972." *Popular Music* 31, no. 3: 383–400.

Haddon, Mimi. 2021. "Matrices of 'Love and Theft': Joan Baez Imitates Bob Dylan." *Twentieth-Century Music* 18, no. 2: 249–79.

Hair, Ross, and Thomas Ruys Smith. 2018. *Harry Smith's Anthology of American Folk Music: America Changed Through Music*. New York: Routledge.

Halle, John, and Fred Lerdahl. 1993. "A Generative Textsetting Model." *Current Musicology* 5: 3–23.

Hardman, Kristi. 2022. "The Continua of Sound Qualities for Tanya Tagaq's *Katajjaq* Sounds." In *Trends in World Music Analysis: New Directions in World Music Analysis*, edited by Lawrence Beaumont Shuster, Somangshu Mukherji, and Noé Dinnerstein, 85–99. New York: Routledge.

Harvey, Todd. 2001. *The Formative Dylan: Transmission and Stylistic Influences, 1961–1963*. Lanham, MD: The Scarecrow Press, Inc.

Harvey, Todd. 2007. "Never Quite Sung in This Fashion before: Bob Dylan's Man of Constant Sorrow." *Oral Tradition* 22, no. 1: 99–111.

Hasty, Christopher. 1997. *Meter as Rhythm*. New York: Oxford University Press.

Hayes, Bruce. 1995. *Metrical Stress Theory: Principles and Case Studies*. Chicago: University of Chicago Press.

Heidemann, Kate. 2016. "A System for Describing Vocal Timbre in Popular Song." *Music Theory Online* 22, no. 1. https://mtosmt.org/issues/mto.16.22.1/mto.16.22.1.heidem ann.php.

Hesselink, Nathan D. 2013. "Radiohead's 'Pyramid Song': Ambiguity, Rhythm, and Participation." *Music Theory Online* 19, no. 1. https://mtosmt.org/issues/mto.13.19.1/ mto.13.19.1.hesselink.html.

Heylin, Clinton. 2009. *Revolution in the Air: The Songs of Bob Dylan 1957–1973*. Chicago: Chicago Review Press.

Heylin, Clinton. 2001. *Bob Dylan: Behind the Shades Revisited*. New York: Harper Collins.

Horlacher, Gretchen. 1995. "Metric Irregularity in 'Les Noces': The Problem of Periodicity." *Journal of Music Theory* 39, no. 2: 285–309.

Horlacher, Gretchen. 2000/2001. "Multiple Meters and Metrical Processes in the Music of Steve Reich." *Intégral* 14/15: 265–97.

Hosken, Fred. 2021. "The Pocket: A Theory of Beats as Domains." PhD diss., Northwestern University.

Hoskins, Barney, ed. 2017. *Joni: The Anthology*. New York: Picador.

Hughes, Timothy. 2000. "Trapped within the Wheels: Flow and Repetition, Modernism, and Tradition in Stevie Wonder's 'Living for the City.'" In *Expression in Pop-Rock Music: Critical and Analytical Essays*, edited by Walter Everett, 239–65. New York: Garland.

Huron, David. 2006. *Sweet Anticipation: Music and the Psychology of Expectation*. Cambridge, MA: MIT Press.

Huron, David, and Ann Ommen. 2006. "An Empirical Study of Syncopation in American Popular Music, 1890–1939." *Music Theory Spectrum* 28, no. 2: 211–31.

Imbrie, Andrew. 1973. "Extra Measures and Metrical Ambiguity in Beethoven." In *Beethoven Studies*, edited by Alan Tyson, 45–66. New York: W. W. Norton.

Islam, Yusuf. 2014. *Why I Still Carry a Guitar: The Spiritual Journey of Cat Stevens to Yusuf*. London: Motivate Publishing.

Ito, John Paul. 2013. "Hypermetrical Schemas, Metrical Orientation, and Cognitive-Linguistic Paradigms." *Journal of Music Theory* 57, no. 1: 47–85.

Ito, John Paul. 2020. *Focal Impulse Theory: Musical Expression, Meter, and the Body*. Bloomington: Indiana University Press.

Jeganathan, Jeyan, and Carla Lucchetta. 2021. "'Felt through the Generations': A Timeline of Residential Schools in Canada." *TVO*. June 21, 2021. https://www.tvo.org/article/felt-throughout-generations-a-timeline-of-residential-schools-in-canada.

Jimoh, A. Yemisi. 2002. *Spiritual, Blues, and Jazz People in African American Fiction: Living in Paradox*. Knoxville: University of Tennessee Press.

Johnson, Brian D., and Danylo Hawalsheka. 1997. "Joni's Secret." *Maclean's*. April 21, 1997, 48–52.

Jones, Mari Reiss, Heather Moynihan, Noah MacKenzie, and Jennifer Puente. 2002. "Temporal Aspects of Stimulus-Driven Attending in Dynamic Arrays." *Psychological Science* 13, no. 4: 313–19.

King, Bill. 2017. "A Conversation With . . . Buffy Sainte-Marie." *FYI Music News*. October 26, 2017. https://www.fyimusicnews.ca/articles/2017/10/26/conversation-buffy-sainte-marie.

King, Thomas. 2012. *The Inconvenient Indian: A Curious Account of Native People in North America*. Toronto: Doubleday Canada.

Knowles, Kristina. 2016. "The Boundaries of Meter and the Subjective Experience of Time in Post-Tonal Unmetered Music." PhD diss., Northwestern University.

Koozin, Timothy. 2000. "Fumbling Towards Ecstasy: Voice Leading, Tonal Structure, and the Theme of Self Realization in the Music of Sarah McLachlan." In *Expression in Pop-Rock Music: Critical and Analytical Essays*, edited by Walter Everett, 267–84. New York: Garland.

188 BIBLIOGRAPHY

Koozin, Timothy. 2011. "Guitar Voicing in Pop-Rock Music: A Performance-Based Analytical Approach." *Music Theory Online* 17, no. 3. https://mtosmt.org/issues/mto.11.17.3/mto.11.17.3.koozin.html.

Kramer, Jonathan. 1988. *The Time of Music*. New York: Schirmer Books.

Krebs, Harald. 1999. *Fantasy Pieces*. New York: Oxford University Press.

Krebs, Harald. 2005. "Hypermeter and Hypermetric Irregularity in the Songs of Josephine Lang." In *Engaging Music: Essays in Music Analysis*, edited by Deborah Stein, 13–29. New York: Oxford University Press.

Krebs, Harald. 2007. "Text-Expressive Functions of Metrical Dissonance in the Songs of Hugo Wolf." *Musicologica Austraica* 26: 267–98.

Krebs, Harald. 2009. "The Expressive Role of Rhythm and Meter in Schumann's Late Lieder." *Gamut* 2, no. 1: 267–98.

Krebs, Harald. 2010. "Fancy Footwork: Distortions of Poetic Rhythm in Robert Schumann's Late Songs." *Indiana Theory Review* 28: 67–84.

Large, Edward W., and Caroline Palmer. 2002. "Perceiving Temporal Regularity in Music." *Cognitive Science* 26, no. 1: 1–37.

Lawrence, John Y. 2019. "Transacting Musical Time: Where Rhythm Ends and Rubato Begins." Paper presented at the Society for Music Theory Conference, Columbus, Ohio.

Lemire, Chantal. 2013. "At the 'Crossroads': The Interaction Between Speech Rhythm and Musical Rhythm in Tom Waits's Spoken-Word Song." MA thesis, University of British Columbia.

Lerdahl, Fred. 2001. "The Sounds of Poetry Viewed as Music." *Annals of the New York Academy of Sciences* 930, no. 1: 337–54.

Lerdahl, Fred. 2009. "Genesis and Architecture of the GTTM Project." *Music Perception: An Interdisciplinary Journal* 26, no. 3: 187–94.

Lerdahl, Fred, and Ray Jackendoff. 1983. *A Generative Theory of Tonal Music*. Cambridge, MA: The MIT Press.

Lester, Joel. 1986. "Notated and Heard Meter." *Perspectives of New Music* 24, no. 2: 116–28.

London, Justin. 2012. *Hearing in Time*. 2nd ed. New York: Oxford University Press.

London, Justin. 2019. "Metric Entrainment and the Problem(s) of Rhythm Perception." In *The Philosophy of Rhythm: Aesthetics, Music, Poetics*, edited by Peter Cheyne, Andy Hamilton, and Max Paddison, 171–82. New York: Oxford University Press.

Lopez, Gerardo. 2020. "Metric Ambiguity and Meter in Copland's Duo for Flute and Piano." Paper presented at Indiana University Annual Symposium of Research in Music, Bloomington, Indiana.

Losseff, Nicky. 1999. "Cathy's Homecoming and the Other World: Kate Bush's 'Wuthering Heights.'" *Popular Music* 18, no. 2: 227–40.

Lucas, Olivia R. 2018. "'So Complete in Beautiful Deformity': Unexpected Beginnings and Rotated Riffs in Meshuggah's *obZen*." *Music Theory Online* 24, no. 3. https://mtosmt.org/issues/mto.18.24.3/mto.18.24.3.lucas.html.

Malawey, Victoria. 2010. "Harmonic Stasis and Oscillation in Björk's *Medúlla*." *Music Theory Online* 16, no. 1. https://mtosmt.org/issues/mto.10.16.1/mto.10.16.1.malawey.html.

Malawey, Victoria. 2020. *A Blaze of Light in Every Word: Analyzing the Popular Singing Voice*. New York: Oxford University Press.

Malin, Yonatan. 2006. "Metric Displacement Dissonance and Romantic Longing in the German Lied." *Music Analysis* 25, no. 3: 251–88.

Malin, Yonatan. 2008. "Metric Analysis and the Metaphor of Energy: A Way into Selected Songs by Wolf and Schoenberg." *Music Theory Spectrum* 30, no. 1: 61–87.

Malin, Yonatan. 2010. *Songs in Motion: Rhythm and Meter in the German Lied*. Oxford Studies in Music Theory. New York: Oxford University Press.

Marcus, Griel. 1997. "The Old, Weird America." In *A Booklet of Essays, Appreciations, and Annotations Pertaining to the Anthology of American Folk Music*, edited by Harry Smith, 5–25. Washington, DC: Smithsonian Folkways Recordings.

Martens, Peter. 2011. "The Ambiguous Tactus: Tempo, Subdivision Benefit, and Three Listener Strategies." *An Interdisciplinary Journal* 28, no. 5: 433–48.

Martens, Peter. 2012. "Tactus in Performance: Constraints and Possibilities." *Music Theory Online* 8, no. 1. https://mtosmt.org/issues/mto.12.18.1/mto.12.18.1.martens.php.

McKenna, Kristine. 2017. "The Dream Girl Wakes Up." In *Joni: The Anthology*, edited by Barney Hoskins, 143–56. New York: Picador.

Meintjes, Louise. 1990. "Paul Simon's Graceland, South Africa, and the Mediation of Musical Meaning." *Ethnomusicology* 34, no. 1: 37–73.

Mercer, Michelle. 2009. *Will You Take Me As I Am: Joni Mitchell's Blue Period*. New York: Free Press.

Meyer, Leonard. 1956. *Emotion and Meaning in Music*. Chicago: University of Chicago Press.

Milius, Emily. 2021. "Voice as Trauma Recovery: Vocal Timbre in Kesha's 'Praying.'" Paper presented at the Society for Music Theory Virtual Conference.

Mirka, Danuta. 2009. *Metric Manipulations in Haydn and Mozart: Chamber Music for Strings, 1787–1791*. New York: Oxford University Press.

Mitchell, Joni. 2019. *Morning Glory On The Vine: Early Songs and Drawings*. New York: Houghton Mifflin Harcourt.

Mitchell, Nate. 2019. "On Metrical Structure and Cueing Systems in Monroe's 'Muleskinner Blues.'" Paper presented at the Society for Music Theory Conference, Columbus, Ohio.

Monelle, Raymond. 2006. *The Musical Topic: Hunt, Military and Pastoral*. Bloomington: Indiana University Press.

Monk, Katherine. 2012. *Joni: The Creative Odyssey of Joni Mitchell*. Vancouver, BC: Greystone Books.

Moore, Allan. 1992. "Patterns of Harmony." *Popular Music* 11, no. 1: 73–106.

Moore, Allan. 2001. *Rock: The Primary Text*. 2nd ed. Aldershot: Ashgate.

Moore, Allan F. 2012. *Song Means: Analysing and Interpreting Recorded Popular Song*. Burlington, VT: Ashgate Publishing.

Moore, Allan. 2016. "Singer-Songwriters and the English Folk Tradition." In *The Cambridge Companion to the Singer Songwriter*, edited by Katherine Williams and Justin A. Williams, 55–66. Cambridge: Cambridge University Press.

Murphy, Nancy. 2015. "'The Times They Are-A Changin'": Flexible Meter and Text Expression in 1960s and 70s Singer-Songwriter Music." PhD diss., University of British Columbia.

Murphy, Nancy. 2016. "Time Rise, Time Fall: Flexible Meter and Text Expression in Cat Stevens's Song 'Time.'" Paper presented at the Music Theory Midwest, Fayetteville, Arkansas.

Murphy, Nancy. 2018. "'Old, Weird America': Metric Irregularities and Harry Smith's *Anthology of American Folk Music*." Paper presented at the Society for Music Theory Conference, San Antonio, Texas.

190 BIBLIOGRAPHY

Murphy, Nancy. 2019. "Expressive Asynchrony in Buffy Sainte-Marie Performances." Paper presented at the Performance Analysis Interest Group, Society for Music Theory Conference, Columbus, Ohio.

Murphy, Nancy. 2020. "Expressive Timing in 'With God on Our Side.'" *Music Analysis* 39, no. 3: 387–413.

Murphy, Nancy. 2022. "'The Times are A-Changin': Metric Flexibility and Text Expression in 1960s and 1970s Singer-Songwriter Music." *Music Theory Spectrum* 44, no. 1: 17–40.

Neal, Jocelyn. 1998. "The Metric Makings of a Country Hit." In *Reading Country Music*, edited by Cecilia Tichi, 322–37. Durham, NC: Duke University Press.

Neal, Jocelyn. 2000. "Songwriter's Signature, Artist's Imprint: The Metric Structure of a Country Song." In *Country Music Annual*, edited by Charles K. Wolfe and Hames E. Akenson 112–40. Lexington, KY: University Press of Kentucky.

Neal, Jocelyn. 2002. "Song Structure Determinants: Poetic Narrative, Phrase Structure, and Hypermeter in the Music of Jimmie Rodgers." PhD diss., Eastman School of Music.

Neal, Jocelyn. 2007. "Narrative Paradigms, Musical Signifiers, and Form as Function in Country Music." *Music Theory Spectrum* 29, no. 1: 41–72.

Neal, Jocelyn. 2009. *The Songs of Jimmie Rodgers: A Legacy in Country Music*. Bloomington: Indiana University Press.

Nobile, Drew. 2022. "Alanis Morissette's Voices." *Music Theory Online* 27, no. 4. https://mtosmt.org/issues/mto.22.28.4/mto.22.28.4.nobile.html.

NPR. 2017. "The 150 Greatest Albums Made by Women." July 24, 2017. https://www.npr.org/2017/07/24/538387823/turning-the-tables-150-greatest-albums-made-by-women.

O'Brien, Karen. 2001. *Joni Mitchell: Shadows and Light*. London: Virgin Books.

Ogg, Arden. 2021. "My Country 'tis of Thy People You're Dying: Buffy Sainte-Marie." Cree Literacy Network. February 7, 2021. https://creeliteracy.org/2021/02/07/my-country-tis-of-thy-people-youre-dying-buffy-sainte-marie/.

Ohriner, Mitchell. 2012. "Grouping Hierarchy and Trajectories of Pacing in Performances of Chopin's Mazurkas." *Music Theory Online* 18, no. 1. https://mtosmt.org/issues/mto.12.18.1/mto.12.18.1.ohriner.php.

Ohriner, Mitchell. 2019. "Expressive Timing." In *The Oxford Handbook of Critical Concepts in Music Theory*, edited by Alexander Rehding and Steven Rings, 369–94. New York: Oxford University Press.

Oliver, Mary. 1994. *A Poetry Handbook*. San Diego, CA: Harcourt Brace & Co.

Oliver, Paul. 1960. *Blues Fell This Morning: Meaning in the Blues*. New York: Horizon Press.

Osborn, Brad. 2011. "Understanding Through-Composition in Post-Rock, Math-Metal, and Other Post-Millennial Rock Genres." *Music Theory Online* 17, no. 3. https://www.mtosmt.org/issues/mto.11.17.3/mto.11.17.3.osborn.html.

Pareles, Jon, Neil Strauss, Ben Ratliff, and Ann Powers. 2000. "Critics' Choices; Albums as Mileposts in a Musical Century." *New York Times*, January 3, 2000. https://www.nytimes.com/2000/01/03/arts/critics-choices-albums-as-mileposts-in-a-musical-century.html.

Parncutt, Richard. 1994. "A Perceptual Model of Pulse Salience and Metrical Accent in Musical Rhythms." *Music Perception: An Interdisciplinary Journal* 11, no. 4: 409–64.

Pieslak, Jonathan. 2007. "Re-Casting Metal: Rhythm and Meter in the Music of Meshuggah." *Music Theory Spectrum* 29, no. 2: 219–45.

The Pulitzer Prize. 2021. "Bob Dylan." Accessed November 30, 2021. https://www.pulitzer.org/winners/bob-dylan.

BIBLIOGRAPHY 191

Raim, Ethel. 1973. *Anthology of American Folk Music*, edited by Josh Dunson and Ethel Raim. New York: Oak Publications.

Repp, Bruno. 1998. "The Detectability of Local Deviations from a Typically Expressive Timing Pattern." *Music Perception: An Interdisciplinary Journal* 15, no. 3: 265–89.

Repp, Bruno. 2005. "Rate Limits of On-Beat and Off-Beat Tapping with Simple Auditory Rhythms: 2. The Roles of Different Kinds of Accent." *Music Perception: An Interdisciplinary Journal* 23, no. 2: 165–88.

Rings, Steven. 2013."A Foreign Sound to Your Ear: Bob Dylan Performs 'It's Alright, Ma (I'm Only Bleeding).'" *Music Theory Online* 19, no. 4. https://mtosmt.org/issues/mto.13.19.4/mto.13.19.4.rings.php.

Rings, Steven. 2015. "Analyzing the Popular Singing Voice: Sense and Surplus." *Journal of the American Musicological Society* 68, no. 3: 663–71.

Robinson, Dylan. 2020. *Hungry Listening: Resonant Theory for Indigenous Sound Studies*. Minneapolis: University of Minnesota Press.

Rockwell, Joti. 2009. "Banjo Transformations and Bluegrass Rhythm." *Journal of Music Theory* 53, no. 1: 137–62.

Rockwell, Joti. 2011. "Time on the Crooked Road: Isochrony, Meter, and Disruption in Old-Time Country and Bluegrass Music." *Ethnomusicology* 55, no. 1: 55–76.

Roeder, John. 1998."Review of Christopher Hasty, *Meter as Rhythm*." *Music Theory Online* 4, no. 4. https://mtosmt.org/issues/mto.98.4.4/mto.98.4.4.roeder.html.

Roeder, John. 2015. "Durational Projections in World Music: Some Analytical Applications." Paper presented at the Society for Music Analysis Conference, Keele, UK.

Rothstein, William. 1989. *Phrase Rhythm in Tonal Music*. New York: Schirmer Books.

Rothstein, William. 2008. "National Metric Types in Music of the Eighteenth and Early Nineteenth Centuries." In *Communication in Eighteenth-Century Music*, edited by Danuta Mirka and Kofi Agawu, 112–59. Cambridge: Cambridge University Press.

Rothstein, William. 2011. "Metrical Theory and Verdi's Midcentury Operas." *Dutch Journal of Music Theory* 16, no. 2: 93–111.

Rotolo, Suze. 2008. *A Freewheelin' Time: A Memoir of Greenwich Village in the Sixties*. New York: Broadway Books.

Russell, Craig. 1997. "The Idiom of Simon and the Image of Dylan: When Do Stars Cast Shadows?" In *Music in Performance and Society: Essays in Honor of Roland Jackson*, edited by Malcolm Cole and John Koegel, 589–97. Warren, MI: Harmonie Park Press.

Sainte-Marie, Buffy. 2021a. "The Mouthbow: Making Music on a Weapon." Cradleboard. org. Accessed January 15, 2021. http://www.cradleboard.org/curriculum/powwow/supplements/mouthbow.html.

Sainte-Marie, Buffy. 2021b. "My Country 'Tis of Thy People You're Dying." BuffySainte-Marie.com. Accessed January 15, 2021. https://buffysainte-marie.com/?page_id=10878#4.

Schachter, Carl. 1999a. "Aspects of Meter." In *Unfoldings: Essays in Schenkerian Theory and Analysis*, edited by Joseph N. Straus, 79–117. New York: Oxford University Press.

Schachter, Carl. 1999b. "Motive and Text in Four Schubert Songs." In *Unfoldings: Essays in Schenkerian Theory and Analysis*, edited by Joseph N. Straus, 209–20. New York: Oxford University Press.

Seeger, Charles. 1950. "Oral Tradition in Music." In *Funk and Wagnalls Standard Dictionary of Folklore and Legend*, edited by Maria Leach and Jerome Fried, 825–29. New York: Funk and Wagnalls.

192 BIBLIOGRAPHY

Seeger, Charles. 1958. "Prescriptive and Descriptive Music-Writing." *The Musical Quarterly* 44, no. 2: 184–95.

Shelton, Robert. 1961. "Bob Dylan: A Distinctive Folk-Song Stylist: 20-Year-Old Singer Is Bright New Face at Gerde's Club." *New York Times*, September 29, 1961, 31.

Shelton, Robert. 1963. "Old Music Taking On New Color: An Indian Girl Sings Her Compositions and Folk Songs." *New York Times*, August 17, 1963, 11.

Shumway, David R. 2016. "The Emergence of the Singer-Songwriter." In *The Cambridge Companion to the Singer-Songwriter*, edited by Katherine Williams and Justin A. Williams, 11–20. Cambridge: Cambridge University Press.

Sonenberg, Daniel. 2003. "'Who in the World She Might Be': A Contextual and Stylistic Approach to the Early Music of Joni Mitchell." PhD diss., City University of New York.

Spicer, Mark, and John Covach, eds. 2010. *Sounding Out Pop: Analytical Essays in Rock Music*. Ann Arbor: University of Michigan Press.

Stephan-Robinson, Anna. 2009. "Form in Paul Simon's Music." PhD diss., University of Rochester, Eastman School of Music.

Stephenson, Ken. 2002. *What to Listen for in Rock: A Stylistic Analysis*. New Haven, CT: Yale University Press.

Stevens, Cat. 2020. "Life." CatStevens.com. Accessed March 19, 2020. https://catstevens.com/life/.

Stoia Nicholas. 2013. "The Common Stock of Schemes in Early Blues and Country Music." *Music Theory Spectrum* 35, no. 2: 194–234.

Stonechild, Blair. 2012. *Buffy Sainte-Marie: It's My Way*. Markham, Ontario: Fifth House Ltd.

Sullivan, James. 2018. "Meter, Melodic Parallelism, and Metric Manipulation in Post-Tonal Music." PhD diss., Eastman School of Music.

Temperley, David. 1999. "Syncopation in Rock: A Perceptual Perspective." *Popular Music* 18, no. 1: 19–40.

Temperley, David. 2000. "Meter and Grouping in African Music: A View from Music Theory." *Ethnomusicology* 44, no. 1: 65–96.

Temperley, David. 2001. *The Cognition of Basic Musical Structures*. Cambridge, MA: MIT Press.

Temperley, David. 2007. "The Melodic-Harmonic 'Divorce' in Rock." *Popular Music* 26, no. 2: 323–42.

Temperley, David. 2008. "Hypermetrical Transitions." *Music Theory Spectrum* 30, no. 2: 305–25.

Temperley, David, and Christopher Bartelle. 2002. "Parallelism as a Factor in Metrical Analysis." *Music Perception: An Interdisciplinary Journal* 20, no. 2: 117–49.

Tochka, Nicholas. 2020. "John Lennon's Plastic Ono Band as 'First-Person Music': Notes on the Politics of Self-Expression in Rock Music since 1970." *Popular Music* 39, no. 3–4: 504–22.

Truth and Reconciliation Commission of Canada. 2015. *Honouring the Truth, Reconciling for the Future: Summary of the Final Report of the Truth and Reconciliation Commission of Canada*. Government of Canada.

Unterberger, Richie. 2002. *Turn! Turn! Turn: The '60s Folk-Rock Revolution*. Milwaukee, WI: Backbeat Books.

Walser, Robert. 1995. "Rhythm, Rhyme, and Rhetoric in the Music of Public Enemy." *Ethnomusicology* 39, no. 2: 193–217.

BIBLIOGRAPHY 193

Warner, Andrea. 2018. *Buffy Sainte-Marie: The Authorized Biography*. Vancouver: Greystone Books.

Whitesell, Lloyd. 2002. "Harmonic Palette in Early Joni Mitchell." *Popular Music* 21, no. 2: 173–93.

Whitesell, Lloyd. 2008. *The Music of Joni Mitchell*. New York: Oxford University Press.

Williams, Katherine, and Justin A. Williams, eds. 2016a. *The Cambridge Companion to the Singer-Songwriter*. Cambridge: Cambridge University Press.

Williams, Katherine, and Justin A. Williams. 2016b. "Introduction." In *The Cambridge Companion to the Singer-Songwriter*, edited by Katherine Williams and Justin A. Williams, 1–7. Cambridge: Cambridge University Press.

Winkler, Allan M. 2009. *"To Everything There Is a Season": Pete Seeger and the Power of Song*. New York: Oxford University Press.

Winkler, Peter. 1997. "Writing Ghost Notes: The Poetics and Politics of Transcription." In *Keeping the Score: Music, Disciplinarity, Culture*, edited by David Schwarz, Anahid Kassabian, and Lawrence Siegel, 169–203. Charlottesville: University Press of Virginia.

Yaffe, David. 2017. *Reckless Daughter: A Portrait of Joni Mitchell*. New York: Sarah Crichton Books.

Yeston, Maury. 1976. *The Stratification of Musical Rhythm*. New Haven: Yale University Press.

Yorgason, Brent. 2009. "Expressive Asynchrony and Meter: A Study of Dispersal, Downbeat Space, and Metric Drift." PhD diss., Indiana University.

Youens, Susan. 1984. "Poetic Rhythm and Musical Metre in Schubert's 'Winterreise.'" *Music & Letters* 65, no. 1: 28–40.

Zak, Albin. 2004. "Bob Dylan and Jimi Hendrix: Juxtaposition and Transformation 'All Along the Watchtower.'" *Journal of the American Musicological Society* 57, no. 3: 599–644.

Zak, Albin. 2010. "'Only the Lonely': Roy Orbison's Sweet West Texas Style." In *Sounding out Pop: Analytical Essays in Rock Music*, edited by Mark Stuart Spicer and John Covach, 18–41. Ann Arbor: University of Michigan Press.

Zak, Albin J. 2001. *The Poetics of Rock: Cutting Tracks, Making Records*. Berkeley: University of California Press.

Zbikowski, Lawrence M. 2002. *Conceptualizing Music: Cognitive Structure, Theory, and Analysis*. New York: Oxford University Press.

Discography

Baez, Joan. 1962. *Joan Baez in Concert*. Vanguard VRS 9112.

Baez, Joan. 1963. *Joan Baez in Concert, Part 2*. Vanguard VRS 9113.

Behan, Dominic. 1957. *Songs of the Irish Republican Army*. Riverside RLP 12-820.

Bush, Kate. 1978. *The Kick Inside*. EMI EMC 3223.

The Carter Family. 1961. *Songs of the Famous Carter Family*. Columbia CS 8464.

The Clancy Brothers. 1959. *Come Fill Your Glass with Us*. Tradition Records TLP 1032.

The Clancy Brothers and Tommy Makem. 1963. *In Person at Carnegie Hall*. Columbia CS 8750.

Costello, Elvis. 1982. *Imperial Bedroom*. FCT 38157.

Dylan, Bob. 1962. *Bob Dylan*. Columbia CS 8579.

Dylan, Bob. 1963. *The Freewheelin' Bob Dylan*. Columbia CS 8786.

194 BIBLIOGRAPHY

Dylan, Bob. 1964a. *The Times They Are A-Changin'*. Columbia CS 8905.
Dylan, Bob. 1964b. *Another Side of Bob Dylan*. Columbia CS 8993.
Dylan, Bob. 1965. *Bringing It All Back Home*. Columbia CS 9128.
Dylan, Bob. 1991. *The Bootleg Series, Vols. 1–3*. Columbia C3K 47382.
Dylan, Bob. 2004. *The Bootleg Series, Vol 6: Bob Dylan Live 1964, The Concert at Philharmonic Hall*. Columbia/Legacy C2K 86882.
Dylan, Bob. 2013. *50th Anniversary Collection 1963*. Columbia 88883799701.
Dylan, Bob. 2015. *50th Anniversary Collection 1964*. Columbia 88875040861.
Guthrie, Woody. 1951. *This Land Is My Land*. Folkways FP 27.
Guthrie, Woody. 2009. *The Asch Recordings, Vols. 1–4*. Smithsonian Folkways SF CD 4010.
Hurley, Michael. 1964. *First Songs*. Folkways Records FG 3581.
Hurley, Michael. 1971. *Armchair Boogie*. WS 1915 #6.
Johnson, Robert. 1961. *King of the Delta Blues Singers*. Columbia CL 1654.
Johnson, Robert. 1998. *Robert Johnson: The Complete Collection*. Prism Leisure PLATCD 278.
Krall, Diana. 2002. *Live in Paris*. Verve Records 440 065 109-2.
Krall, Diana. 2004. *The Girl in the Other Room*. B0000182612.
McClennan, Tommy. [1940] 1960. "New Highway No. 51." *The Rural Blues: A Study of the Vocal and Instrumental Resources*. Matrix 044986-1.
Mitchell, Joni. 1969. *Clouds*. Reprise Records. RS 6341.
Mitchell, Joni. 1970. *Ladies of the Canyon*. Reprise Records RS 6376.
Mitchell, Joni. 1971. *Blue*. Reprise Records. MS 2038.
Mitchell, Joni. 1972. *For the Roses*. Asylum Records SD 5057.
Mitchell, Joni. 1974. *Court and Spark*. Asylum Records 7E-1001.
Mitchell, Joni. 1976. *Hejira*. Asylum Records 7E-1087.
Mitchell, Joni. 1977. *Don Juan's Reckless Daughter*. Asylum Records BB-701.
Mitchell, Joni. 1979. *Mingus*. Asylum Records 5E-505.
Ochs, Phil. 1964. *All the News That's Fit to Sing*. Elektra. EKL 269.
Ochs, Phil. 1966. *Phil Ochs in Concert*. Elektra. EKS-7310.
Odetta. 1960. *Odetta at Carnegie Hall*. Vanguard VSD 2072.
Rodgers, Jimmie. 1960. *My Rough and Rowdy Ways*. RCA Victor LPM-2112.
Sainte-Marie, Buffy. 1964. *It's My Way*. Vanguard VSD-79142.
Sainte-Marie, Buffy. 1965. *Many a Mile*. Vanguard VSD-89171.
Sainte-Marie, Buffy. 1966. *Little Wheel Spin and Spin*. Vanguard VRS 9211.
Sainte-Marie, Buffy. 2017. *Medicine Songs*. True North TND681.
Seeger, Mike. 1962. *Old Time Country Music*. Folkways FA 2325.
Seeger, Pete. 1954. *American Folk Songs*. Folkways FA 2005.
Seeger, Pete. 1958. *American Favorite Ballads, Vol. 2*. Folkways 2321.
Simon & Garfunkel. 1964. *Wednesday Morning, 3 A.M.* Columbia CL 2249.
Simon & Garfunkel. 1966a. *The Sounds of Silence*. Columbia CL 2469.
Simon & Garfunkel. 1966b. *Parsley, Sage, Rosemary and Thyme*. Columbia CL 2563.
Simon, Paul. 1965. *The Paul Simon Songbook*. CBS BPG 62579.
Simon, Paul. 1986. *Graceland*. W8-25447.
Simone, Nina. 1964. *Nina Simone in Concert*. Philips Records PHM 200-135.
Smith, Harry. 1997. *Anthology of American Folk Music*. Smithsonian Folkways SFW 40090.
Stevens, Cat. 1970a. *Mona Bone Jakon*. A&M Records SP 4260.
Stevens, Cat. 1970b. *Tea for the Tillerman*. A&M Records CS-4280.
Stevens, Cat. 1971. *Teaser and the Firecat*. Island Records ILPS 9154.

Van Ronk, Dave. 1989. *Dave Van Ronk, Folksinger*. Fantasy FCD-24701-2.
Various. 1964. *Newport Broadside*. Vanguard VRS 9144.
Waters, Muddy. 1964. *Folk Singer* LP-1483, 1964.

Videography

1966. "Buffy Sainte-Marie." *Rainbow Quest*. Channel 47.

1969. *The Dick Cavett Show*. New York: ABC, August 19, 1969.

1976. "Buffy Sings 'Cripple Creek' with Fred the Wonder Horse." *Sesame Street*. PBS, May 5, 1976.

Coulter, Philip. 2012. *Still This Love Goes On: The Songs of Buffy Sainte-Marie*. CBC Music.

Lacy, Susan. 2003. *Joni Mitchell: Woman of Heart and Mind: A Life Story*. Eagle Rock Entertainment.

Lerner, Murray. 2007. *Bob Dylan: The Other Side of the Mirror*. Sony Legacy.

Pennebaker, D. A. 2011. *Bob Dylan; Don't Look Back*. Docudrama.

Prowse, Joan. 2014. *Buffy Sainte-Marie: A Multimedia Life*. Toronto: True North.

Scorsese, Martin. 2005. *No Direction Home*. Hollywood: Paramount.

Yentob, Alan. 2006. *Yusuf: The Artist Formerly Known as Cat Stevens*. London: Imagine, BBC1.

Index

For the benefit of digital users, indexed terms that span two pages (e.g., 52–53) may, on occasion, appear on only one of those pages.

Figures are indicated by *f* following the page number

1960s counterculture, 11–12
1970s, individualism of, 13–14, 99–100

a cappella singing, 1, 4, 5–7.
    See also "Fiddle and the Drum, The"
    (Mitchell)
added beats
  in "All I Want" (Mitchell), 60–62, 61*f*
  in "A Case of You" (Mitchell), 58–60, 59*f*
  defined, 34–36, 35*f*, 46, 57–58
  in "Lesson in Survival" (Mitchell), 36*f*,
    36–37, 76–77
  in "The Sound of Silence" (Simon),
    37–38, 38*f*
  See also omitted beats;
    Reinterpreted Meter
"All I Want" (Mitchell), 60–63, 61*f*, 62*f*
Ambiguous Meter
  defined, 25, 28–30, 29*f*, 42–43, 125–26
  in "Down the Highway" (Dylan), 127–
    37, 130*f*, 132*f*, 135*f*
  in "The Fiddle and the Drum"
    (Mitchell), 148–54, 150*f*
  and metric process, 42–46
  in "Restless Farewell" (Dylan), 138,
    139–44, 141*f*, 142*f*, 144*f*, 147–48
  in "Sir Patrick Spens" (Sainte-Marie),
    48–49, 49*f*, 155, 157–61, 158*f*, 160*f*
  Unrealized Durations in, 46–47,
    47*f*, 50–51
antiwar messages, 1–2, 5–7, 11–12. *See*
    also "Fiddle and the Drum, The"
    (Mitchell); "Universal Soldier"
    (Sainte-Marie)
Appalachian ballads, 19–20
"April Come She Will" (Simon), 66, 67*f*

aspects of meter. *See* meter: aspects of
asynchrony, 139–41, 143–44
authenticity, perceptions of, 10, 14–26,
    99–100, 123, 138, 146–47

Baez, Joan, 11n.25, 15n.37, 161–62
ballad tradition, 9–10, 19–20, 156. *See also*
    "Sir Patrick Spens" (Sainte-Marie)
Behan, Dominic, 137
Benjamin, William, 39–40
Bentley, Christa Anne, 11n.25, 13nn.30–
    31, 17–18
Berry, Wallace, 27–28
"Blue" (Mitchell)
  formal structure of, 113–15, 115*f*
  Lost Meter in, 47–48, 48*f*, 110–11, 112–
    21, 117*f*, 119*f*, 121*f*
  lyrics of, 110–15, 118, 120
  Regular Meter in, 110–15, 116–18,
    121, 122–23
  Reinterpreted Meter in, 112, 113*f*,
    114*f*, 118–20
  theme of freedom in, 121–23
Blue (Mitchell), 13, 23, 55, 84–85, 110,
    122–24. *See also* "All I Want"; "Blue";
    "Case of You, A"; "Little Green"
blues, 9–10, 18–21, 127–28, 134–37. *See*
    also "Down the Highway" (Dylan)

Campbell, Olive Dame, 19–20
"Case of You, A" (Mitchell), 58–60, 58*f*, 59*f*
Child ballads, 19nn.52–53, 156. *See also*
    "Sir Patrick Spens" (Sainte-Marie)
civil rights movement, 11–12, 87, 97–98.
    See also "Only a Pawn in Their Game"
    (Dylan)

198 INDEX

Clancy Brothers, The, 137, 138–39, 139*f*
confessional songwriting
  in Mitchell's work, 13–14, 22–23, 55–57,
    84–85, 110, 122–24
  shift toward, 13–14, 99–100, 164
  in Stevens's work, 13–14, 22–23, 67–68,
    73–74, 85, 99–100, 109
country music, 9–10, 66n.21

De La Beckwith, Byron, 87, 94–97. *See
  also* "Only a Pawn in Their Game"
  (Dylan)
Delta blues. *See* blues
Dick Cavett Show, The, 1–3, 21–22,
  153–54
dot notation, introduced, 31–32, 32*f*,
  33*f*, 35*f*
"Down the Highway" (Dylan)
  Ambiguous Meter in, 126, 127–37, 130*f*,
    132*f*, 135*f*
  blues style of, 127–29, 128*f*, 129*f*, 133,
    134–37, 136*f*
  guitar in, 127, 129–34
  lyrics of, 128–29, 128*f*, 129*f*
dramatization through metric flexibility,
  91–97, 98–99
drums. *See* percussion
duration, defined, 50–52, 51*f*, 52*f*. *See
  also* Realized Durations; Unrealized
  Durations
Dylan, Bob
  as "authentic," 10, 15, 18–21,
    138, 146–47
  blues influence on, 20–21, 127–29, 128*f*,
    129*f*, 133, 134–37, 136*f*
  and flexible meter, 10, 18–21, 18n.44
  and the folk revival, 18–21, 22–
    23, 137–48
  "Freight Train Blues," 40n.32
  "With God on Our Side," 57n.9, 137
  going electric, 165–66
  influence of, 10, 22–23
  "The Lonesome Death of Hattie
    Carroll," 11, 97–98n.17
  performance aesthetic of, 18n.44, 88–
    91, 94–95, 98–99, 128, 136–48
  as "protest singer," 2n.4, 11, 87, 97–98
  reception of, 18n.44

"Talkin' New York," 18–19, 138
"The Times They Are A-Changin',"
  11, 97–98
vocal production techniques of,
  4, 18–19
See also "Down the Highway"; "Only
  a Pawn in Their Game"; "Restless
  Farewell"

emerging meter, 24, 49, 52, 116, 125–26,
  144–146, 148–54, 159–61
ensemble textures, 23, 26, 139, 164–67
entrainment, 31–32, 39–40, 46
Everett, Walter, 17n.43, 23n.60, 33nn.16–17,
  99n.19
Evers, Medgar, 11–12, 87, 94–97. *See
  also* "Only a Pawn in Their Game"
  (Dylan)

"Fiddle and the Drum, The" (Mitchell)
  on the Dick Cavett Show, 1–4, 153–54
  fragmentation in, 149–51, 150*f*, 152*f*
  political message of, 1–2, 3–4, 126–27,
    148–49, 153–54
  and self-expression, 2–5, 21–22
  shift from Ambiguous to Regular Meter
    in, 5–8, 6*f*, 28–30, 126–27, 148–54,
    150*f*, 152*f*
  studio recording of, 148–53, 150*f*, 152*f*
flexible meter
  contrasted with regular meter, 6–7, 8
  definition of, 5
  and dramatization, 91–97, 98–99
  and the folk revival, 18–21, 161–63
  in other genres, 181–82
  and self-accompaniment, 5, 94–95,
    164–65
  as self-expression, 5, 21–26, 84–85,
    123–24, 162–63, 167–68, 181–82
  shift away from, 23, 26, 164–67
  and the singer-songwriter aesthetic,
    8–10, 164–67
  theory of, 24–26, 27–30, 52–53,
    123–24
  types of, 24–26, 27–30, 49–50
  See also Ambiguous Meter; Ideal
    Meter; Lost Meter; Regular Meter;
    Reinterpreted Meter

INDEX 199

folk revival
  and "authenticity," 15, 17–18
  and the Delta blues, 20–21
  in dialogue with singer-songwriter
    music, 2–3, 9–10, 11n.25, 21–23
  Dylan's position in, 10, 18–21, 137–48
  and the music industry, 161–62
  Sainte-Marie's position in, 154–55,
    161–62
folk rock, 12nn.28–29, 63, 165–67
For the Roses (Mitchell), 165–66
"Freight Train Blues" (Dylan), 40n.32
Frith, Simon, 15–16

Gioia, Ted, 20–21
Green, Mitchell S., 14
Greenwich Village folk scene, 8–9, 11–12,
  18, 138, 154–55, 161–62
grouping, 31–32, 34, 37–38, 63–66, 71–72,
  72*f*, 73*f*
grouping parallelism. *See* parallelism
guitar
  in "A Case of You" (Mitchell), 59*f*, 59–60
  in "Down the Highway" (Dylan), 127,
    129–34, 130*f*, 132*f*, 135*f*
  in "Katmandu" (Stevens), 71–72,
    72*f*, 73*f*
  in "Little Green" (Mitchell), 55–56, 56*f*
  in "My Country 'Tis of Thy People
    You're Dying" (Sainte-Marie), 172
  in "Only a Pawn in Their Game"
    (Dylan), 91–94, 92*f*, 93*f*, 95, 96*f*
  on *The Paul Simon Songbook*, 11–12
  in "Restless Farewell" (Dylan), 138,
    139–41, 141*f*, 142*f*, 142, 143–46,
    144*f*
  in "Time" (Stevens), 100, 101–3,
    102*f*, 104*f*
Guthrie, Woody, 4, 11, 18–19, 137n.22

Harvey, Todd, 137n.23, 137n.25,
  138n.26
Hasty, Christopher, 7, 42–43, 45*f*.
  See also metric process
hiatus, 44–46, 47–48, 47*f*, 48*f*, 116
Horlacher, Gretchen, 7, 34–35, 39–40
hypermeter, 31–32, 63–66, 79–84,
  112, 144–46

Ideal Meter, 28, 29*f*, 30
Indigenous people
  mistreatment of, 11–12, 161–62,
    167–70, 176–77, 180–81
  and Sainte-Marie's heritage, 12n.26,
    156–57, 167–69
  See also Sainte-Marie, Buffy
inter-onset intervals (IOIs), perceptual
  limits of, 39–40
"Into White" (Stevens), 68–71, 70*f*,
  73–74
introspection. *See* confessional
  songwriting
Islam, Yusuf. *See* Stevens, Cat

Jackendoff, Ray, 7, 31, 32n.13, 34, 37n.23,
  39, 42–43
Johnson, Robert, 11n.23, 85n.33, 127n.5,
  136n.18

"Katmandu" (Stevens), 71–72, 72*f*, 73*f*
Kramer, Jonathan, 39

Ladies of the Canyon (Mitchell), 165–66
Lerdahl, Fred, 7, 31, 32n.13, 34, 37n.23,
  39, 42–43
"Lesson in Survival" (Mitchell)
  analysis of, 36, 36*f*, 75–84, 76*f*, 78*f*, 79*f*,
    80*f*, 81*f*, 83*f*, 84*f*
  lyrics of, 74–81, 75*f*, 82–84
  overview of, 74–75, 84–85
  piano in, 76–77, 79–81
  structure of, 74–75, 75*f*
Lilith Fair, 166–67
"Little Green" (Mitchell), 25, 55–57, 56*f*
Little Wheel Spin and Spin (Sainte-Marie),
  167–68, 171. *See also* "My Country
  'Tis of Thy People You're Dying"
London, Justin, 27n.2, 39–40
"Lonesome Death of Hattie Carroll, The"
  (Dylan), 11, 97–98n.17
Lost Meter
  in "Blue" (Mitchell), 110–11, 112–21,
    117*f*, 119*f*, 121*f*
  defined, 25, 28–30, 29*f*, 38–40, 50–51,
    86
  hiatus in, 46–47, 47*f*, 86
  and metric process, 42–43

200 INDEX

Lost Meter (*cont.*)
 in "My Country 'Tis of Thy People
  You're Dying" (Sainte-Marie), 172–
  74, 173*f*, 177–79, 178*f*, 179*f*, 180*f*
 in "Only a Pawn in Their Game"
  (Dylan), 91–97, 92*f*, 93*f*, 98–99
 as temporary, 86–87, 91–94, 95–97
 in "Time" (Stevens), 100, 103–10, 106*f*
 in "Woodstock" (Mitchell), 40–42, 41*f*
lyrics
 as commentary, 11–12 (*see also* "My
  Country 'Tis of Thy People You're
  Dying" [Sainte-Marie]; "Only a Pawn
  in Their Game" [Dylan])
 highlighted by flexible meter, 9–10, 58–
  66, 123–24 (*see also* "Blue" [Mitchell];
  "Lesson in Survival" [Mitchell])
 metric emphasis of, 55–57, 56*f*, 68–72
 personal narratives in, 55–57, 99–100,
  110, 128 (*see also* "Lesson in Survival"
  [Mitchell])
 as self-expression, 2–4, 15–16, 167–68,
  169–70
 See also word stresses

Malawey, Victoria, 4nn.11–12, 101n.25,
  177n.36
Malin, Yonatan, 39–40
malleability. *See* flexible meter
March on Washington (1963), 11–12, 90–91
Medicine Songs (Sainte-Marie), 167–68,
  176. *See also* "My Country 'Tis of Thy
  People You're Dying"
meter
 aspects of, 50–53, 51*f*, 52*f*
 theories of, 7–9, 27–28, 44
 See also flexible meter; metric hierarchy;
  metric process (Hasty)
metric accents, 37, 55, 56–57, 63–66
metric cues, defined, 8, 24, 27–30, 42–43,
  125–26. *See also* meter: aspects of
metric emergence. *See* emerging meter
metric flexibility. *See* flexible meter
metric hierarchy
 defined, 31–32, 50–52, 51*f*, 52*f*
 in dot notation, 32*f*, 33*f*, 34–35, 35*f*
 See also Regular Meter
metric loss. *See* Lost Meter

metric potential, 42–43, 49–50, 125–26,
  129, 157–59
metric process (Hasty), 42–46, 45*f*, 103–8,
  106*f*, 159, 160*f*
metric projection. *See* metric process
  (Hasty)
metrical reinterpretations. *See*
  Reinterpreted Meter
Mirka, Danuta, 7n.17, 24n.63, 39n.25,
  44n.43, 46n.49
Mitchell, Joni
 "All I Want," 60–63, 61*f*, 62*f*
 artistic autonomy of, 122–24
 Blue (1971 album), 13, 23, 55, 84–85,
  110, 122–24
 "A Case of You," 58–60, 58*f*, 59*f*
 as confessional songwriter, 13–14, 22–
  23, 55–57, 84–85, 110, 122–24
 on The Dick Cavett Show (1969), 1, 2–3,
  2n.4, 153–54
 as ensemble performer, 165–66
 For the Roses (1972 album), 165–66
 Ladies of the Canyon (1970 album), 165–66
 "Little Green," 25, 55–57, 56*f*
 as political singer, 1–2, 3–4, 148–49,
  153–54
 reception of, 3n.7
 and Reinterpreted Meter, 58–63, 59*f*, 61*f*
 self-presentation of, 3, 148–49, 153–54
 vocal production techniques of, 4
 "Woodstock," 1–2, 40–42, 41*f*
 See also "Blue"; "Fiddle and the Drum,
  The"; "Lesson in Survival"
Moore, Allan, 16
mouthbow, 48–49, 49*f*, 156–61
"My Country 'Tis of Thy People You're
  Dying" (Sainte-Marie)
 1966 performance on *Rainbow Quest*,
  167–68, 175–76
 1966 studio recording, 26, 164–66, 167–
  68, 169–74
 2017 recording, 26, 164–66, 176–81,
  178*f*, 179*f*, 180*f*
 flexible meter in, 26, 167–68, 172–74,
  173*f*, 176–81, 178*f*
 lyrics of, 12n.27, 26, 169–70, 174–77
 vocal performance in, 171–76, 173*f*,
  177–81, 178*f*, 179*f*, 180*f*

INDEX   201

Neal, Jocelyn, 9n.21, 57n.10, 61n.15, 66n.21
Newport Folk Festival, 90–91, 165–66
nostalgia, 58–60, 116–18
"Now That the Buffalo's Gone" (Sainte-Marie), 11–12, 168–69, 176

old-time music, 9–10, 18
omitted beats
  in "All I Want" (Mitchell), 62, 62f
  defined, 34–36, 35f, 46, 57–58
  in "Lesson in Survival" (Mitchell), 36f, 36
  in "Into White" (Stevens), 68–71
  See also added beats; Reinterpreted Meter
"Only a Pawn in Their Game" (Dylan)
  dramatization through metric flexibility in, 91–97, 98–99
  formal flexibility in, 88f, 88–91, 89f, 90f
  Lost Meter in, 91–97, 92f, 93f, 98–99
  lyrics of, 87, 88f, 88, 89f, 90f, 94–97
  and perceived spontaneity, 87–91, 98–99
  performance history of, 11–12, 90–91, 97–98

parallelism, 37–38, 40–42
"Parting Glass, The" (The Clancy Brothers), 137, 138–39, 139f, 142
"Patriot Game, The" (Behan), 137
Paul Simon Songbook, The (Simon), 11–12, 22–23, 63
percussion, 33
piano
  in "Blue" (Mitchell), 47, 48f, 112, 113f, 114f, 116, 117f, 119–20
  in "Lesson in Survival" (Mitchell), 76–77, 79–81
projective meter. See metric process (Hasty)
protest songs, 2n.4, 11–12, 87, 97–98, 167–70, 180–81
pulse, defined, 50–52, 51f, 52f

Rainbow Quest, 167–69, 175–76
Realized Durations, 46–47, 47f, 52, 177, 178f

Regular Meter
  in "Blue" (Mitchell), 110–15, 116–18, 121, 122–23
  defined, 28–30, 29f, 31–34, 54
  disruption of, 25, 34, 38–40
  in "The Fiddle and the Drum" (Mitchell), 148–49, 151–54, 152f
  in later singer-songwriter music, 166–67
  in "Lesson in Survival" (Mitchell), 77
  in "Little Green" (Mitchell), 25, 55–57, 56f
  in "My Country 'Tis of Thy People You're Dying" (Sainte-Marie), 26, 167–68, 172, 174, 177–79
  parallelism in, 37
  Realized Durations in, 46–47, 47f
  in "Restless Farewell" (Dylan), 144–46
  in rock music, 33–34
  in "Time" (Stevens), 108–9, 109f
  in "Woodstock" (Mitchell), 40–42, 41f
Reinterpreted Meter
  in "All I Want" (Mitchell), 60–63, 61f, 62f
  in "April Come She Will" (Simon), 66, 67f
  in "Blue" (Mitchell), 112, 113f, 114f, 118–20
  in "A Case of You" (Mitchell), 58–60, 59f
  defined, 25, 28–30, 29f, 34, 38, 46, 57–58
  effects of, 57–60, 66–67, 74–75, 84–85
  in "Katmandu" (Stevens), 71–72, 72f, 73f
  in later singer-songwriter music, 166–67
  limits of, 103–5
  omitted and added beats, 34–38, 35f, 36f, 38f, 46, 57–58
  in "The Sound of Silence" (Simon), 37–38, 38f, 63–66, 64f, 65f
  in "Time" (Stevens), 100–5, 102f, 104f, 108–10
  in "Into White" (Stevens), 68–71, 70f
  in "The Wind" (Stevens), 68, 69f
  See also "Lesson in Survival" (Mitchell)
"Restless Farewell" (Dylan)
  Ambiguous Meter in, 126, 138, 139–44, 141f, 142f, 144f, 147–48

202 INDEX

"Restless Farewell" (Dylan) *(cont.)*
   asynchrony in, 139–41, 143–44
   and Dylan's persona, 137–48
   guitar in, 138, 139–41, 142, 143–46
   lyrics of, 140*f*, 146–47
   Regular Meter in, 144–46
   source material for, 137, 138–39,
      139*f*, 142
   word stresses in, 136–48, 140*f*
rhythm sections, 33–34
rock music, 33–34. *See also* folk rock
Rockwell, Joti, 7n.17, 24n.63, 44n.43
Roeder, John, 44n.45, 46n.48
Rotolo, Suze, 128
rubato, 27–28, 30

Sainte-Marie, Buffy
   as activist and protest singer, 2n.4,
      11–12, 167–70, 180–81
   background and identity, 12n.26,
      156–57, 167–69
   as ensemble performer, 165–66
   folk-song adaptations by, 22–23,
      154–56, 161–62
   and Indigenous rights, 11–12, 161–62,
      167–70, 176–77, 180–81
   Little Wheel Spin and Spin (1966
      album), 167–68, 171
   Medicine Songs (2017 album), 167–68,
      176
   "Now That the Buffalo's Gone," 11–12,
      168–69, 176
   "Universal Soldier," 2n.5, 11–12, 176
   vocal production techniques of, 4, 171,
      175–76, 177–81
   "Winter Boy," 99n.20
   See also "My Country 'Tis of Thy People
      You're Dying"; "Sir Patrick Spens"
Seeger, Pete, 11, 19n.51, 175–76.
      See also *Rainbow Quest*
self-accompaniment, 14, 16, 94–95,
      122–23, 164–65
self-expression
   and "authenticity," 14–18
   definitions of, 14, 167–68
   flexible meter as, 5, 21–26, 84–85, 123–
      24, 162–63, 167–68, 181–82
   and protest songs, 21–26, 148–49

   self-presentation as, 3, 153–54, 167–68,
      169
Sharp, Cecil, 19–20
Shelton, Robert, 12n.26, 18n.44
Simon, Paul
   "April Come She Will," 66, 67*f*
   Dylan's influence on, 22–23
   limited use of flexible meter, 85
   The Paul Simon Songbook (1965 album),
      11–12, 22–23, 63
   Simon & Garfunkel, 12nn.28–29,
      22–23, 63–64, 165–66
   singer-songwriter period of,
      12n.29, 66–67
   "The Sound of Silence," 38*f*, 41*f*, 63–66,
      64*f*, 65*f*
singer-songwriter tradition
   after 1972, 164–67
   components of self-expression in, 2–5,
      14, 164 (*see also* self-expression)
   definitions of, 2–3, 10–11, 13n.31, 14
   role of flexible meter in, 8–14, 22–26,
      33–34, 164–65
"Sir Patrick Spens" (Sainte-Marie)
   Ambiguous Meter in, 48–49, 49*f*, 126–
      27, 155, 157–61, 158*f*, 160*f*
   as folk-song adaptation, 154–57, 161–62
"Sound of Silence, The" (Simon), 37–38,
      38*f*, 63–66, 64*f*, 65*f*
spontaneity, perceived, 9–10, 14, 21,
      87–91, 98–99, 125
Stevens, Cat
   as confessional songwriter, 13–14,
      22–23, 67–68, 73–74, 85, 99–100,
      109
   as ensemble performer, 165–66
   illness of, 67–68, 73–74, 99–100, 108–9
   "Katmandu," 71–72, 72*f*, 73*f*
   "Into White," 68–71, 70*f*, 73–74
   "The Wind," 68, 69*f*, 73–74
stress, defined, 50–52, 51*f*, 52*f*
strong-weak organization, 50, 51–52,
      51*f*, 52*f*

"Talkin' New York" (Dylan), 18–19, 138
television, performances on, 1–2, 3,
      168–69, 175–76. *See also* Dick Cavett
      Show, The; *Rainbow Quest*

temporality
  in "Katmandu" (Stevens), 71–72, 73–74
  in "Time" (Stevens), 100, 101–9
texture, 16, 33–34, 165–66.
    See also ensemble textures;
    self-accompaniment
"Time" (Stevens)
  as Lost Meter, 100, 103–10, 106*f*
  Regular Meter in, 108–9, 109*f*
  as Reinterpreted Meter, 100–5, 102*f*,
    104*f*, 108–10
  and Stevens's illness, 99–100, 108–9
  temporality in, 100, 101–9
"Times They Are A-Changin,' The"
  (Dylan), 11, 97–98
transcription, approach to, 53
Troubadour (Los Angeles), 17

Ungrouped Beats, 48–49, 49*f*, 126–27,
  155, 157–61
"Universal Soldier" (Sainte-Marie), 2n.5,
  11–12, 176
unmediated performance, impression
  of, 16–17, 181. *See also* authenticity,
  perceptions of
unpredictability, 5–6, 88–91, 88*f*, 94–95,
  98–99. *See also* Ambiguous Meter;
  flexible meter; Lost Meter
Unrealized Durations
  defined, 28, 29*f*, 46–47, 50–51
  in "The Fiddle and the Drum"
    (Mitchell), 28–30, 149, 150*f*

in "Sir Patrick Spens" (Sainte-Marie),
  48–49, 49*f*, 126–27, 155, 159

Vanguard Records, 154–55, 161–62
Vietnam War, opposition to, 1–2
vocal production as self-expression, 4,
  18–19, 167–68, 171, 175–81.
    See also word stresses
vocal stresses. *See* word stresses

Warner, Andrea, 2n.5, 162n.67, 168n.11,
  170n.21
Whitesell, Lloyd, 60, 110–11, 111n.38,
  148n.42
"Wind, The" (Stevens), 68, 69*f*, 73–74
"Winter Boy" (Sainte-Marie), 99n.20
"With God on Our Side" (Dylan),
  57n.9, 137
"Woodstock" (Mitchell), 1–2, 40–42,
  41*f*
Woodstock festival, 1–2
word stresses
  in "Down the Highway" (Dylan), 129,
    129*f*, 131–33, 136–37
  in "The Fiddle and the Drum"
    (Mitchell), 5–6, 8, 149–51
  in "The Parting Glass" (The Clancy
    Brothers), 138–39, 139*f*
  in "Restless Farewell" (Dylan), 139–46,
    140*f*
  in "Sir Patrick Spens" (Sainte-Marie),
    159–61, 160*f*